ORLANDO BLOOM HAS
RUINED EVERYTHING

Other FoxTrot Books by Bill Amend

FoxTrot • Pass the Loot • Black Bart Says Draw • Eight Yards, Down and Out
Bury My Heart at Fun-Fun Mountain • Say Hello to Cactus Flats • May the Force Be with Us, Please
Take Us to Your Mall • The Return of the Lone Iguana • At Least This Place Sells T-shirts
Come Closer, Roger, There's a Mosquito on Your Nose • Welcome to Jasorassic Park
I'm Flying, Jack . . . I Mean, Roger • Think iFruity • Death by Field Trip
Encyclopedias Brown and White • His Code Name Was The Fox
Your Momma Thinks Square Roots Are Vegetables • Who's Up for Some Bonding?
Am I a Mutant or What!

Anthologies

FoxTrot: The Works • FoxTrot en masse • Enormously FoxTrot • Wildly FoxTrot
FoxTrot Beyond a Doubt • Camp FoxTrot • Assorted FoxTrot • FoxTrot: Assembled with Care
FoxTrotius Maximus

ORLANDO BLOOM HAS RUINED EVERYTHING

A FoxTrot Collection by Bill Amend

**Andrews McMeel
Publishing**

Kansas City

FoxTrot is distributed internationally by Universal Press Syndicate.

Orlando Bloom Has Ruined Everything copyright © 2005 by Bill Amend. All rights reserved. Printed in the United States of America. No part of this book may be used or reproduced in any manner whatsoever without written permission except in the case of reprints in the context of reviews. For information, write Andrews McMeel Publishing, 4520 Main Street, Kansas City, Missouri 64111.

05 06 07 08 09 BBG 10 9 8 7 6 5 4 3 2 1

ISBN: 0-7407-4999-4

Library of Congress Control Number: 2004113772

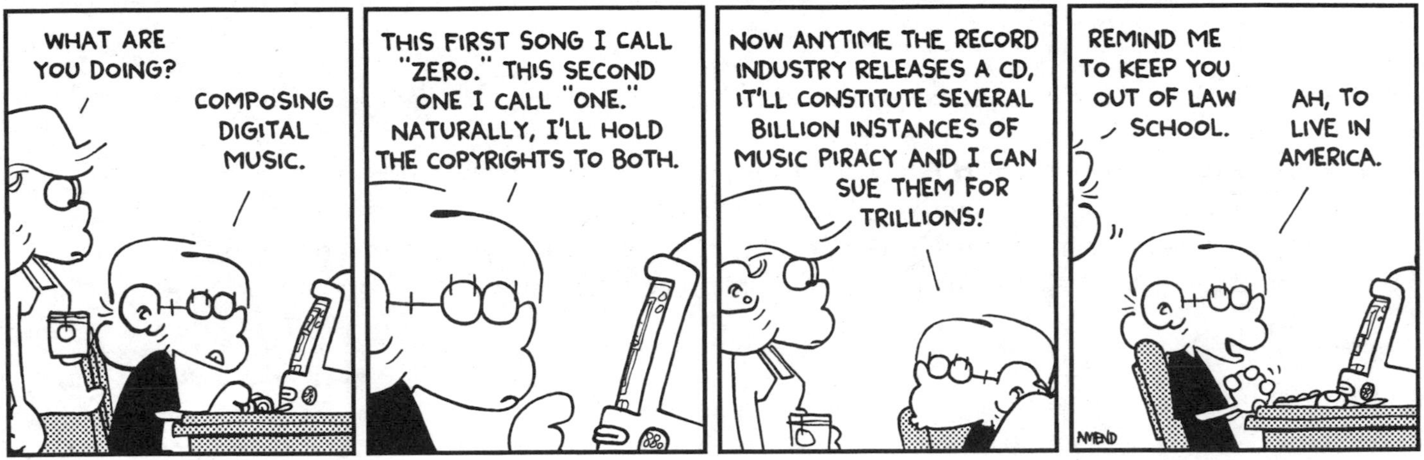
WHAT ARE YOU DOING?
COMPOSING DIGITAL MUSIC.
THIS FIRST SONG I CALL "ZERO." THIS SECOND ONE I CALL "ONE." NATURALLY, I'LL HOLD THE COPYRIGHTS TO BOTH.
NOW ANYTIME THE RECORD INDUSTRY RELEASES A CD, IT'LL CONSTITUTE SEVERAL BILLION INSTANCES OF MUSIC PIRACY AND I CAN SUE THEM FOR TRILLIONS!
REMIND ME TO KEEP YOU OUT OF LAW SCHOOL.
AH, TO LIVE IN AMERICA.
AMEND

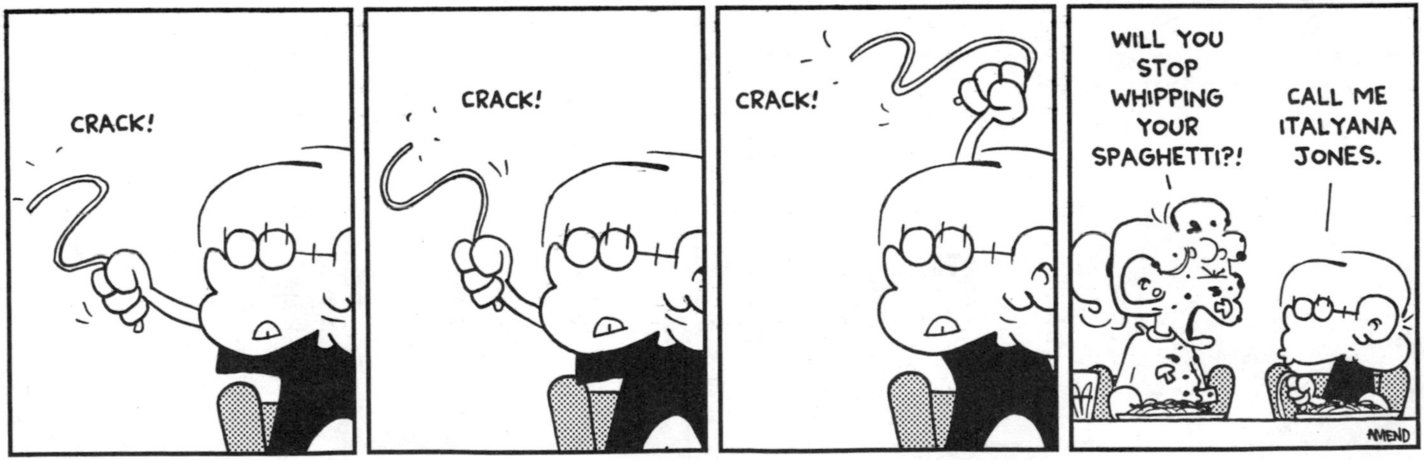
CRACK!
CRACK!
CRACK!
WILL YOU STOP WHIPPING YOUR SPAGHETTI?!
CALL ME ITALYANA JONES.
AMEND

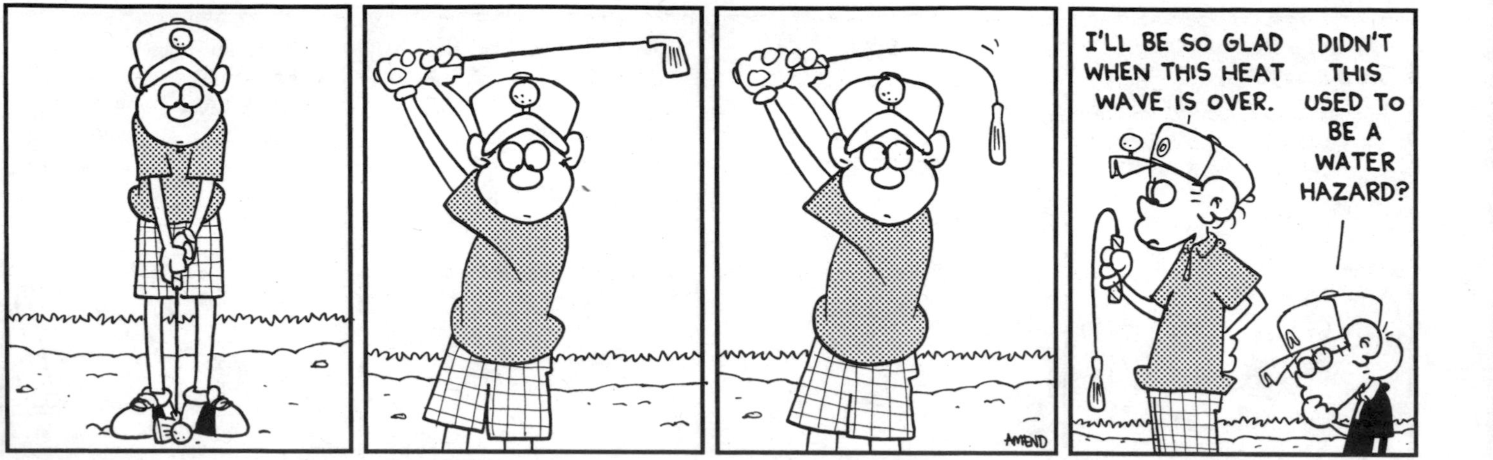
AMEND
I'LL BE SO GLAD WHEN THIS HEAT WAVE IS OVER.
DIDN'T THIS USED TO BE A WATER HAZARD?

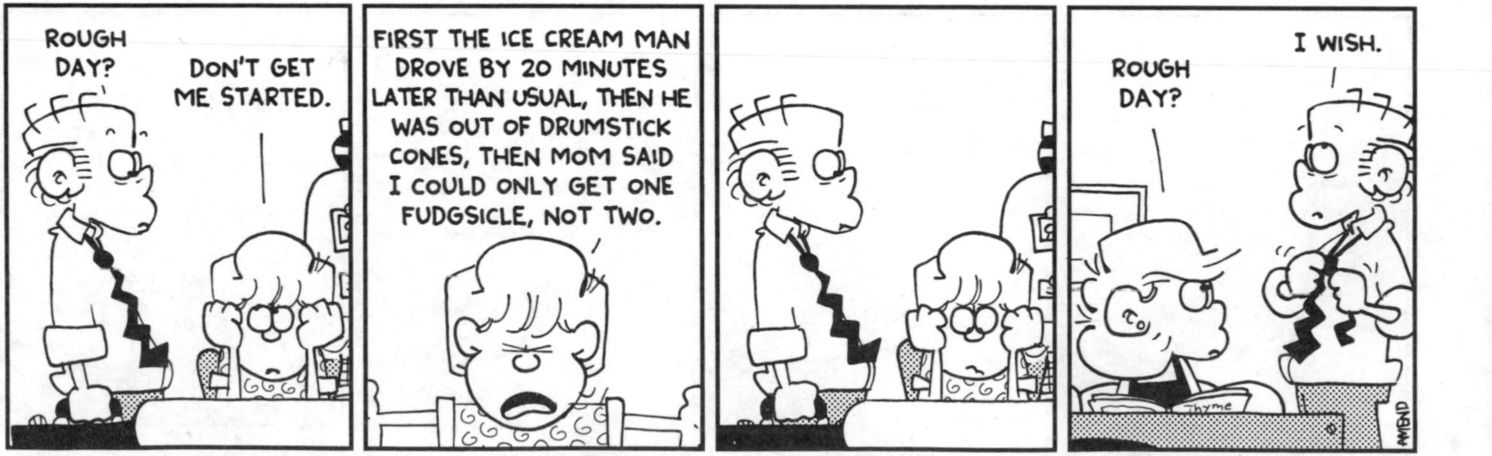
ROUGH DAY?
DON'T GET ME STARTED.
FIRST THE ICE CREAM MAN DROVE BY 20 MINUTES LATER THAN USUAL, THEN HE WAS OUT OF DRUMSTICK CONES, THEN MOM SAID I COULD ONLY GET ONE FUDGSICLE, NOT TWO.
ROUGH DAY?
I WISH.
Thyme
AMEND

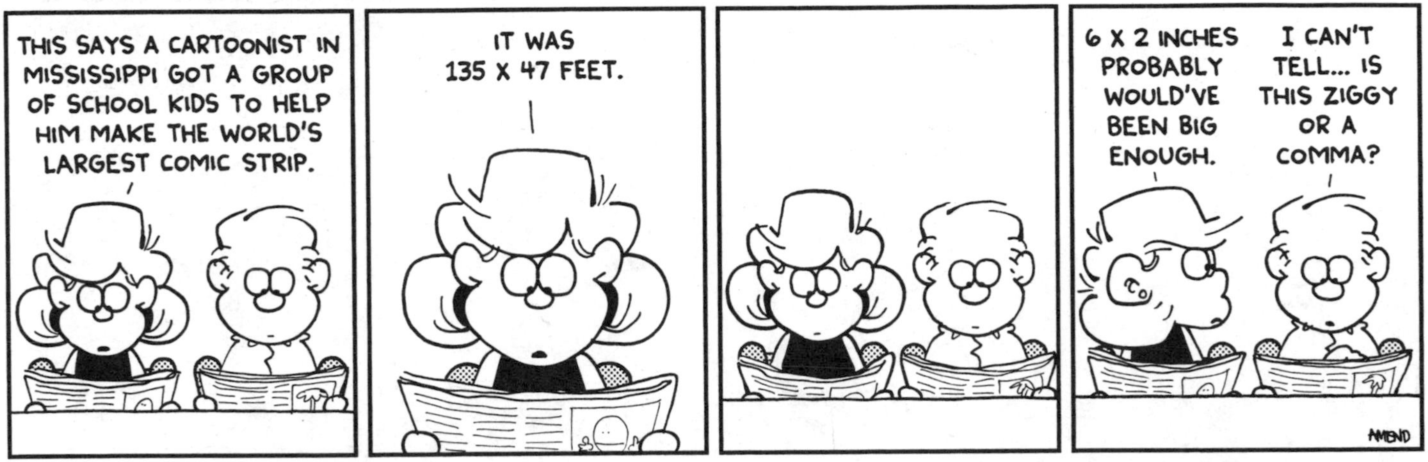
THIS SAYS A CARTOONIST IN MISSISSIPPI GOT A GROUP OF SCHOOL KIDS TO HELP HIM MAKE THE WORLD'S LARGEST COMIC STRIP.
IT WAS 135 X 47 FEET.
6 X 2 INCHES PROBABLY WOULD'VE BEEN BIG ENOUGH.
I CAN'T TELL... IS THIS ZIGGY OR A COMMA?
AMEND

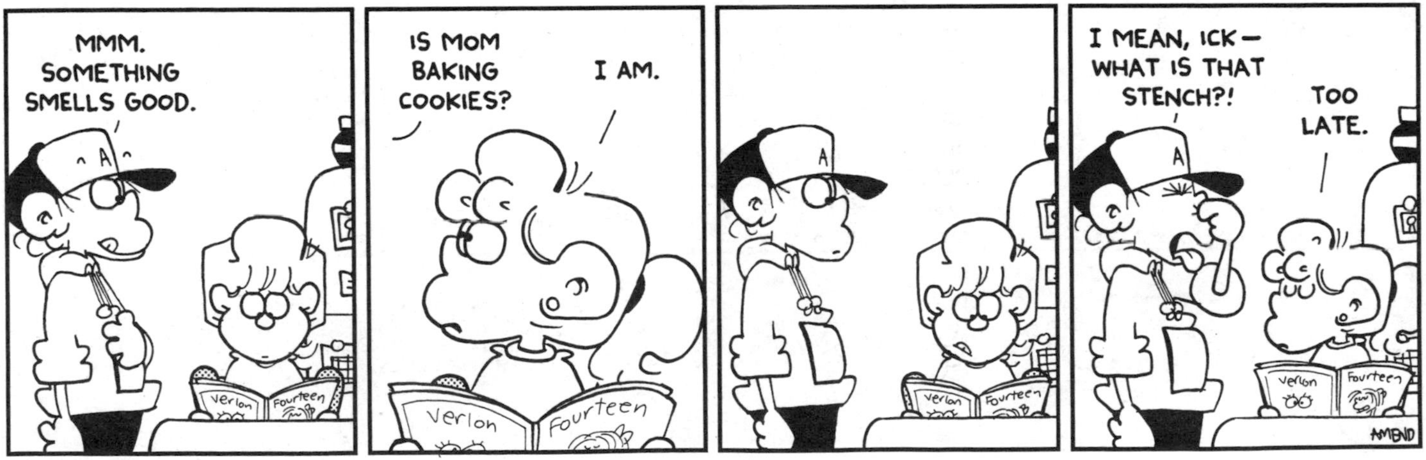
MMM. SOMETHING SMELLS GOOD.
Verlon
Fourteen
IS MOM BAKING COOKIES?
I AM.
I MEAN, ICK— WHAT IS THAT STENCH?!
TOO LATE.
AMEND

BRRR! IT'S 35 DEGREES!
BRRR! IT'S 35 DEGREES!
BRRR! IT'S 35 DEGREES!
GLAM
CELSIUS, YOU LUNATIC!
YOU STAY COOL YOUR WAY, I STAY COOL MINE.
AMEND

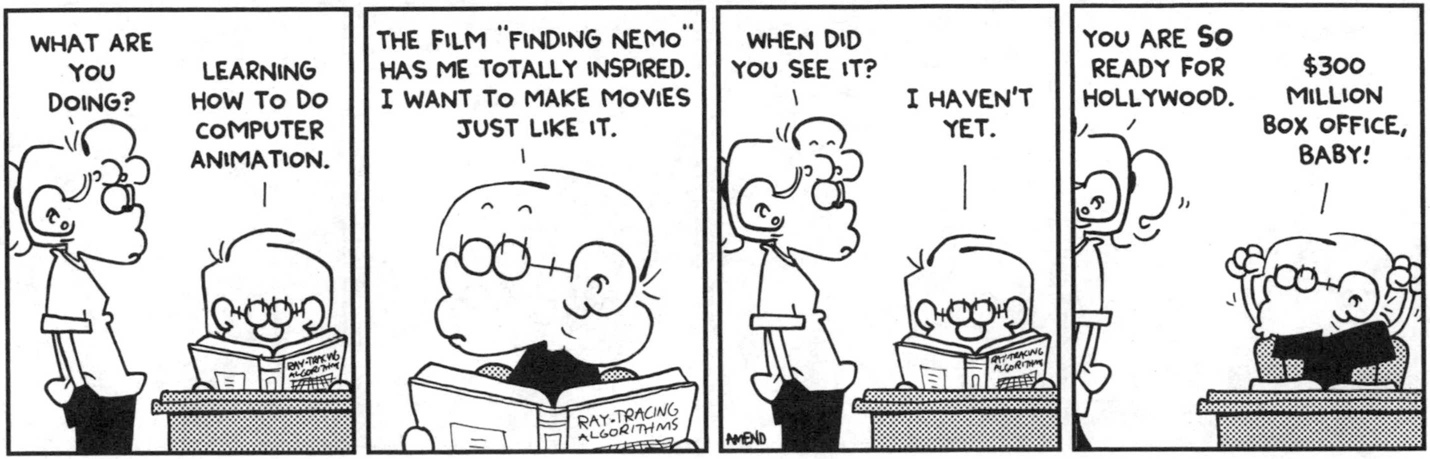
WHAT ARE YOU DOING?
LEARNING HOW TO DO COMPUTER ANIMATION.
RAY-TRACING ALGORITHMS
THE FILM "FINDING NEMO" HAS ME TOTALLY INSPIRED. I WANT TO MAKE MOVIES JUST LIKE IT.
RAY-TRACING ALGORITHMS
WHEN DID YOU SEE IT?
I HAVEN'T YET.
AMEND
YOU ARE SO READY FOR HOLLYWOOD.
$300 MILLION BOX OFFICE, BABY!

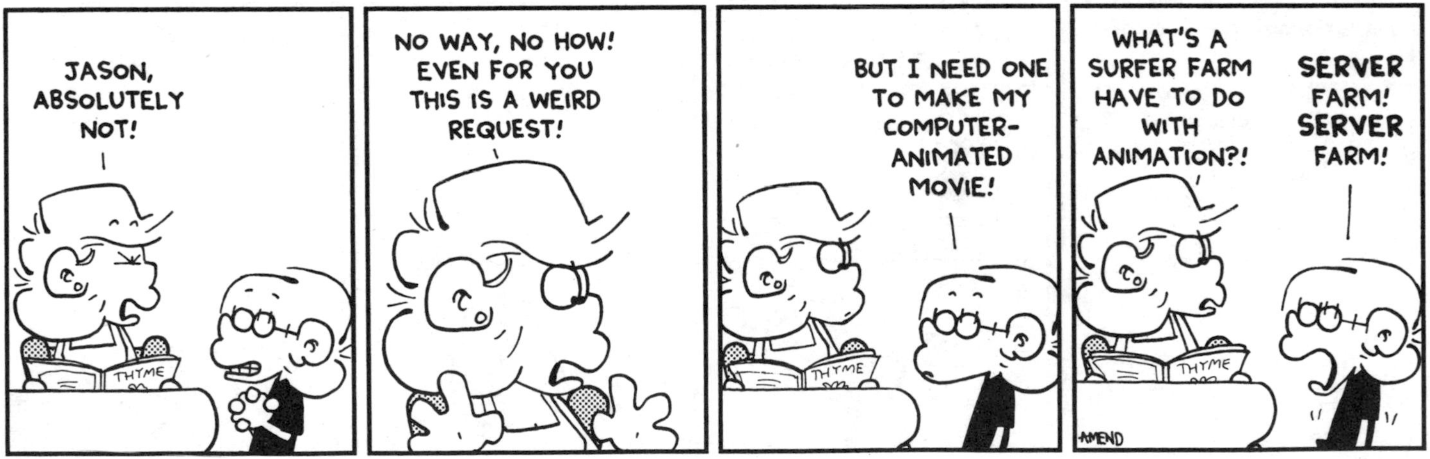
JASON, ABSOLUTELY NOT!
THYME
NO WAY, NO HOW! EVEN FOR YOU THIS IS A WEIRD REQUEST!
BUT I NEED ONE TO MAKE MY COMPUTER-ANIMATED MOVIE!
THYME
WHAT'S A SURFER FARM HAVE TO DO WITH ANIMATION?!
SERVER FARM! SERVER FARM!
THYME
AMEND

I HEAR YOU'RE MAKING AN ANIMATED MOVIE.

YUP.

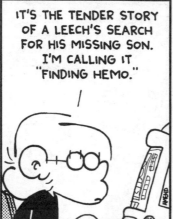

IT'S THE TENDER STORY OF A LEECH'S SEARCH FOR HIS MISSING SON. I'M CALLING IT "FINDING HEMO."

YOU CAN'T DO THAT! IT'S A TOTAL RIPOFF OF PIXAR!

SO?

SO THAT'S DREAMWORKS' TURF.

GOOD POINT. I'D HATE TO MAKE THEM MAD.

YOU'RE MAKING A MOVIE ABOUT **LEECHES**?!

"FINDING HEMO." AND YOU KNOW WHAT'S THE BEST PART?

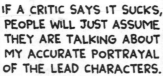

IF A CRITIC SAYS IT SUCKS, PEOPLE WILL JUST ASSUME THEY ARE TALKING ABOUT MY ACCURATE PORTRAYAL OF THE LEAD CHARACTERS.

AM I BRILLIANT, OR WHAT?

I'LL GO WITH "WHAT."

I'VE ALSO GOT A SKUNK CAMEO, IN CASE THEY ALSO SAY IT STINKS.

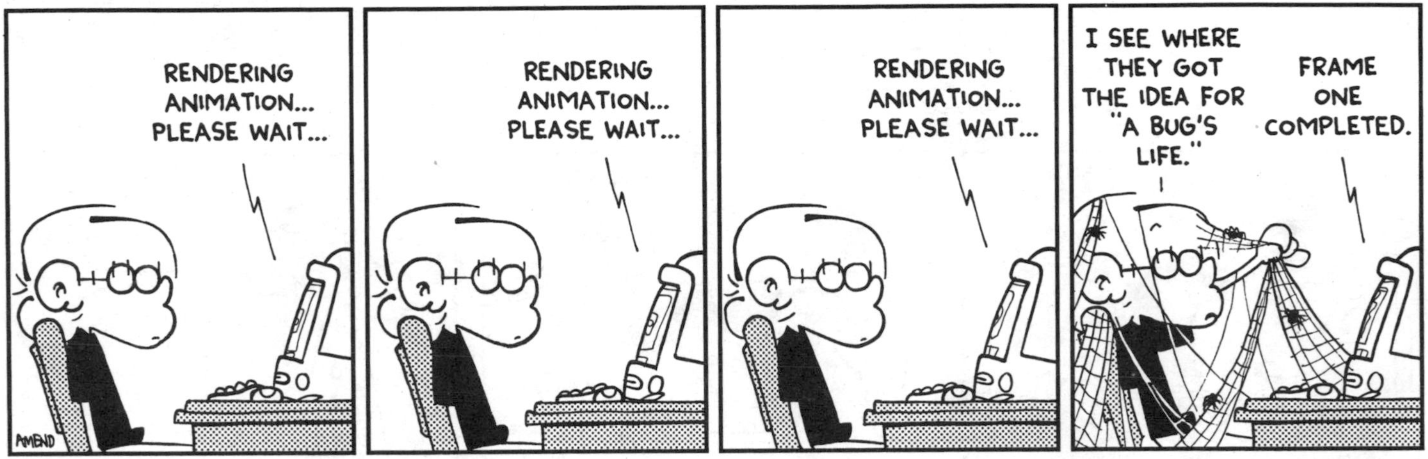
AMEND
RENDERING ANIMATION... PLEASE WAIT...
RENDERING ANIMATION... PLEASE WAIT...
RENDERING ANIMATION... PLEASE WAIT...
I SEE WHERE THEY GOT THE IDEA FOR "A BUG'S LIFE."
FRAME ONE COMPLETED.

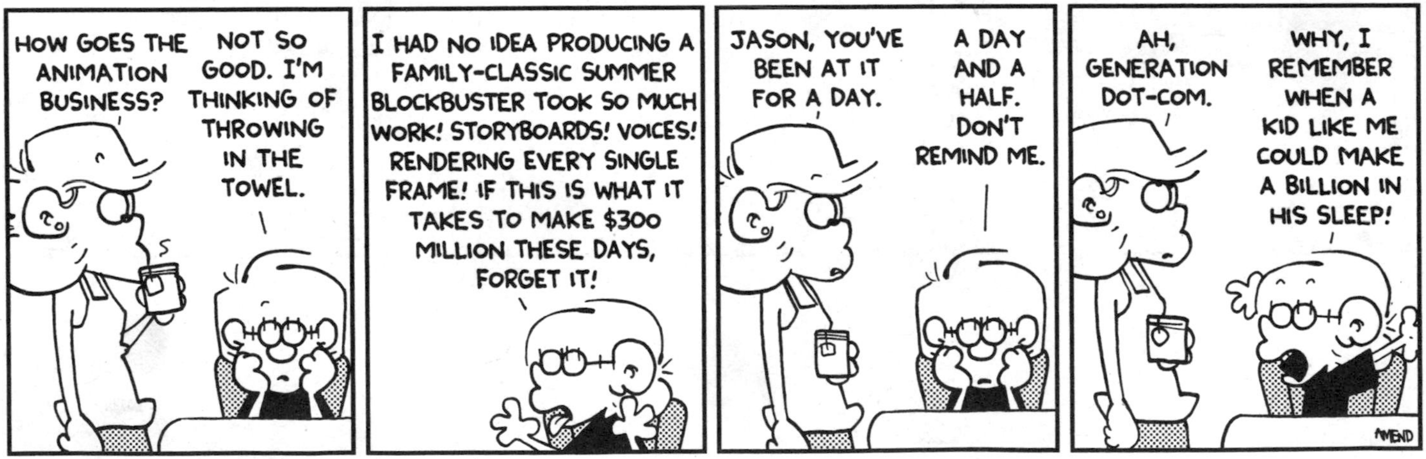
HOW GOES THE ANIMATION BUSINESS?
NOT SO GOOD. I'M THINKING OF THROWING IN THE TOWEL.
I HAD NO IDEA PRODUCING A FAMILY-CLASSIC SUMMER BLOCKBUSTER TOOK SO MUCH WORK! STORYBOARDS! VOICES! RENDERING EVERY SINGLE FRAME! IF THIS IS WHAT IT TAKES TO MAKE $300 MILLION THESE DAYS, FORGET IT!
JASON, YOU'VE BEEN AT IT FOR A DAY.
A DAY AND A HALF. DON'T REMIND ME.
AH, GENERATION DOT-COM.
WHY, I REMEMBER WHEN A KID LIKE ME COULD MAKE A BILLION IN HIS SLEEP!
AMEND

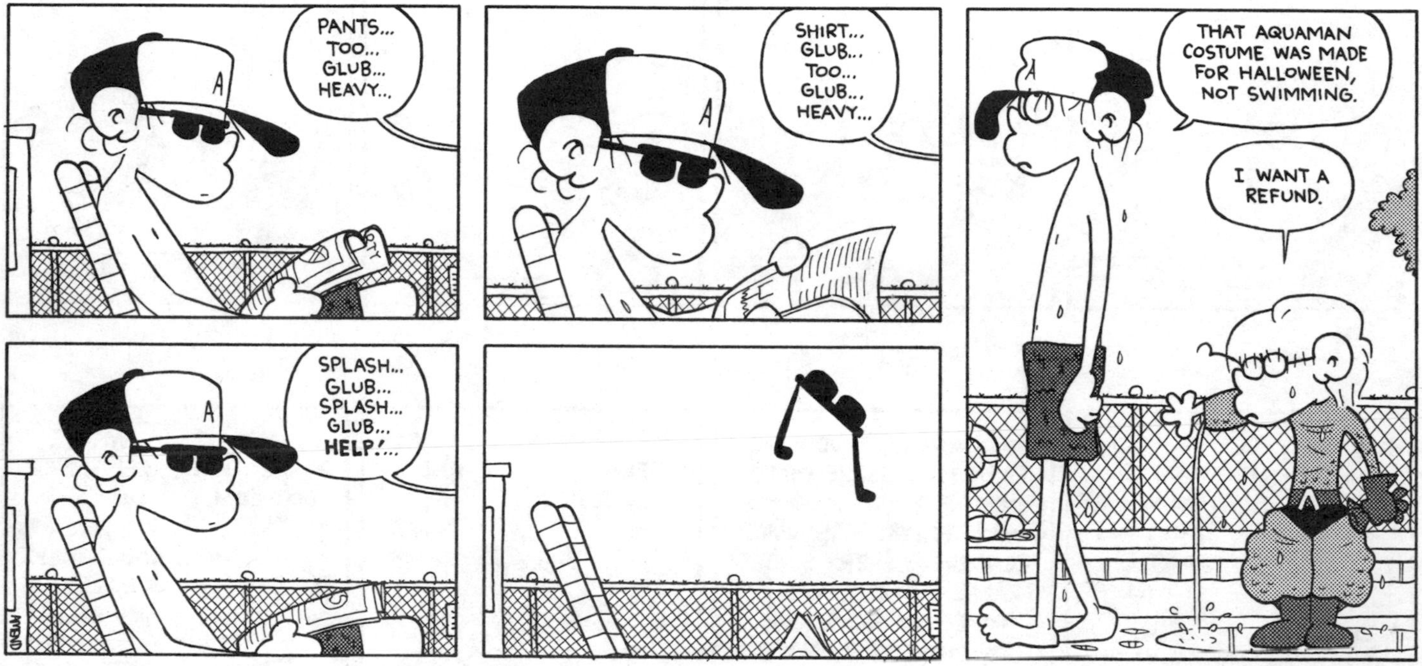
PANTS... TOO... GLUB... HEAVY...
SHIRT... GLUB... TOO... GLUB... HEAVY...
SPLASH... GLUB... SPLASH... GLUB... **HELP!**...
THAT AQUAMAN COSTUME WAS MADE FOR HALLOWEEN, NOT SWIMMING.
I WANT A REFUND.

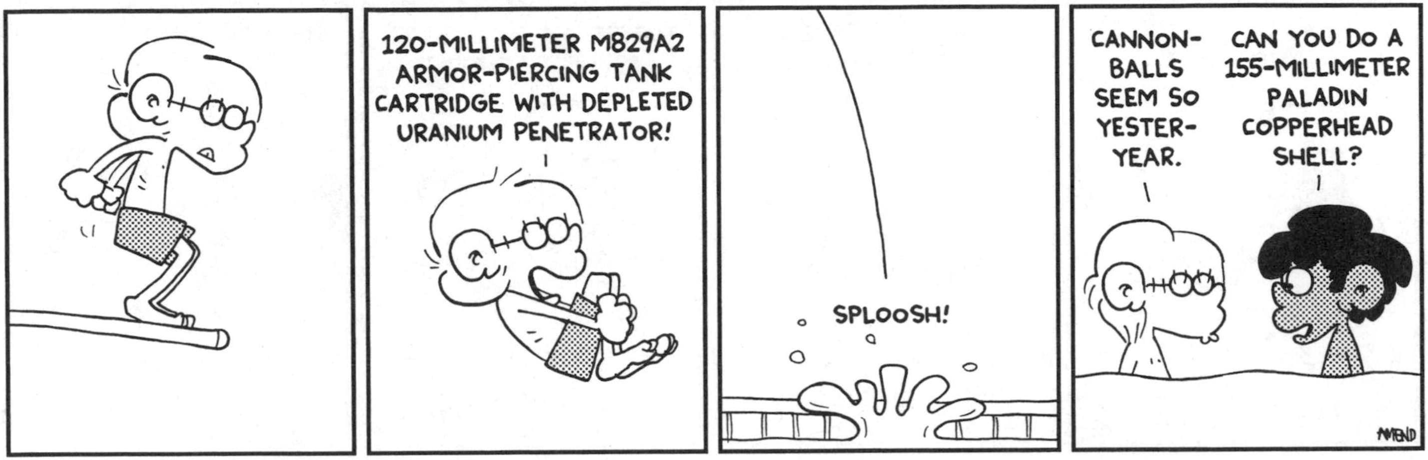
120-MILLIMETER M829A2 ARMOR-PIERCING TANK CARTRIDGE WITH DEPLETED URANIUM PENETRATOR!
SPLOOSH!
CANNON-BALLS SEEM SO YESTER-YEAR.
CAN YOU DO A 155-MILLIMETER PALADIN COPPERHEAD SHELL?
AMEND

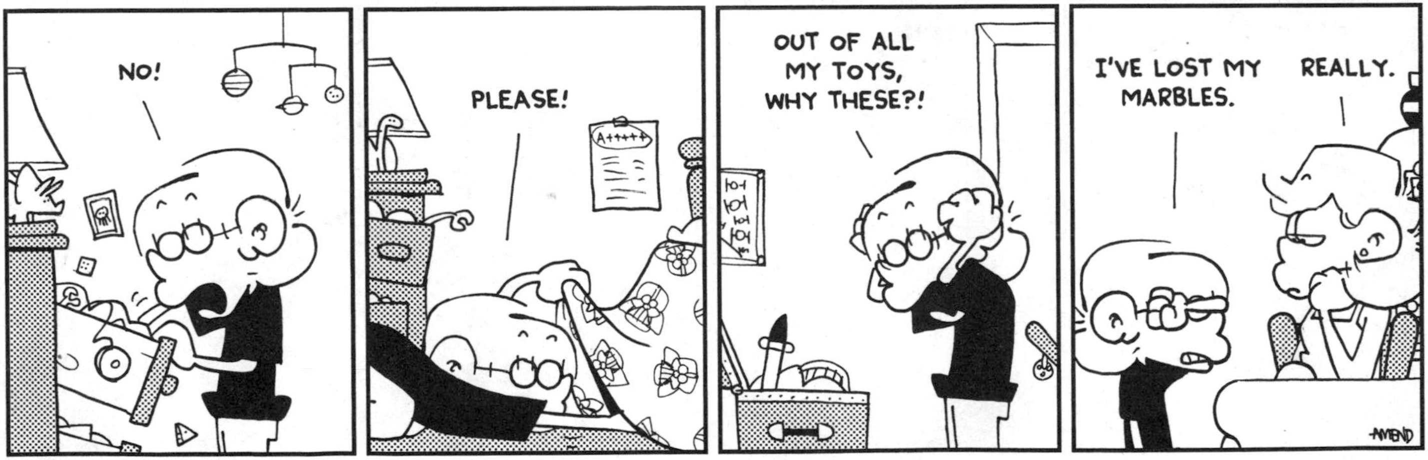
NO!
PLEASE!
A+++++
OUT OF ALL MY TOYS, WHY THESE?!
I'VE LOST MY MARBLES.
REALLY.
AMEND

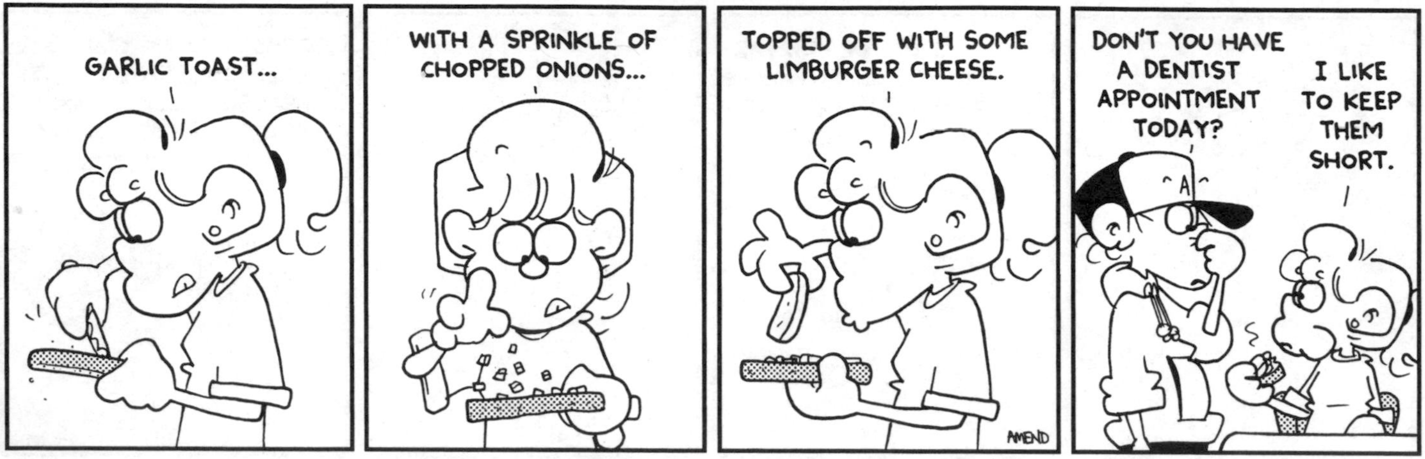
GARLIC TOAST...
WITH A SPRINKLE OF CHOPPED ONIONS...
TOPPED OFF WITH SOME LIMBURGER CHEESE.
AMEND
DON'T YOU HAVE A DENTIST APPOINTMENT TODAY?
I LIKE TO KEEP THEM SHORT.

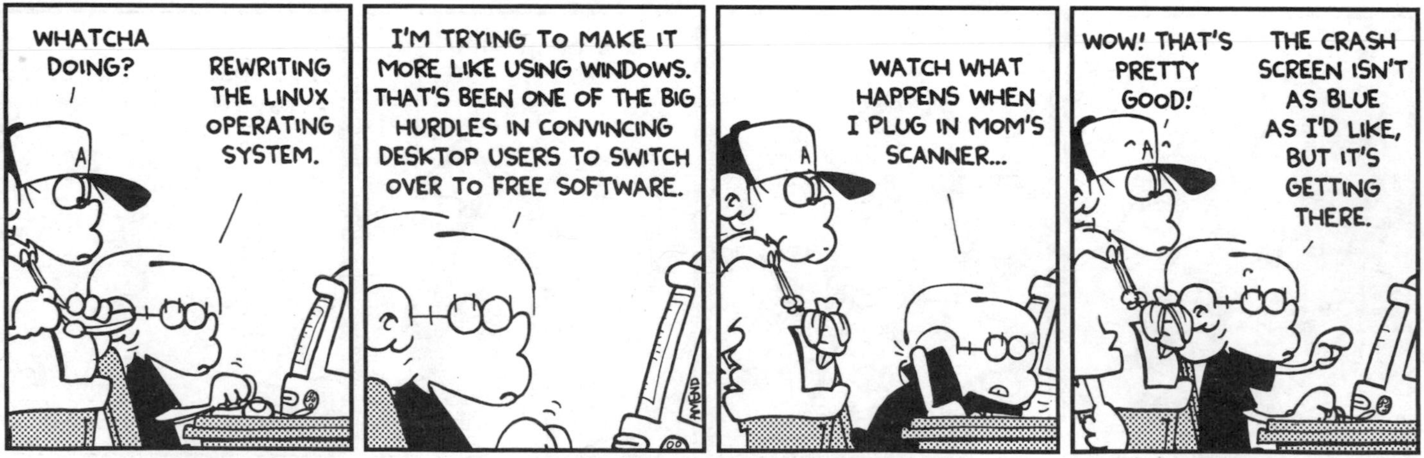
WHATCHA DOING?
REWRITING THE LINUX OPERATING SYSTEM.
I'M TRYING TO MAKE IT MORE LIKE USING WINDOWS. THAT'S BEEN ONE OF THE BIG HURDLES IN CONVINCING DESKTOP USERS TO SWITCH OVER TO FREE SOFTWARE.
AMEND
WATCH WHAT HAPPENS WHEN I PLUG IN MOM'S SCANNER...
WOW! THAT'S PRETTY GOOD!
THE CRASH SCREEN ISN'T AS BLUE AS I'D LIKE, BUT IT'S GETTING THERE.

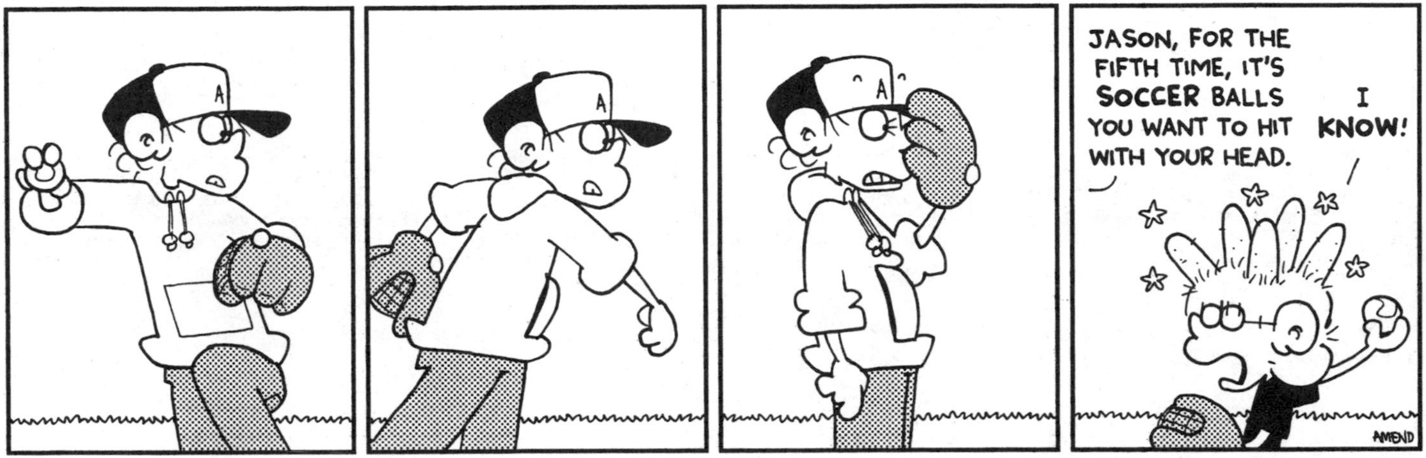
JASON, FOR THE FIFTH TIME, IT'S **SOCCER** BALLS YOU WANT TO HIT WITH YOUR HEAD.
I **KNOW!**
AMEND

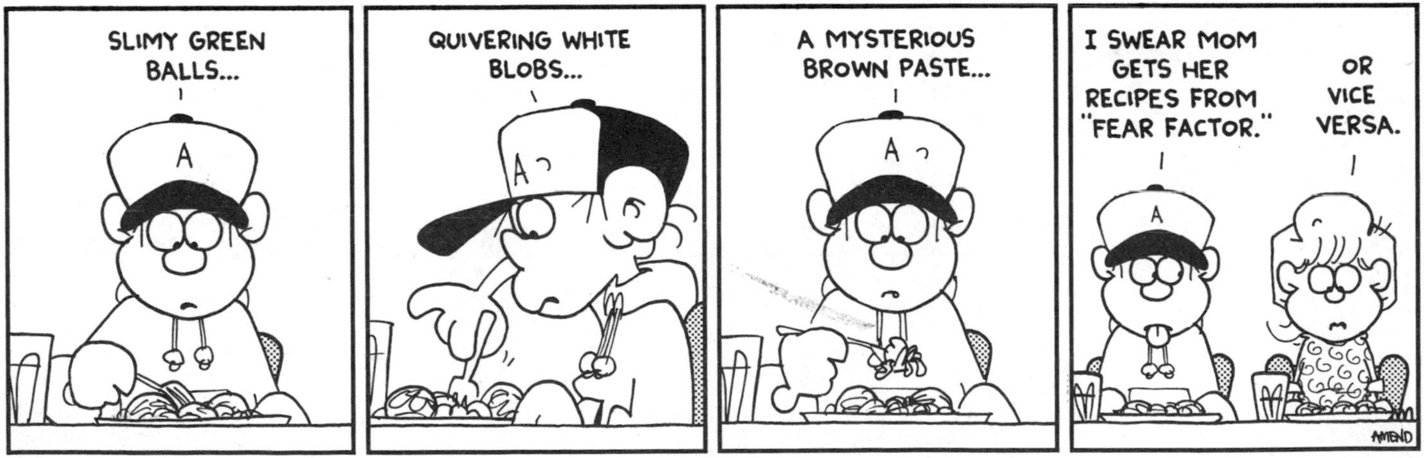
SLIMY GREEN BALLS...
QUIVERING WHITE BLOBS...
A MYSTERIOUS BROWN PASTE...
I SWEAR MOM GETS HER RECIPES FROM "FEAR FACTOR."
OR VICE VERSA.
AMEND

IN WASHINGTON, THE JUSTICE DEPARTMENT TODAY CHARACTERIZED THE FIRST, FOURTH, FIFTH AND SIXTH AMENDMENTS TO THE CONSTITUTION AS "TYPOS."

IN SPORTS, THE NCAA HAS DETERMINED THAT ITS ANNUAL MEN'S BASKETBALL TOURNAMENT IS DISRUPTIVE TO ACADEMIC SCHEDULES AND WILL BE ABOLISHED.

IN TECH NEWS, MICROSOFT CHAIRMAN BILL GATES HAS CHALLENGED LINUX CREATOR LINUS TORVALDS TO A WINNER-TAKE-ALL STEEL-CAGE JUDO DEATHMATCH.

AND ON THE BUSINESS FRONT, ANALYSTS ARE PREDICTING A MAJOR SPIKE IN THE ECONOMY AS PAIGE FOX PURCHASES HER BACK-TO-SCHOOL PIMPLE CREAM.

WILL YOU STOP HACKING THE CNN TELEPROMPTER?!

WOLF BLITZER'S ABOUT TO SAY "FEAR ME" IN KLINGON.

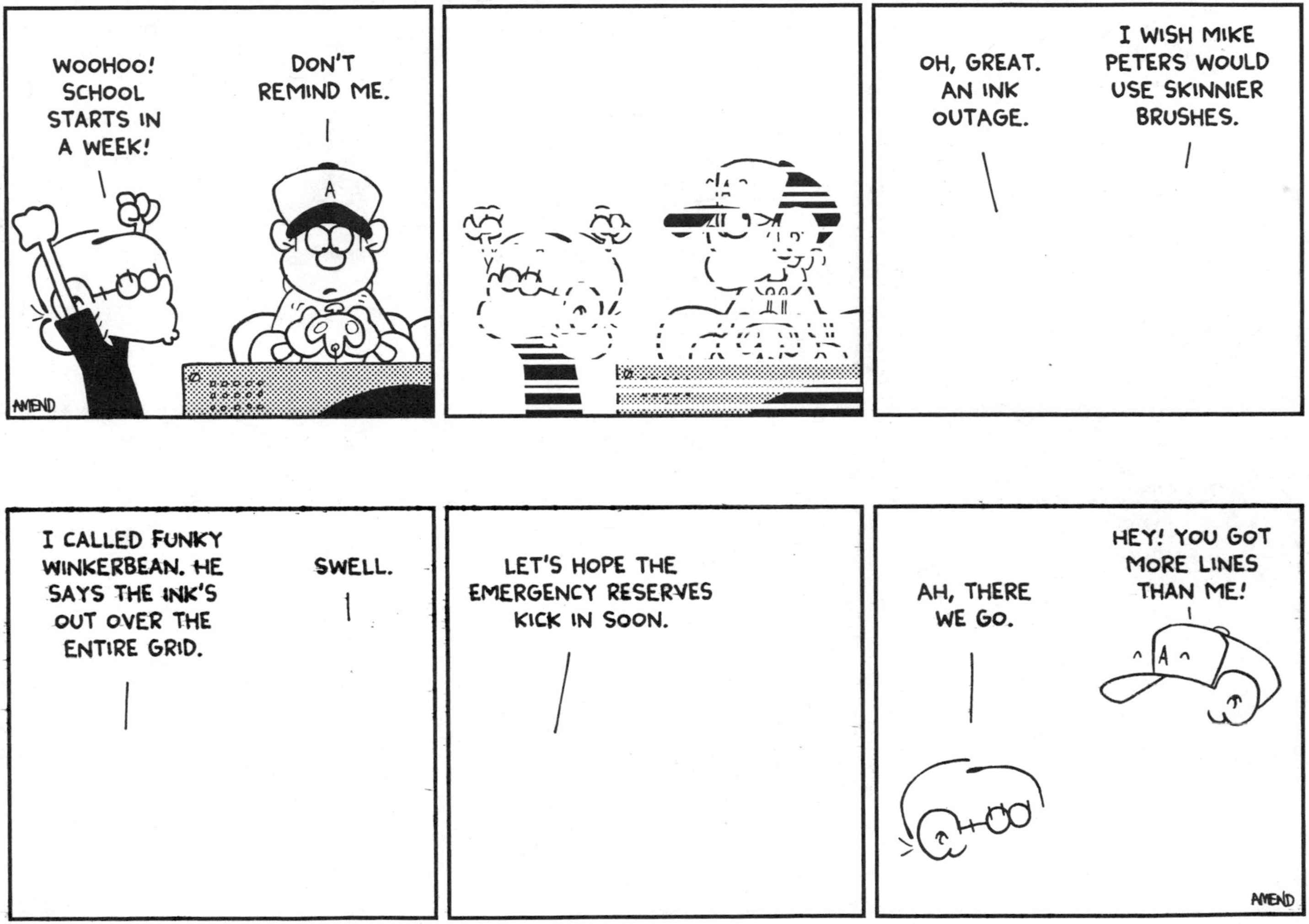
WOOHOO! SCHOOL STARTS IN A WEEK!
DON'T REMIND ME.
AMEND
OH, GREAT. AN INK OUTAGE.
I WISH MIKE PETERS WOULD USE SKINNIER BRUSHES.
I CALLED FUNKY WINKERBEAN. HE SAYS THE INK'S OUT OVER THE ENTIRE GRID.
SWELL.
LET'S HOPE THE EMERGENCY RESERVES KICK IN SOON.
AH, THERE WE GO.
HEY! YOU GOT MORE LINES THAN ME!
AMEND

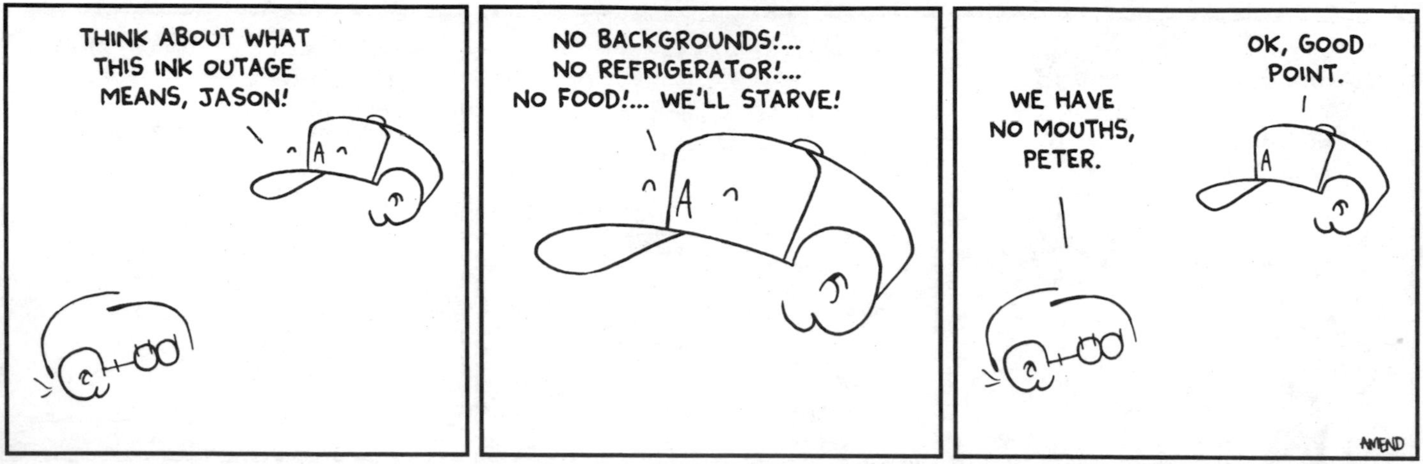
THINK ABOUT WHAT THIS INK OUTAGE MEANS, JASON!
NO BACKGROUNDS!... NO REFRIGERATOR!... NO FOOD!... WE'LL STARVE!
WE HAVE NO MOUTHS, PETER.
OK, GOOD POINT.
AMEND

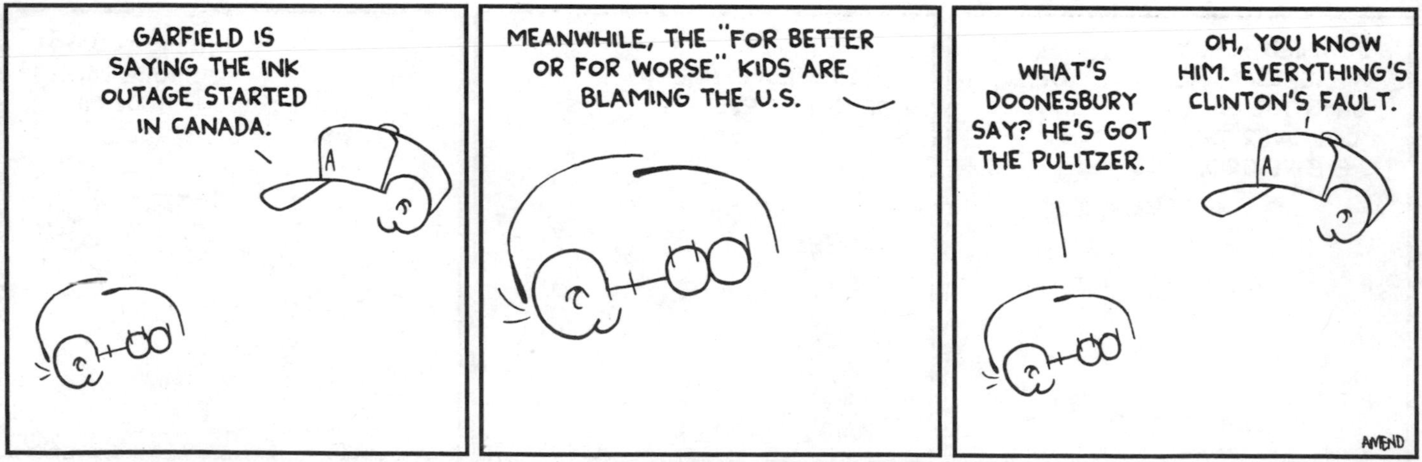
GARFIELD IS SAYING THE INK OUTAGE STARTED IN CANADA.
MEANWHILE, THE "FOR BETTER OR FOR WORSE" KIDS ARE BLAMING THE U.S.
WHAT'S DOONESBURY SAY? HE'S GOT THE PULITZER.
OH, YOU KNOW HIM. EVERYTHING'S CLINTON'S FAULT.
AMEND

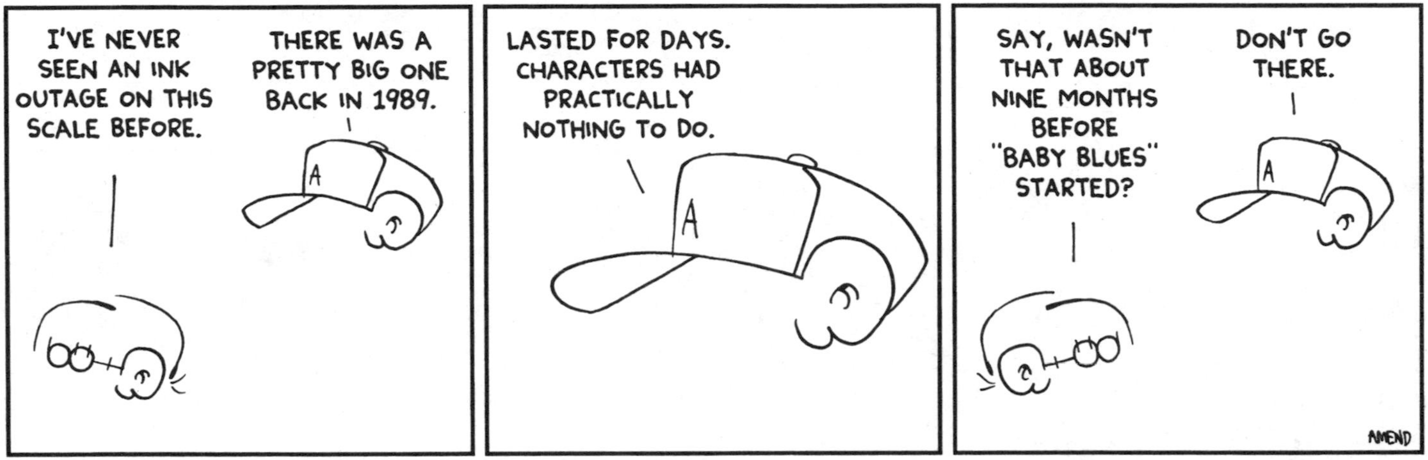
I'VE NEVER SEEN AN INK OUTAGE ON THIS SCALE BEFORE.
THERE WAS A PRETTY BIG ONE BACK IN 1989.
LASTED FOR DAYS. CHARACTERS HAD PRACTICALLY NOTHING TO DO.
SAY, WASN'T THAT ABOUT NINE MONTHS BEFORE "BABY BLUES" STARTED?
DON'T GO THERE.
AMEND

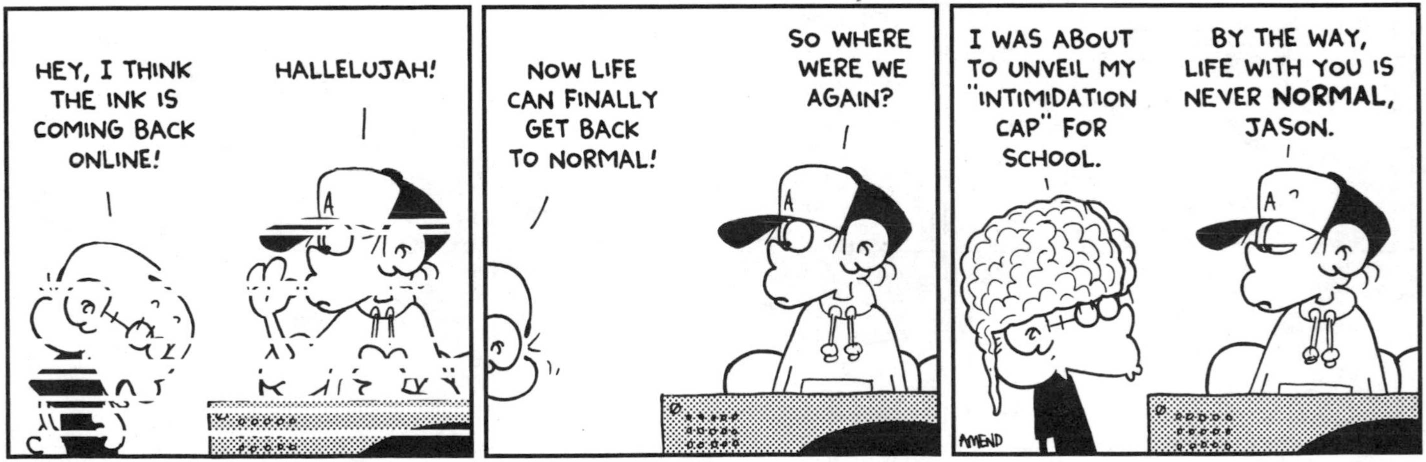
HEY, I THINK THE INK IS COMING BACK ONLINE!
HALLELUJAH!
NOW LIFE CAN FINALLY GET BACK TO NORMAL!
SO WHERE WERE WE AGAIN?
I WAS ABOUT TO UNVEIL MY "INTIMIDATION CAP" FOR SCHOOL.
BY THE WAY, LIFE WITH YOU IS NEVER **NORMAL**, JASON.
AMEND

WHAT'S THIS?
BAG LUNCH SUGGESTIONS FOR THE NEW SCHOOL YEAR.
MY GRADES LAST YEAR WEREN'T AS GOOD AS THEY COULD HAVE BEEN, AND I BLAME IT ALL ON THE BORING AND UNINSPIRING PEANUT BUTTER AND JELLY SANDWICHES YOU ALWAYS MADE ME. THIS YEAR, I'D LIKE MORE INTERESTING FARE, SUCH AS REUBENS AND CHEESESTEAKS AND FOOT-LONG MEATBALL GRINDERS.
DID I MENTION THAT THIS YEAR YOU KIDS WILL BE MAKING YOUR OWN LUNCHES?
AMEND
WHAT'D YOU BRING TODAY?
PEANUT BUTTER AND JELLY.

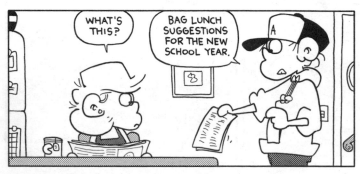

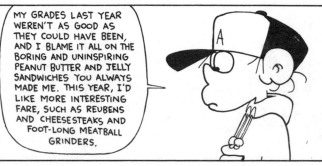

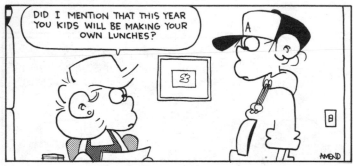

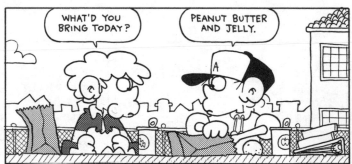

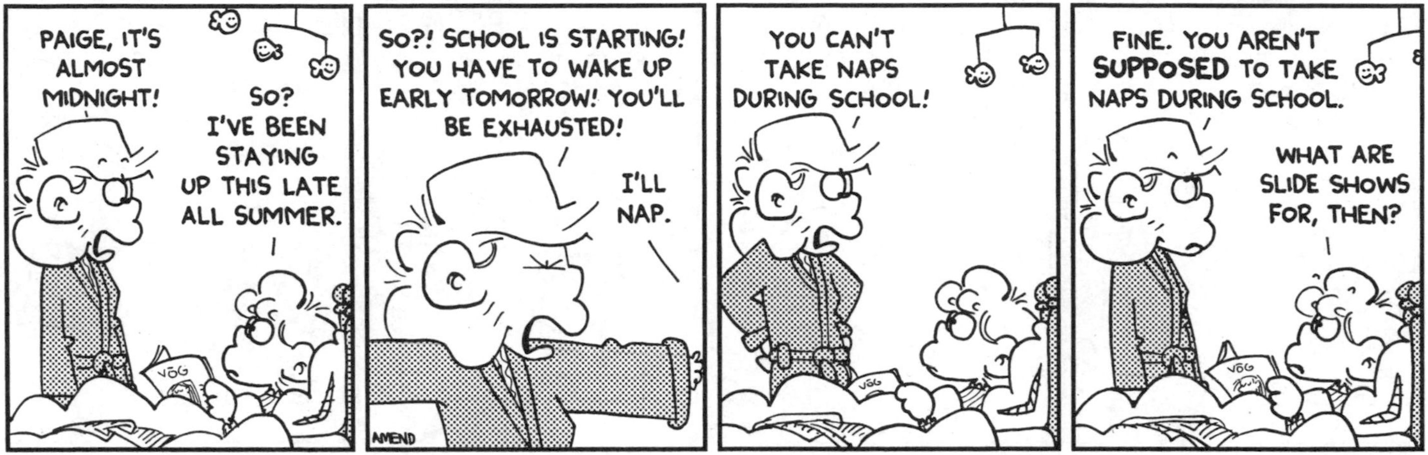
PAIGE, IT'S ALMOST MIDNIGHT!
SO? I'VE BEEN STAYING UP THIS LATE ALL SUMMER.
SO?! SCHOOL IS STARTING! YOU HAVE TO WAKE UP EARLY TOMORROW! YOU'LL BE EXHAUSTED!
I'LL NAP.
AMEND
YOU CAN'T TAKE NAPS DURING SCHOOL!
FINE. YOU AREN'T **SUPPOSED** TO TAKE NAPS DURING SCHOOL.
WHAT ARE SLIDE SHOWS FOR, THEN?

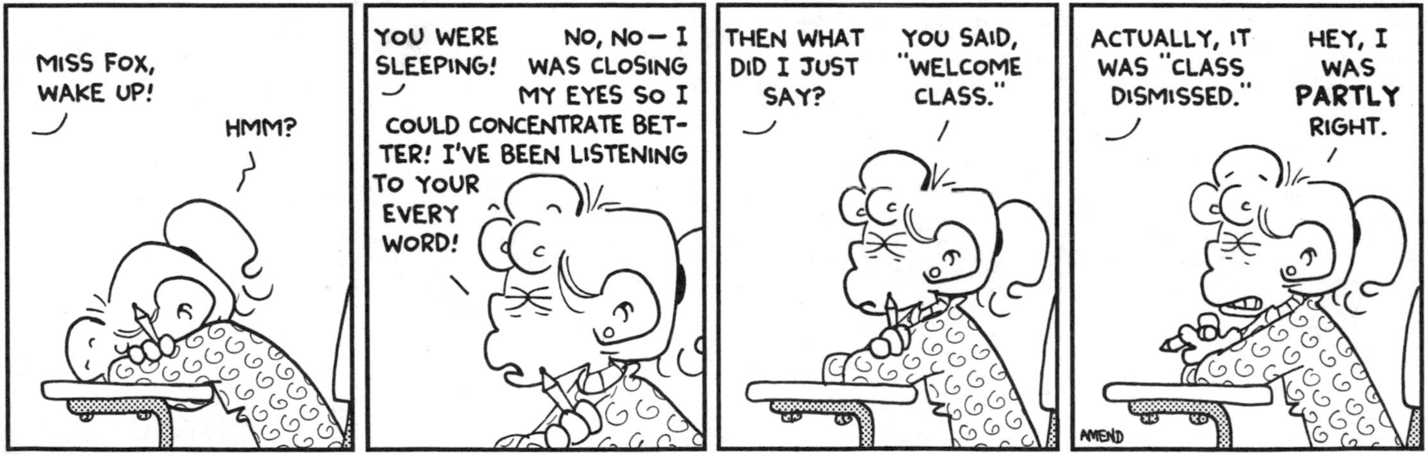
MISS FOX, WAKE UP!
HMM?
YOU WERE SLEEPING!
NO, NO — I WAS CLOSING MY EYES SO I COULD CONCENTRATE BETTER! I'VE BEEN LISTENING TO YOUR EVERY WORD!
THEN WHAT DID I JUST SAY?
YOU SAID, "WELCOME CLASS."
ACTUALLY, IT WAS "CLASS DISMISSED."
HEY, I WAS **PARTLY** RIGHT.
AMEND

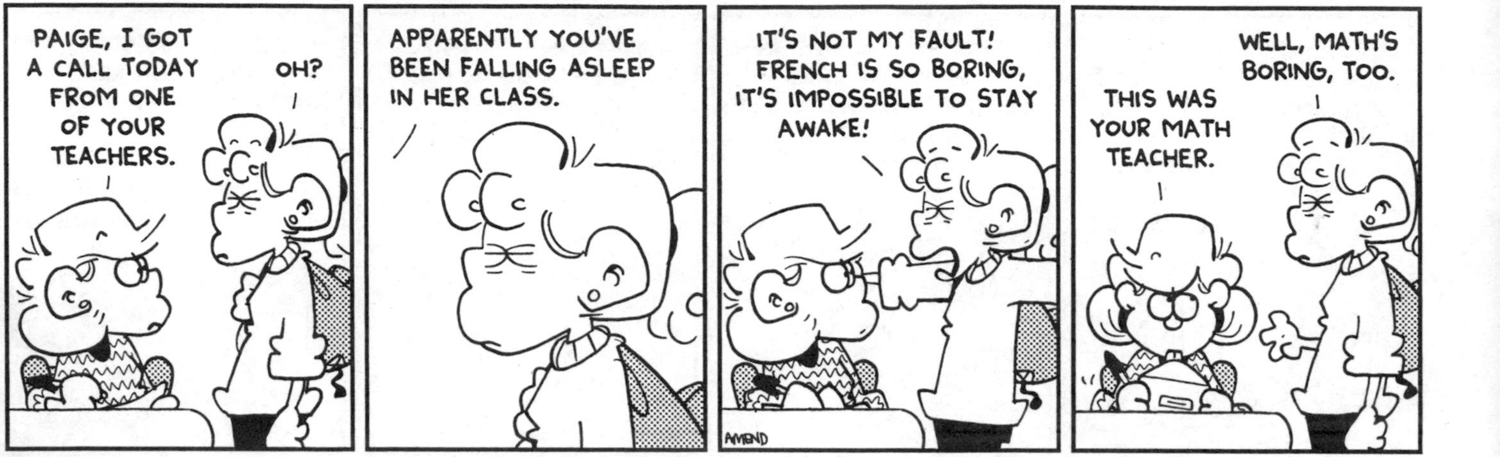
PAIGE, I GOT A CALL TODAY FROM ONE OF YOUR TEACHERS.
OH?
APPARENTLY YOU'VE BEEN FALLING ASLEEP IN HER CLASS.
IT'S NOT MY FAULT! FRENCH IS SO BORING, IT'S IMPOSSIBLE TO STAY AWAKE!
AMEND
THIS WAS YOUR MATH TEACHER.
WELL, MATH'S BORING, TOO.

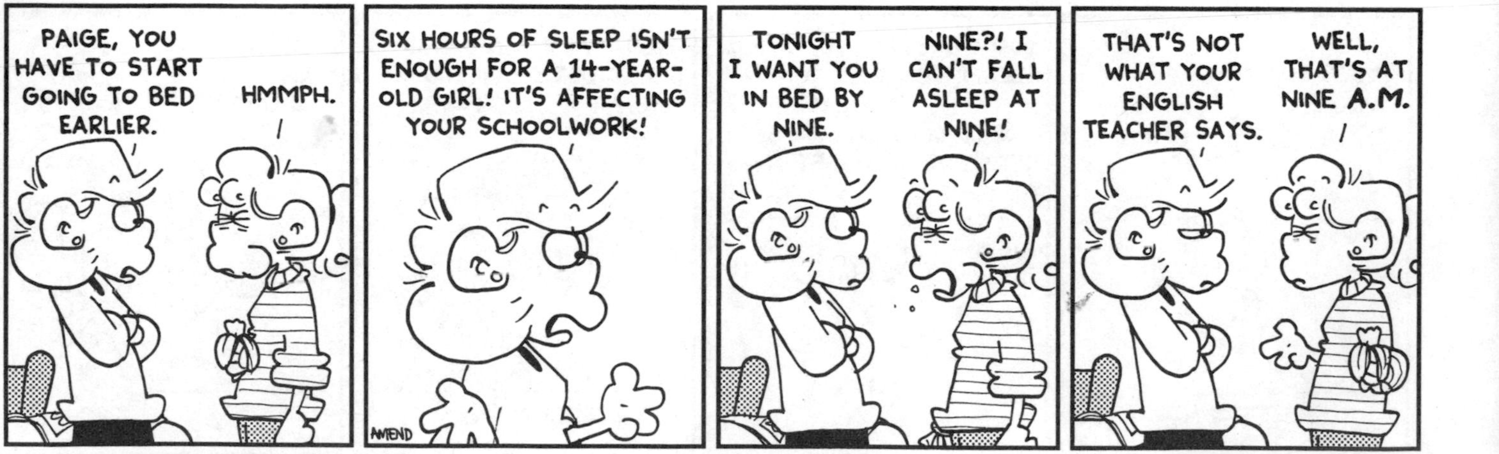
PAIGE, YOU HAVE TO START GOING TO BED EARLIER.
HMMPH.
SIX HOURS OF SLEEP ISN'T ENOUGH FOR A 14-YEAR-OLD GIRL! IT'S AFFECTING YOUR SCHOOLWORK!
AMEND
TONIGHT I WANT YOU IN BED BY NINE.
NINE?! I CAN'T FALL ASLEEP AT NINE!
THAT'S NOT WHAT YOUR ENGLISH TEACHER SAYS.
WELL, THAT'S AT NINE A.M.

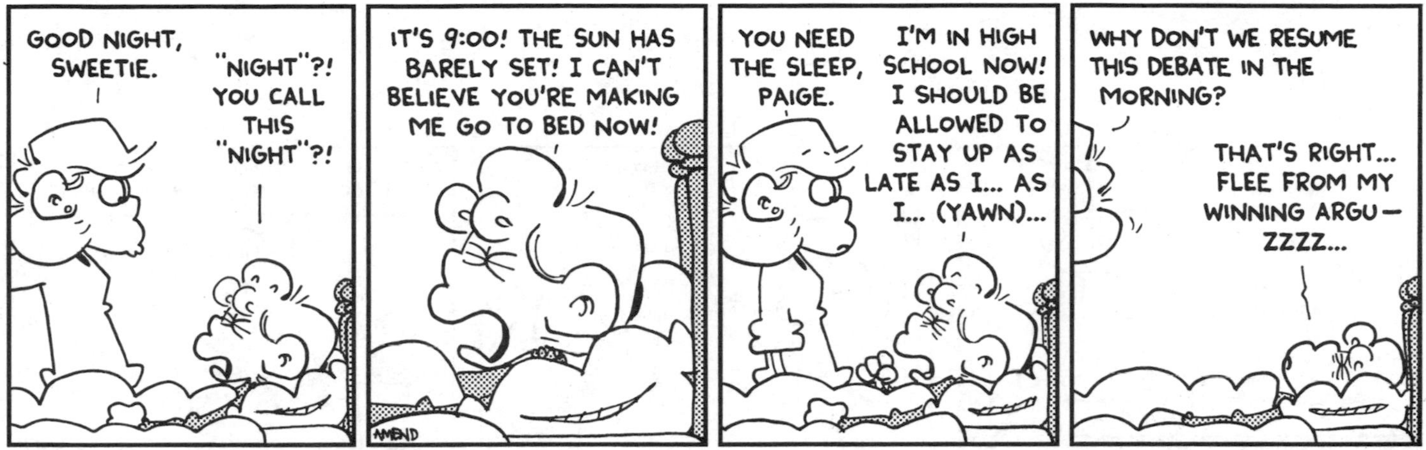
GOOD NIGHT, SWEETIE.
"NIGHT"?! YOU CALL THIS "NIGHT"?!
IT'S 9:00! THE SUN HAS BARELY SET! I CAN'T BELIEVE YOU'RE MAKING ME GO TO BED NOW!
AMEND
YOU NEED THE SLEEP, PAIGE.
I'M IN HIGH SCHOOL NOW! I SHOULD BE ALLOWED TO STAY UP AS LATE AS I... AS I... (YAWN)...
WHY DON'T WE RESUME THIS DEBATE IN THE MORNING?
THAT'S RIGHT... FLEE FROM MY WINNING ARGU— ZZZZ...

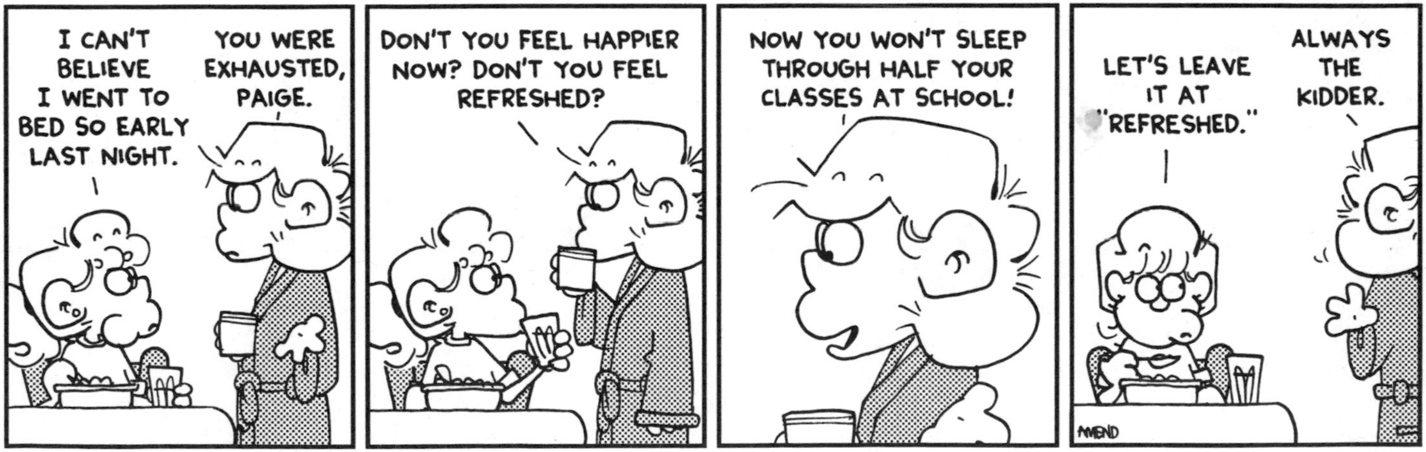
I CAN'T BELIEVE I WENT TO BED SO EARLY LAST NIGHT.
YOU WERE EXHAUSTED, PAIGE.
DON'T YOU FEEL HAPPIER NOW? DON'T YOU FEEL REFRESHED?
NOW YOU WON'T SLEEP THROUGH HALF YOUR CLASSES AT SCHOOL!
LET'S LEAVE IT AT "REFRESHED."
ALWAYS THE KIDDER.
AMEND

CAN OUR DAUGHTER SCREAM ANY LOUDER?
I'LL GO CHECK ON HER.
PAIGE, WHAT'S WRONG?
MY ENGLISH TEACHER IS A PSYCHO!
THE SCHOOL YEAR JUST STARTED AND HE'S ALREADY BURYING US IN HOMEWORK!
LOOK AT THIS ASSIGNMENT, MOTHER! LOOK AT IT!
YOU HAVE TO READ 70 PAGES BY TUESDAY. SO?
70? I THOUGHT IT SAID 10...
I GUESS SHE **CAN** SCREAM LOUDER.
HOW MANY MORE WEEKS UNTIL SUMMER?

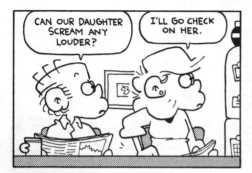

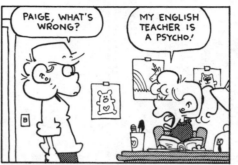

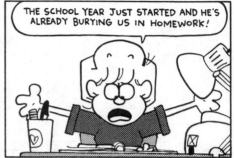

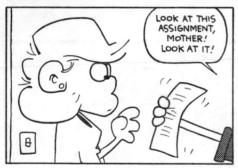

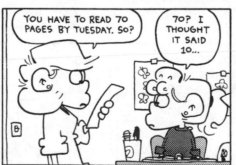

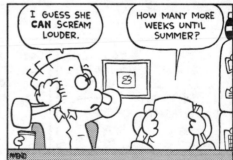

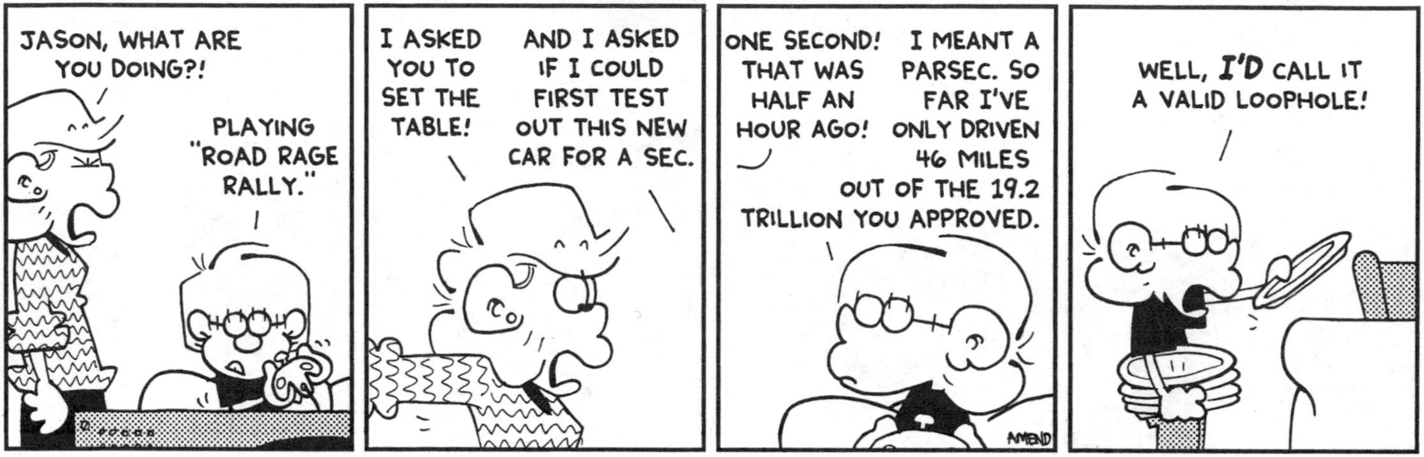
JASON, WHAT ARE YOU DOING?!
PLAYING "ROAD RAGE RALLY."
I ASKED YOU TO SET THE TABLE!
AND I ASKED IF I COULD FIRST TEST OUT THIS NEW CAR FOR A SEC.
ONE SECOND! THAT WAS HALF AN HOUR AGO!
I MEANT A PARSEC. SO FAR I'VE ONLY DRIVEN 46 MILES OUT OF THE 19.2 TRILLION YOU APPROVED.
AMEND
WELL, ***I'D*** CALL IT A VALID LOOPHOLE!

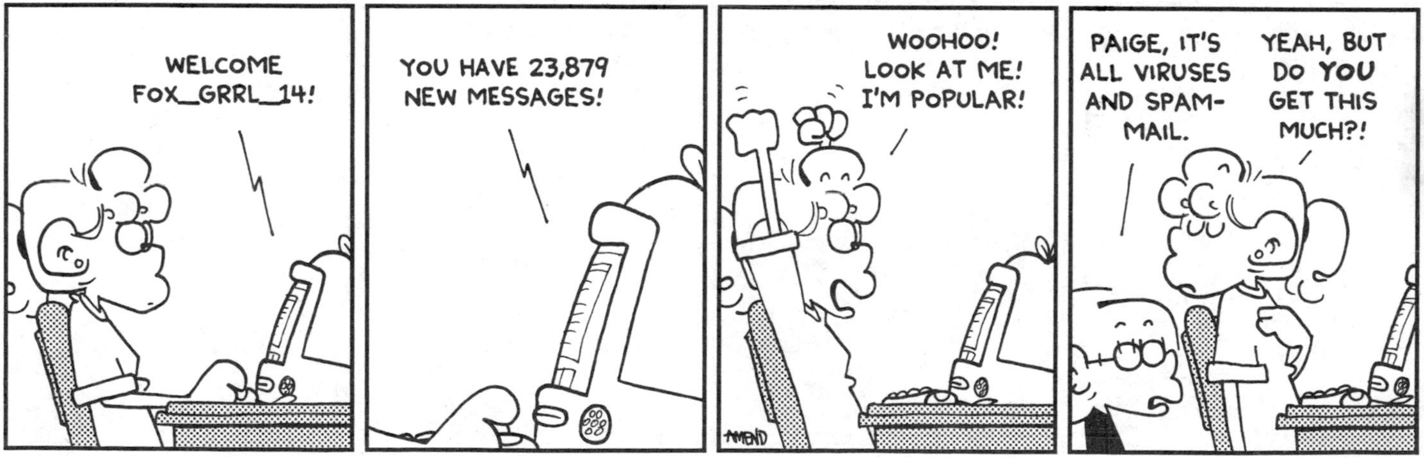
WELCOME FOX_GRRL_14!
YOU HAVE 23,879 NEW MESSAGES!
WOOHOO! LOOK AT ME! I'M POPULAR!
AMEND
PAIGE, IT'S ALL VIRUSES AND SPAM-MAIL.
YEAH, BUT DO ***YOU*** GET THIS MUCH?!

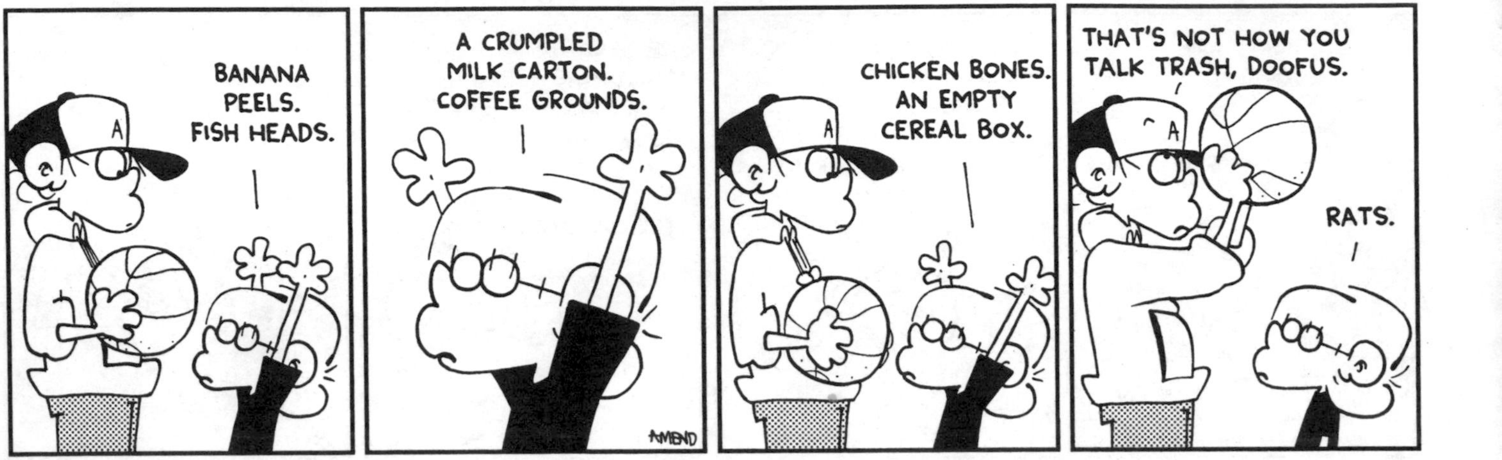
BANANA PEELS. FISH HEADS.
A CRUMPLED MILK CARTON. COFFEE GROUNDS.
AMEND
CHICKEN BONES. AN EMPTY CEREAL BOX.
THAT'S NOT HOW YOU TALK TRASH, DOOFUS.
RATS.

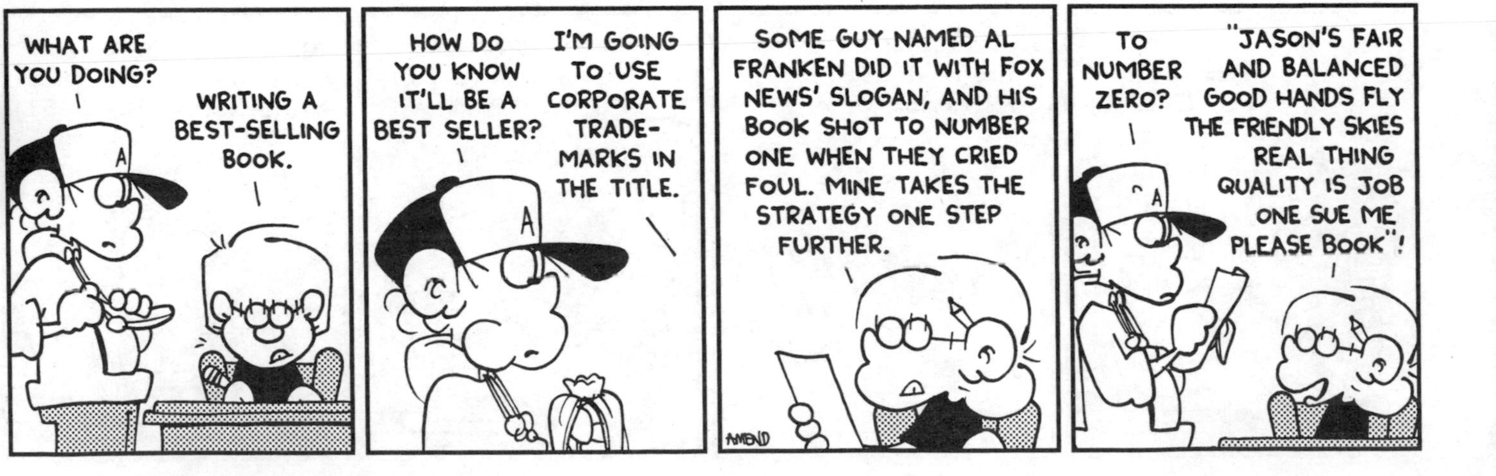
WHAT ARE YOU DOING?
WRITING A BEST-SELLING BOOK.
HOW DO YOU KNOW IT'LL BE A BEST SELLER?
I'M GOING TO USE CORPORATE TRADE-MARKS IN THE TITLE.
SOME GUY NAMED AL FRANKEN DID IT WITH FOX NEWS' SLOGAN, AND HIS BOOK SHOT TO NUMBER ONE WHEN THEY CRIED FOUL. MINE TAKES THE STRATEGY ONE STEP FURTHER.
AMEND
TO NUMBER ZERO?
"JASON'S FAIR AND BALANCED GOOD HANDS FLY THE FRIENDLY SKIES REAL THING QUALITY IS JOB ONE SUE ME PLEASE BOOK"!

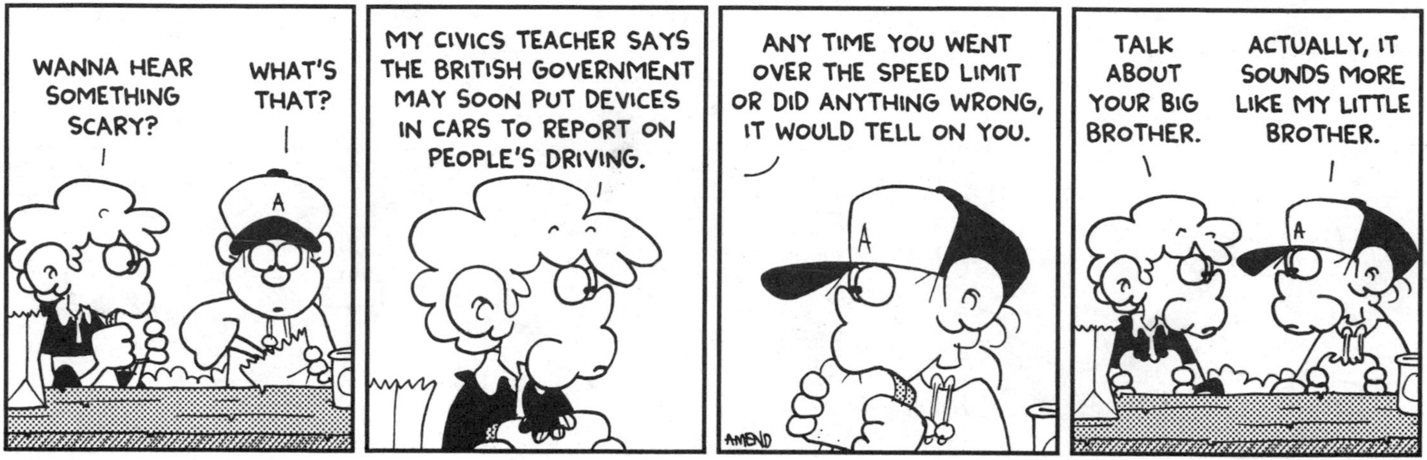
WANNA HEAR SOMETHING SCARY?
WHAT'S THAT?
MY CIVICS TEACHER SAYS THE BRITISH GOVERNMENT MAY SOON PUT DEVICES IN CARS TO REPORT ON PEOPLE'S DRIVING.
ANY TIME YOU WENT OVER THE SPEED LIMIT OR DID ANYTHING WRONG, IT WOULD TELL ON YOU.
AMEND
TALK ABOUT YOUR BIG BROTHER.
ACTUALLY, IT SOUNDS MORE LIKE MY LITTLE BROTHER.

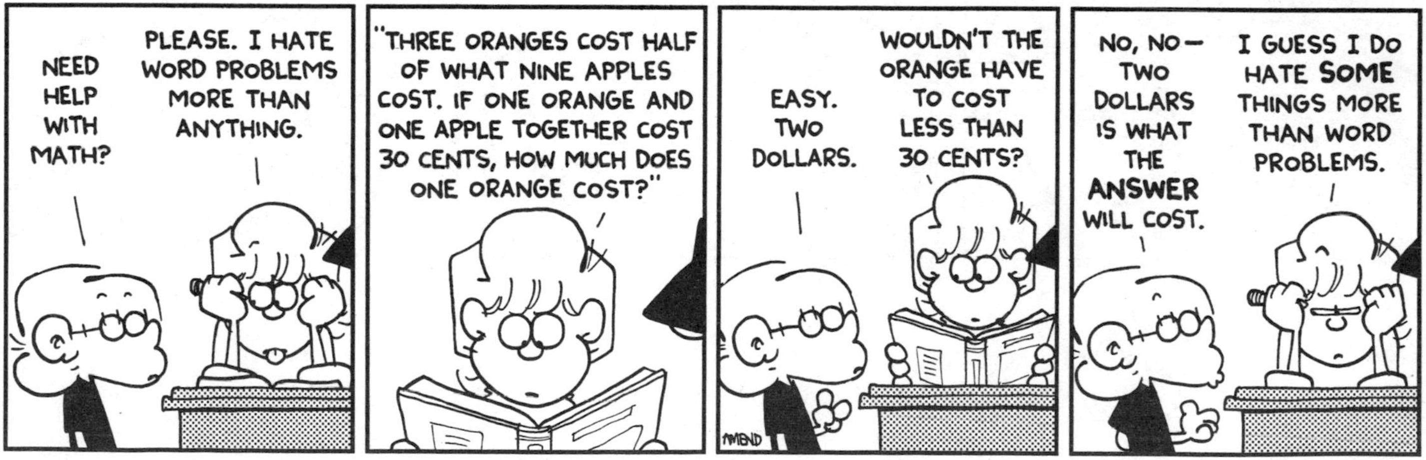
NEED HELP WITH MATH?
PLEASE. I HATE WORD PROBLEMS MORE THAN ANYTHING.
"THREE ORANGES COST HALF OF WHAT NINE APPLES COST. IF ONE ORANGE AND ONE APPLE TOGETHER COST 30 CENTS, HOW MUCH DOES ONE ORANGE COST?"
EASY. TWO DOLLARS.
WOULDN'T THE ORANGE HAVE TO COST LESS THAN 30 CENTS?
AMEND
NO, NO— TWO DOLLARS IS WHAT THE **ANSWER** WILL COST.
I GUESS I DO HATE **SOME** THINGS MORE THAN WORD PROBLEMS.

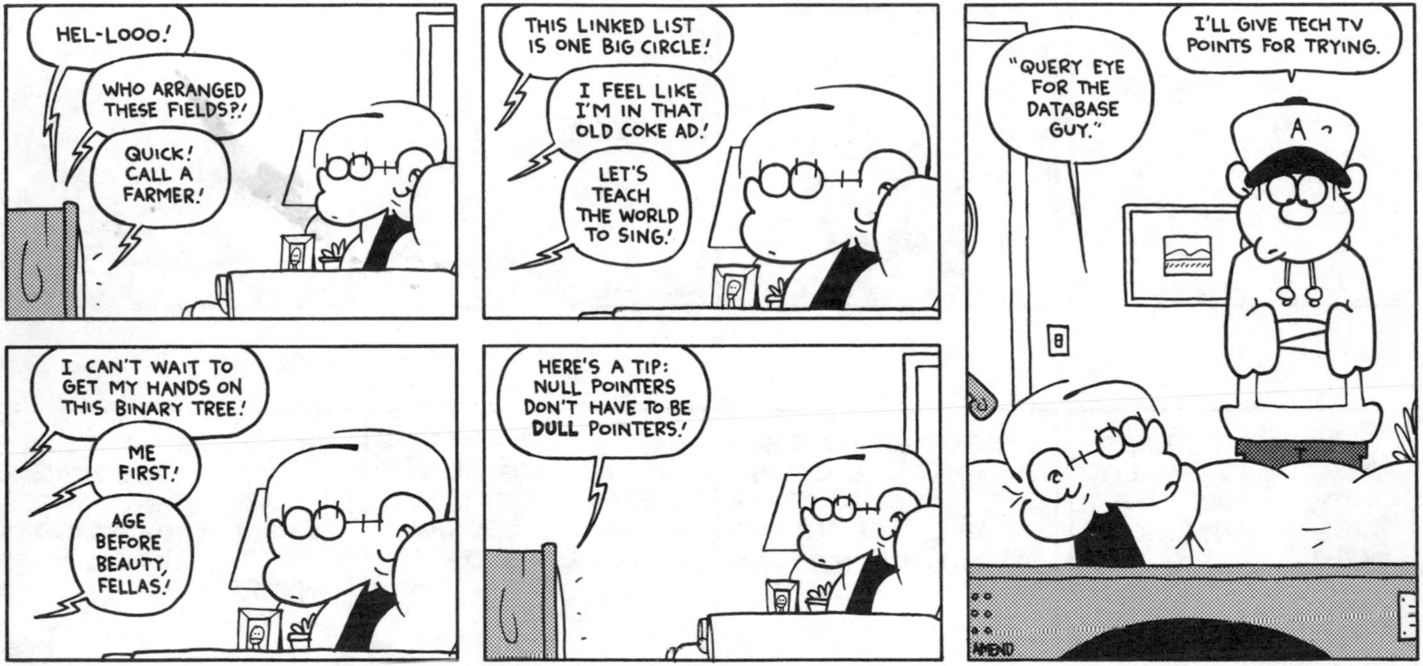
HEL-LOOO!
WHO ARRANGED THESE FIELDS?!
QUICK! CALL A FARMER!
THIS LINKED LIST IS ONE BIG CIRCLE!
I FEEL LIKE I'M IN THAT OLD COKE AD!
LET'S TEACH THE WORLD TO SING!
I CAN'T WAIT TO GET MY HANDS ON THIS BINARY TREE!
ME FIRST!
AGE BEFORE BEAUTY, FELLAS!
HERE'S A TIP: NULL POINTERS DON'T HAVE TO BE DULL POINTERS!
"QUERY EYE FOR THE DATABASE GUY."
I'LL GIVE TECH TV POINTS FOR TRYING.
AMEND

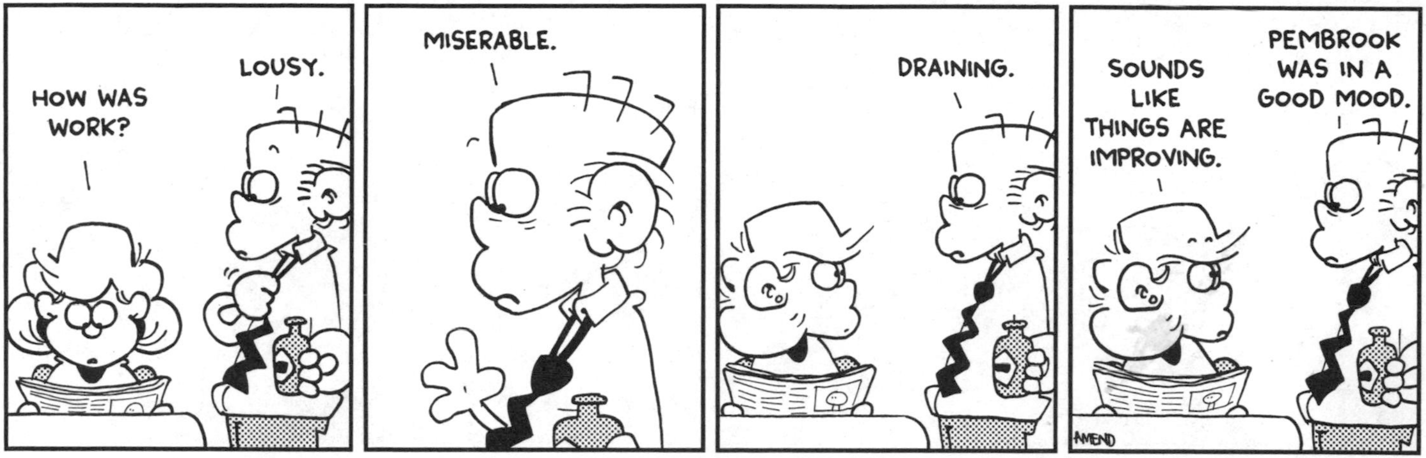
HOW WAS WORK?
LOUSY.
MISERABLE.
DRAINING.
SOUNDS LIKE THINGS ARE IMPROVING.
PEMBROOK WAS IN A GOOD MOOD.
AMEND

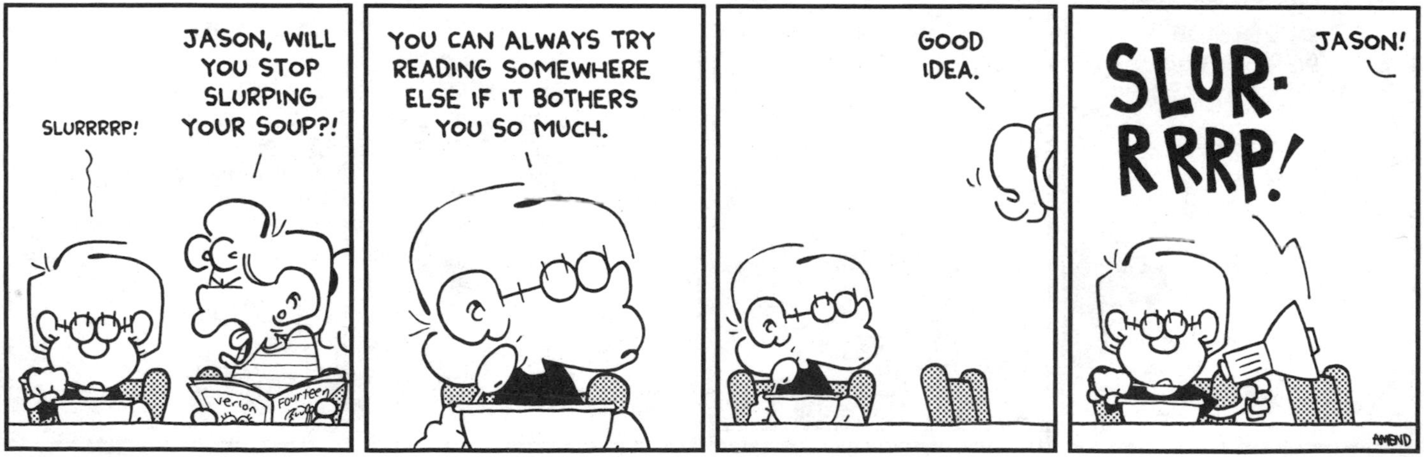
SLURRRRP!
JASON, WILL YOU STOP SLURPING YOUR SOUP?!
YOU CAN ALWAYS TRY READING SOMEWHERE ELSE IF IT BOTHERS YOU SO MUCH.
GOOD IDEA.
SLUR-RRRP!
JASON!
AMEND

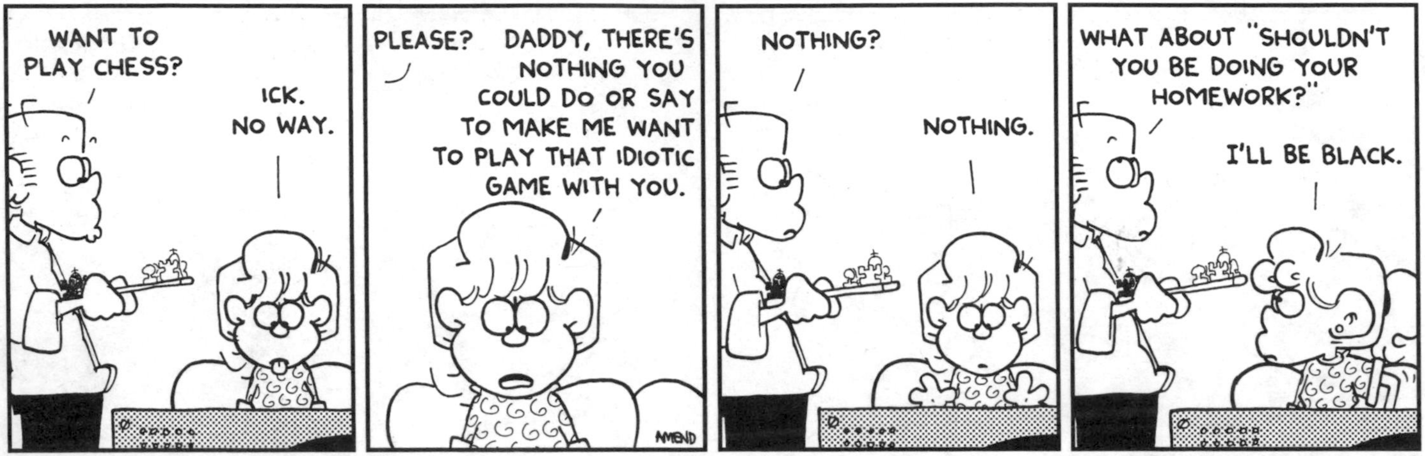
WANT TO PLAY CHESS?
ICK. NO WAY.
PLEASE?
DADDY, THERE'S NOTHING YOU COULD DO OR SAY TO MAKE ME WANT TO PLAY THAT IDIOTIC GAME WITH YOU.
AMEND
NOTHING?
NOTHING.
WHAT ABOUT "SHOULDN'T YOU BE DOING YOUR HOMEWORK?"
I'LL BE BLACK.

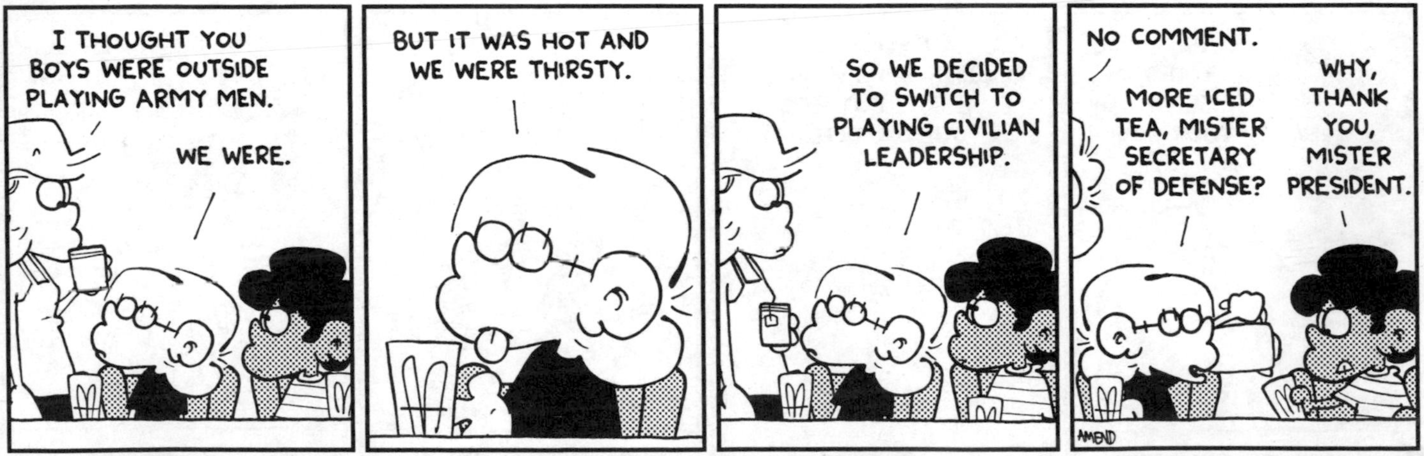
I THOUGHT YOU BOYS WERE OUTSIDE PLAYING ARMY MEN.
WE WERE.
BUT IT WAS HOT AND WE WERE THIRSTY.
SO WE DECIDED TO SWITCH TO PLAYING CIVILIAN LEADERSHIP.
NO COMMENT.
MORE ICED TEA, MISTER SECRETARY OF DEFENSE?
WHY, THANK YOU, MISTER PRESIDENT.
AMEND

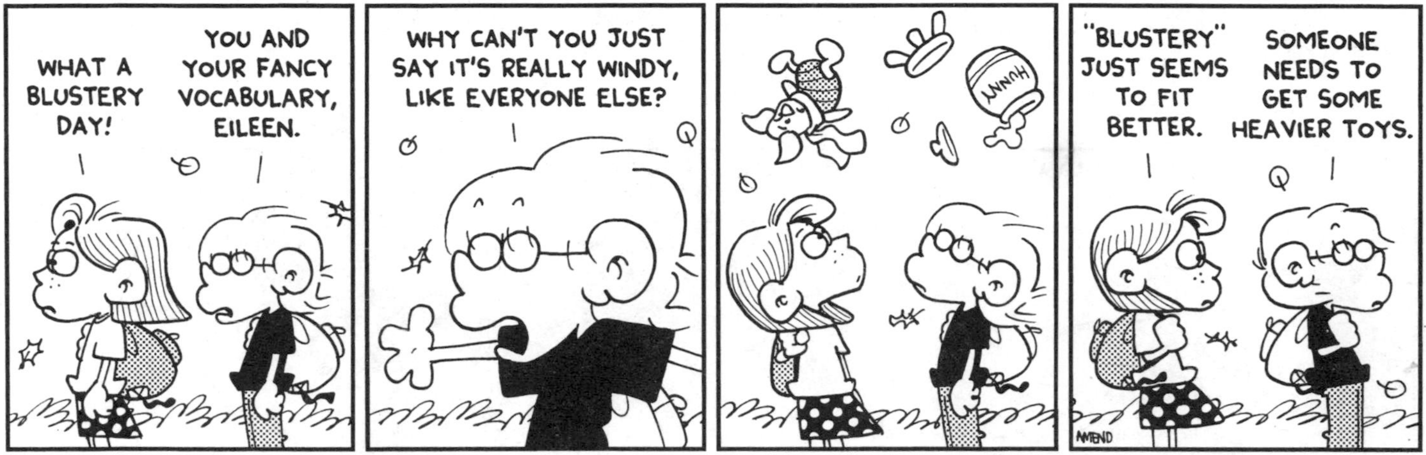
WHAT A BLUSTERY DAY!
YOU AND YOUR FANCY VOCABULARY, EILEEN.
WHY CAN'T YOU JUST SAY IT'S REALLY WINDY, LIKE EVERYONE ELSE?
"BLUSTERY" JUST SEEMS TO FIT BETTER.
SOMEONE NEEDS TO GET SOME HEAVIER TOYS.
AMEND

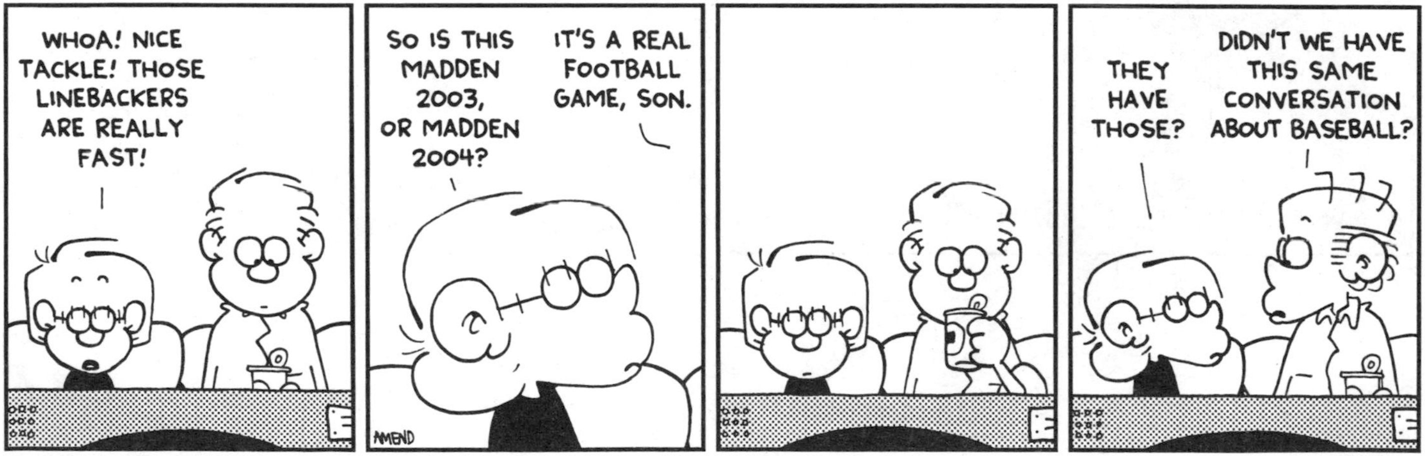
WHOA! NICE TACKLE! THOSE LINEBACKERS ARE REALLY FAST!
SO IS THIS MADDEN 2003, OR MADDEN 2004?
IT'S A REAL FOOTBALL GAME, SON.
AMEND
THEY HAVE THOSE?
DIDN'T WE HAVE THIS SAME CONVERSATION ABOUT BASEBALL?

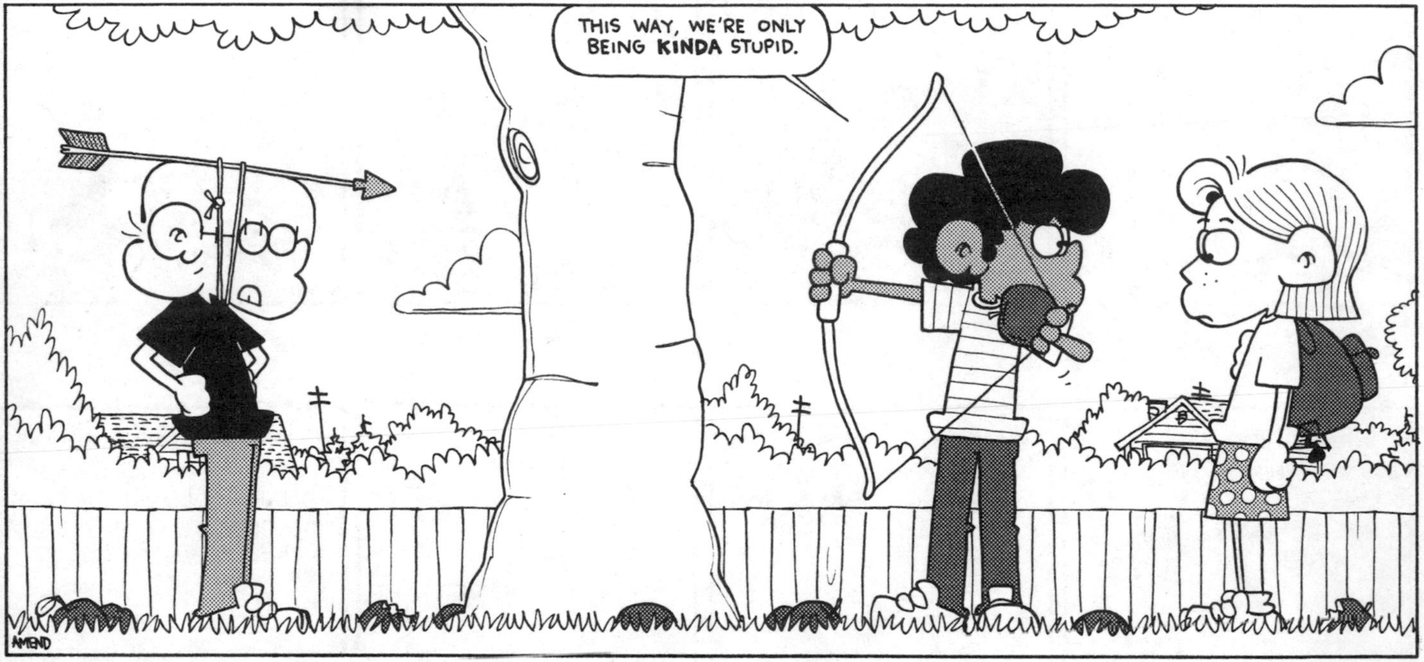
THIS WAY, WE'RE ONLY BEING KINDA STUPID.
AMEND

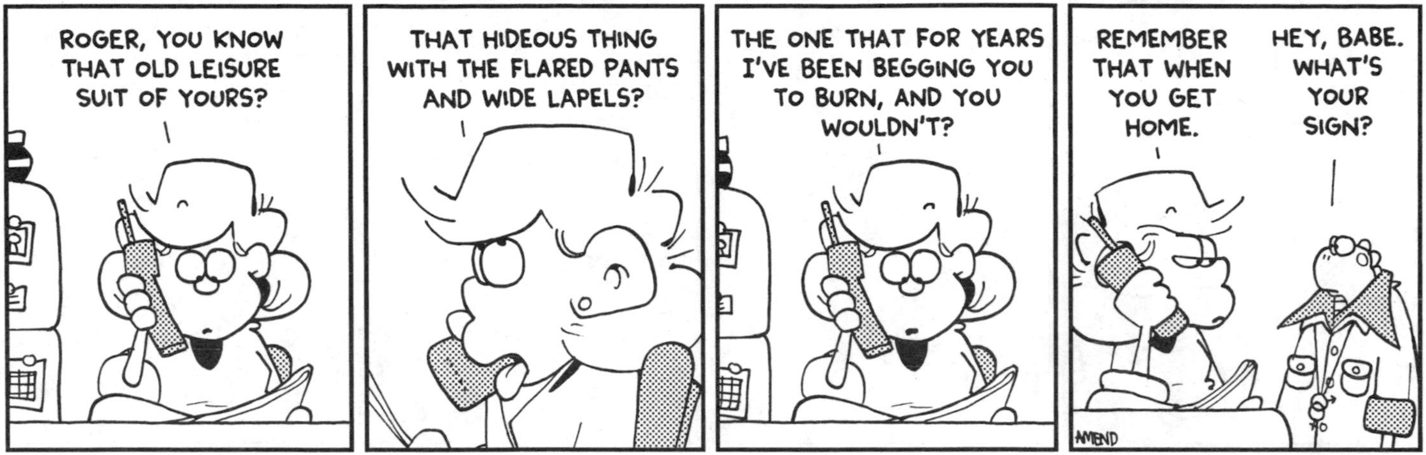
ROGER, YOU KNOW THAT OLD LEISURE SUIT OF YOURS?
THAT HIDEOUS THING WITH THE FLARED PANTS AND WIDE LAPELS?
THE ONE THAT FOR YEARS I'VE BEEN BEGGING YOU TO BURN, AND YOU WOULDN'T?
REMEMBER THAT WHEN YOU GET HOME.
HEY, BABE. WHAT'S YOUR SIGN?
AMEND

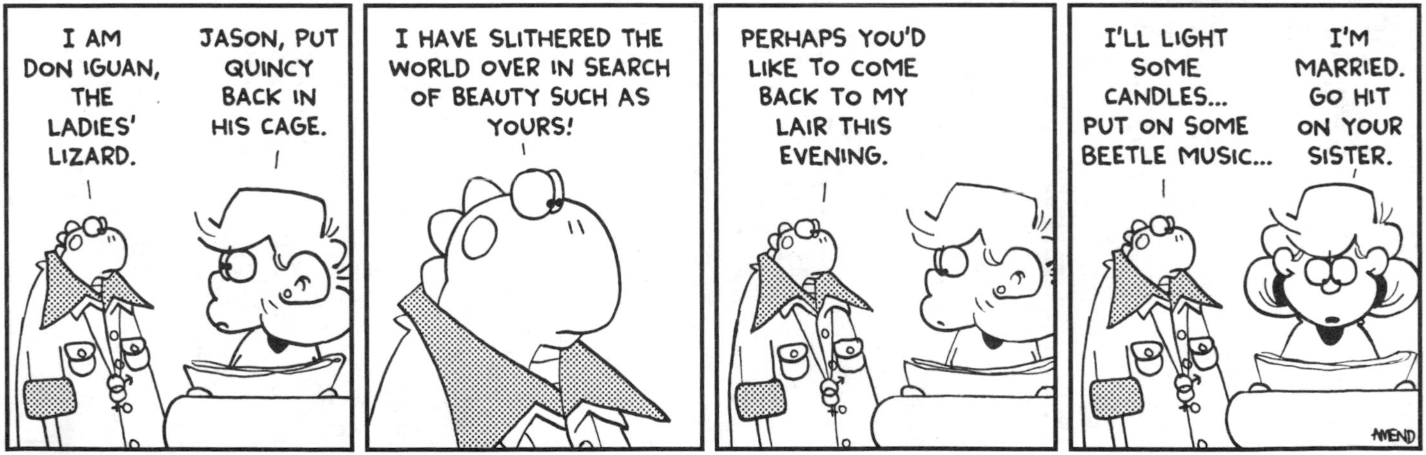
I AM DON IGUAN, THE LADIES' LIZARD.
JASON, PUT QUINCY BACK IN HIS CAGE.
I HAVE SLITHERED THE WORLD OVER IN SEARCH OF BEAUTY SUCH AS YOURS!
PERHAPS YOU'D LIKE TO COME BACK TO MY LAIR THIS EVENING.
I'LL LIGHT SOME CANDLES... PUT ON SOME BEETLE MUSIC...
I'M MARRIED. GO HIT ON YOUR SISTER.
AMEND

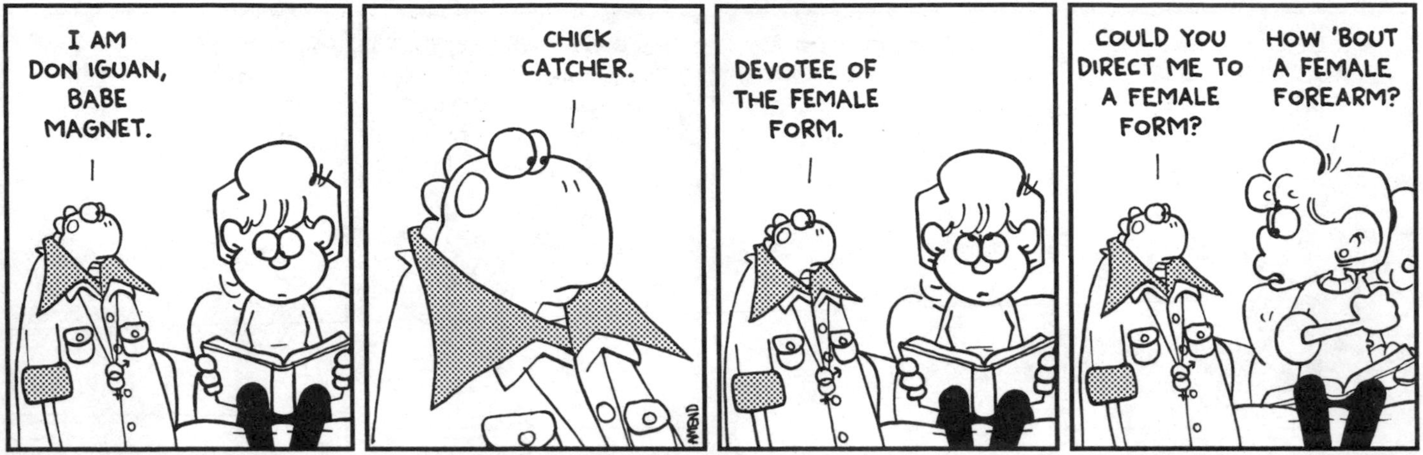
I AM DON IGUAN, BABE MAGNET.
CHICK CATCHER.
DEVOTEE OF THE FEMALE FORM.
COULD YOU DIRECT ME TO A FEMALE FORM?
HOW 'BOUT A FEMALE FOREARM?
AMEND

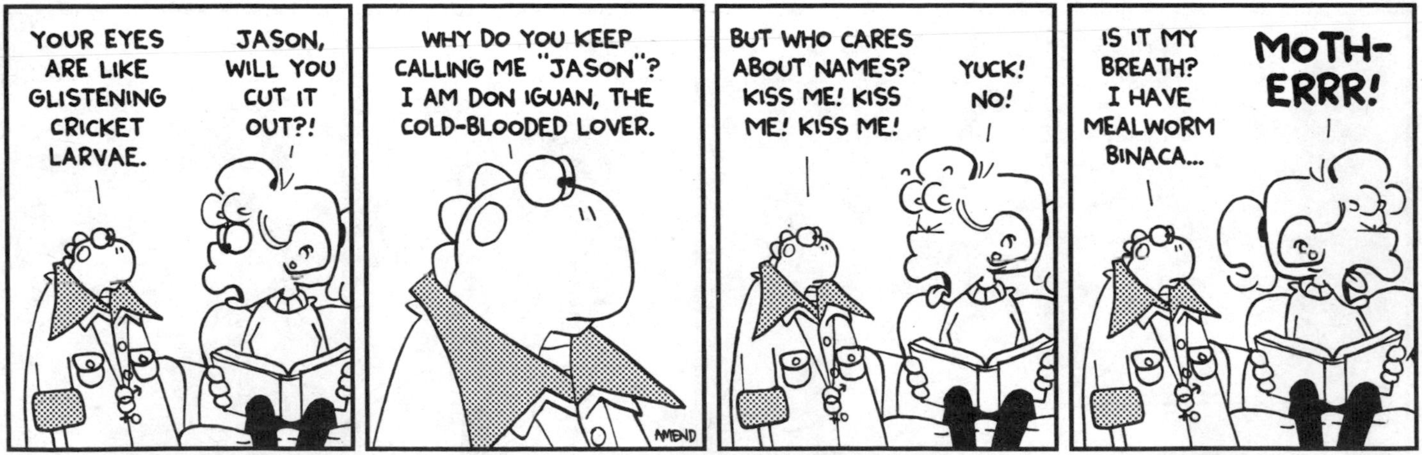
YOUR EYES ARE LIKE GLISTENING CRICKET LARVAE.
JASON, WILL YOU CUT IT OUT?!
WHY DO YOU KEEP CALLING ME "JASON"? I AM DON IGUAN, THE COLD-BLOODED LOVER.
AMEND
BUT WHO CARES ABOUT NAMES? KISS ME! KISS ME! KISS ME!
YUCK! NO!
IS IT MY BREATH? I HAVE MEALWORM BINACA...
MOTH-ERRR!

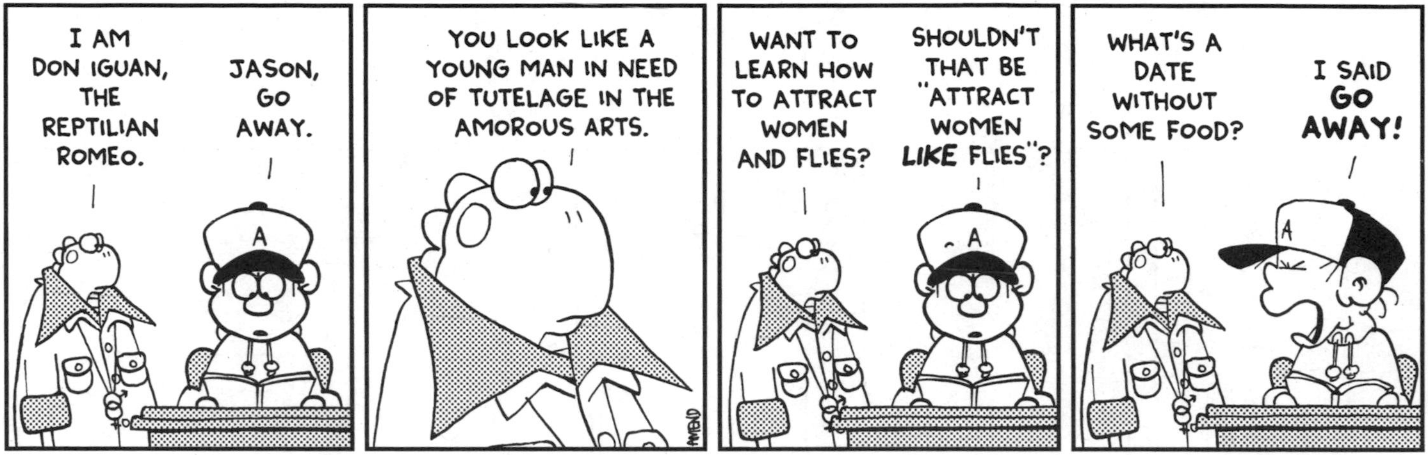
I AM DON IGUAN, THE REPTILIAN ROMEO.
JASON, GO AWAY.
YOU LOOK LIKE A YOUNG MAN IN NEED OF TUTELAGE IN THE AMOROUS ARTS.
WANT TO LEARN HOW TO ATTRACT WOMEN AND FLIES?
SHOULDN'T THAT BE "ATTRACT WOMEN **LIKE** FLIES"?
WHAT'S A DATE WITHOUT SOME FOOD?
I SAID **GO AWAY!**
AMEND

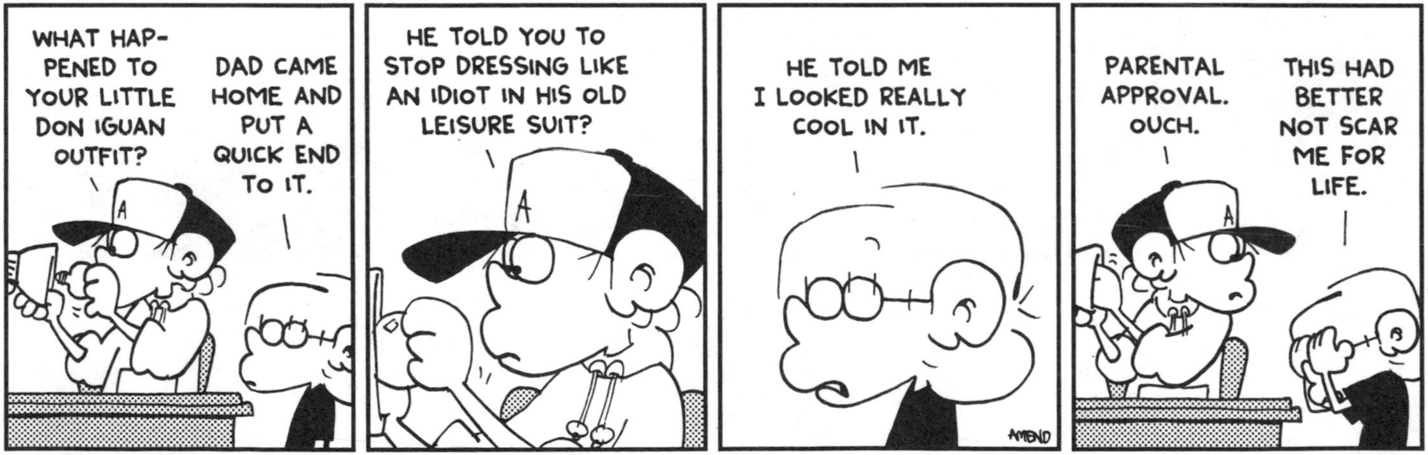
WHAT HAP-PENED TO YOUR LITTLE DON IGUAN OUTFIT?
DAD CAME HOME AND PUT A QUICK END TO IT.
HE TOLD YOU TO STOP DRESSING LIKE AN IDIOT IN HIS OLD LEISURE SUIT?
HE TOLD ME I LOOKED REALLY COOL IN IT.
PARENTAL APPROVAL. OUCH.
THIS HAD BETTER NOT SCAR ME FOR LIFE.
AMEND

TEEN
AMEND
I HAVE MY FIRST GEOMETRY TEST TOMORROW.
DAMOCLES MEETS ISOSCELES. I'VE BEEN THERE.
MR. CHIPS

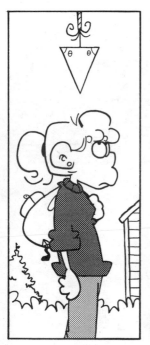

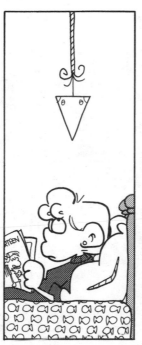

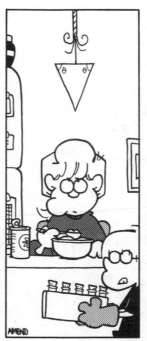

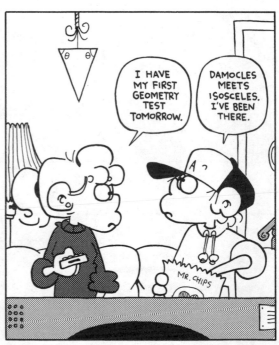

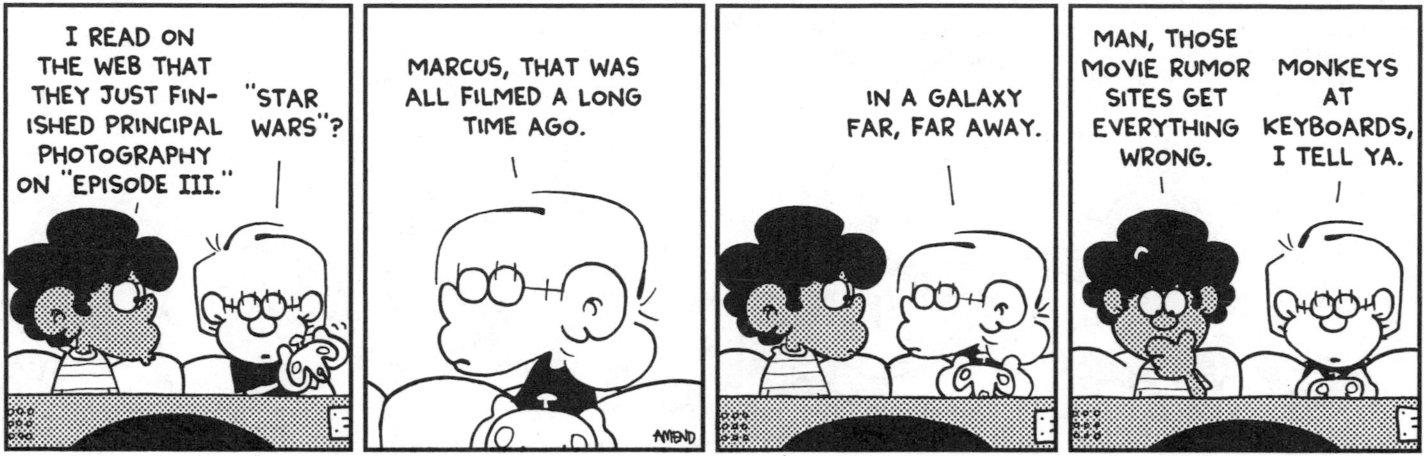
I READ ON THE WEB THAT THEY JUST FIN-ISHED PRINCIPAL PHOTOGRAPHY ON "EPISODE III."
"STAR WARS"?
MARCUS, THAT WAS ALL FILMED A LONG TIME AGO.
AMEND
IN A GALAXY FAR, FAR AWAY.
MAN, THOSE MOVIE RUMOR SITES GET EVERYTHING WRONG.
MONKEYS AT KEYBOARDS, I TELL YA.

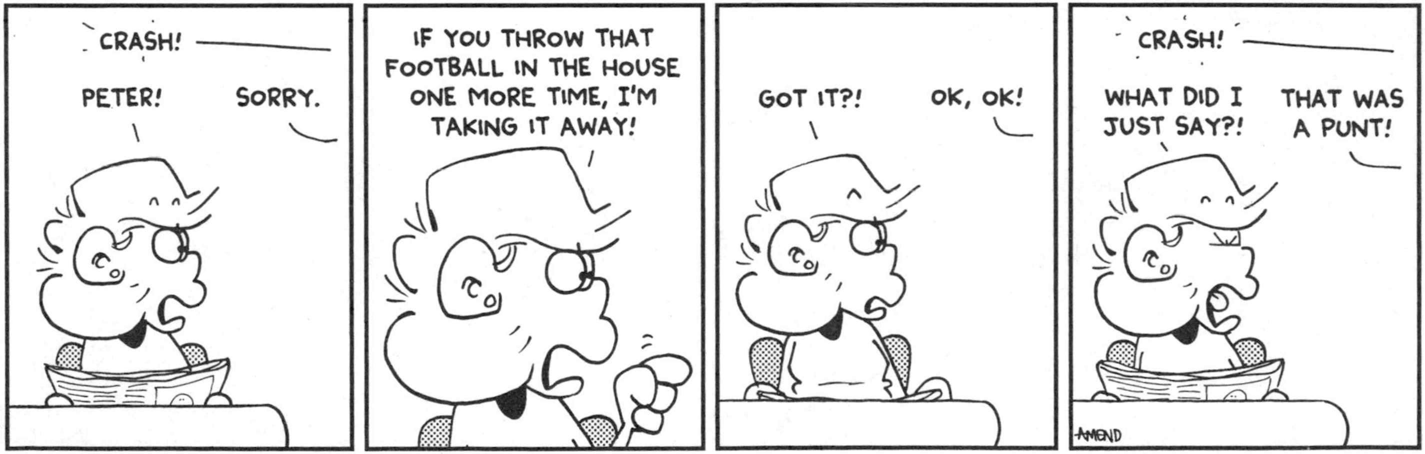
CRASH!
PETER!
SORRY.
IF YOU THROW THAT FOOTBALL IN THE HOUSE ONE MORE TIME, I'M TAKING IT AWAY!
GOT IT?!
OK, OK!
CRASH!
WHAT DID I JUST SAY?!
THAT WAS A PUNT!
AMEND

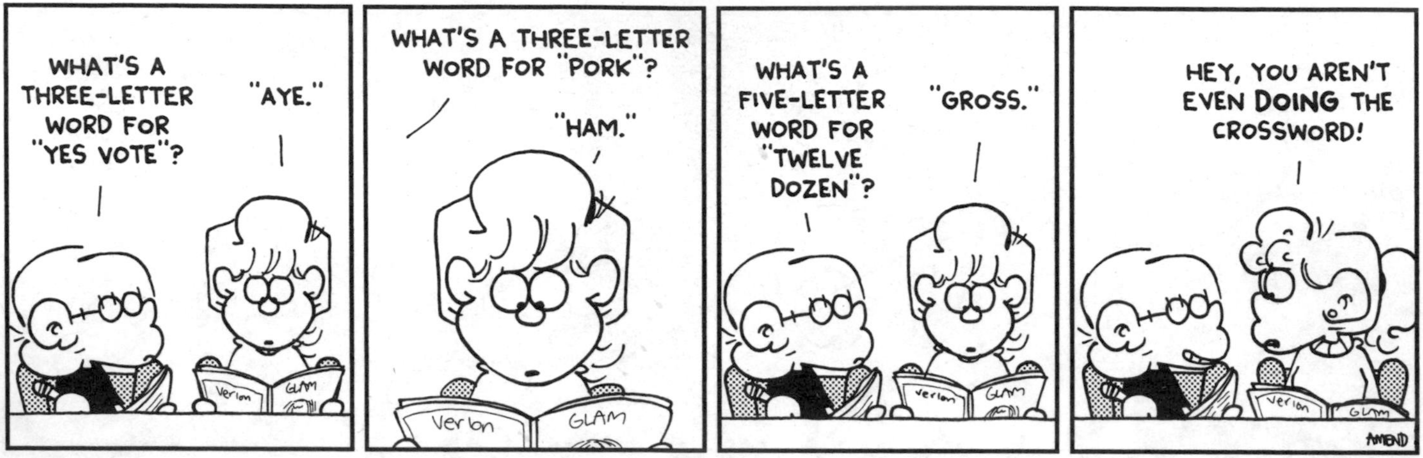
WHAT'S A THREE-LETTER WORD FOR "YES VOTE"?
"AYE."
WHAT'S A THREE-LETTER WORD FOR "PORK"?
"HAM."
WHAT'S A FIVE-LETTER WORD FOR "TWELVE DOZEN"?
"GROSS."
HEY, YOU AREN'T EVEN DOING THE CROSSWORD!

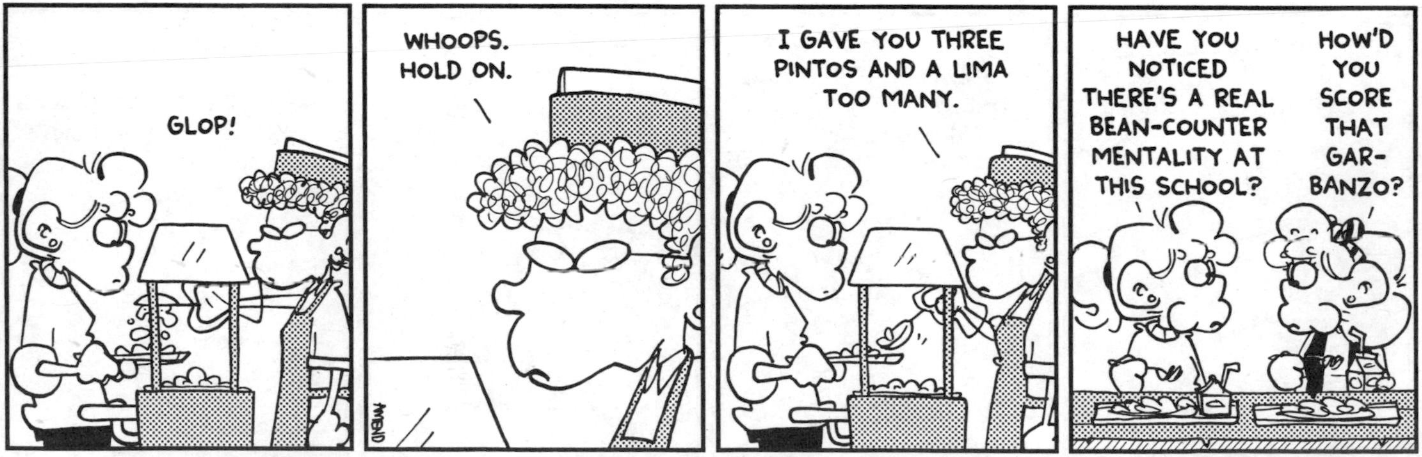
GLOP!
WHOOPS. HOLD ON.
I GAVE YOU THREE PINTOS AND A LIMA TOO MANY.
HAVE YOU NOTICED THERE'S A REAL BEAN-COUNTER MENTALITY AT THIS SCHOOL?
HOW'D YOU SCORE THAT GAR-BANZO?

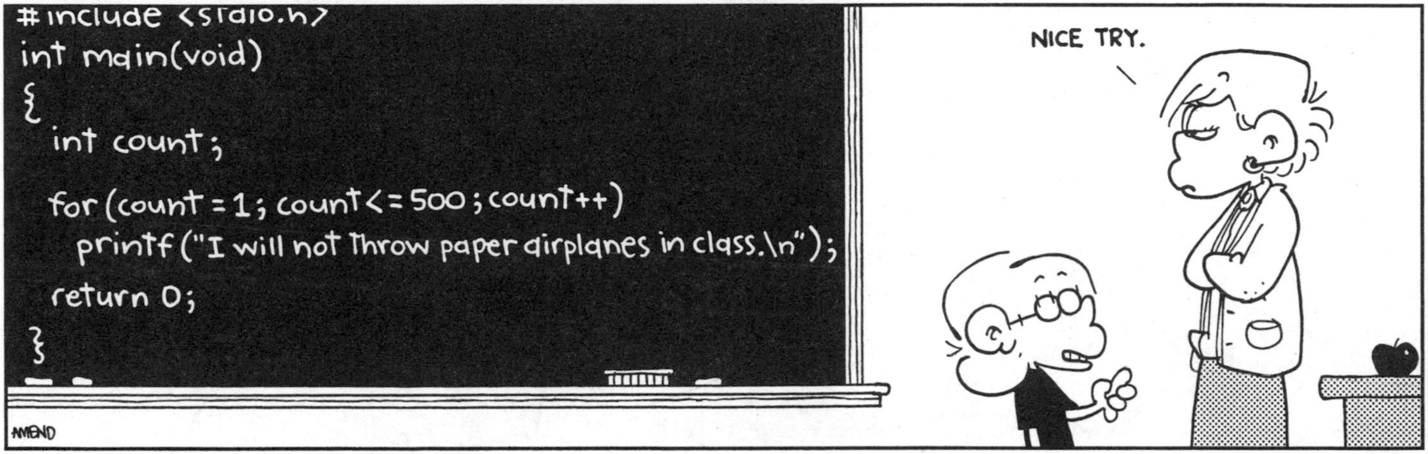
#include <stdio.h>
int main(void)
{
int count;
for (count = 1; count<=500; count++)
printf("I will not throw paper airplanes in class.\n");
return 0;
}
AMEND
NICE TRY.

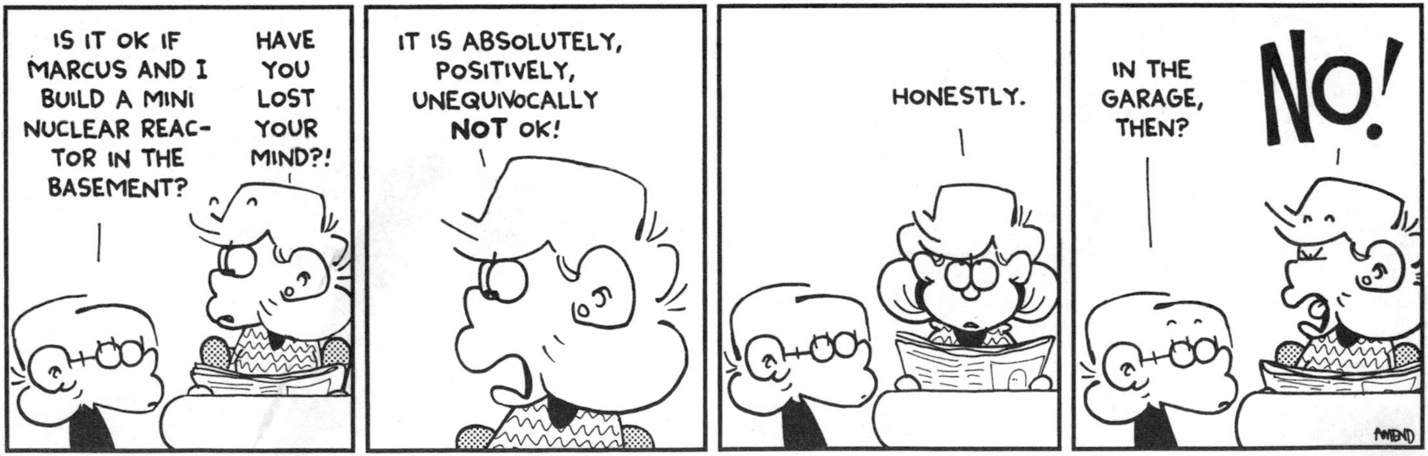
IS IT OK IF MARCUS AND I BUILD A MINI NUCLEAR REACTOR IN THE BASEMENT?
HAVE YOU LOST YOUR MIND?!
IT IS ABSOLUTELY, POSITIVELY, UNEQUIVOCALLY **NOT** OK!
HONESTLY.
IN THE GARAGE, THEN?
NO!
AMEND

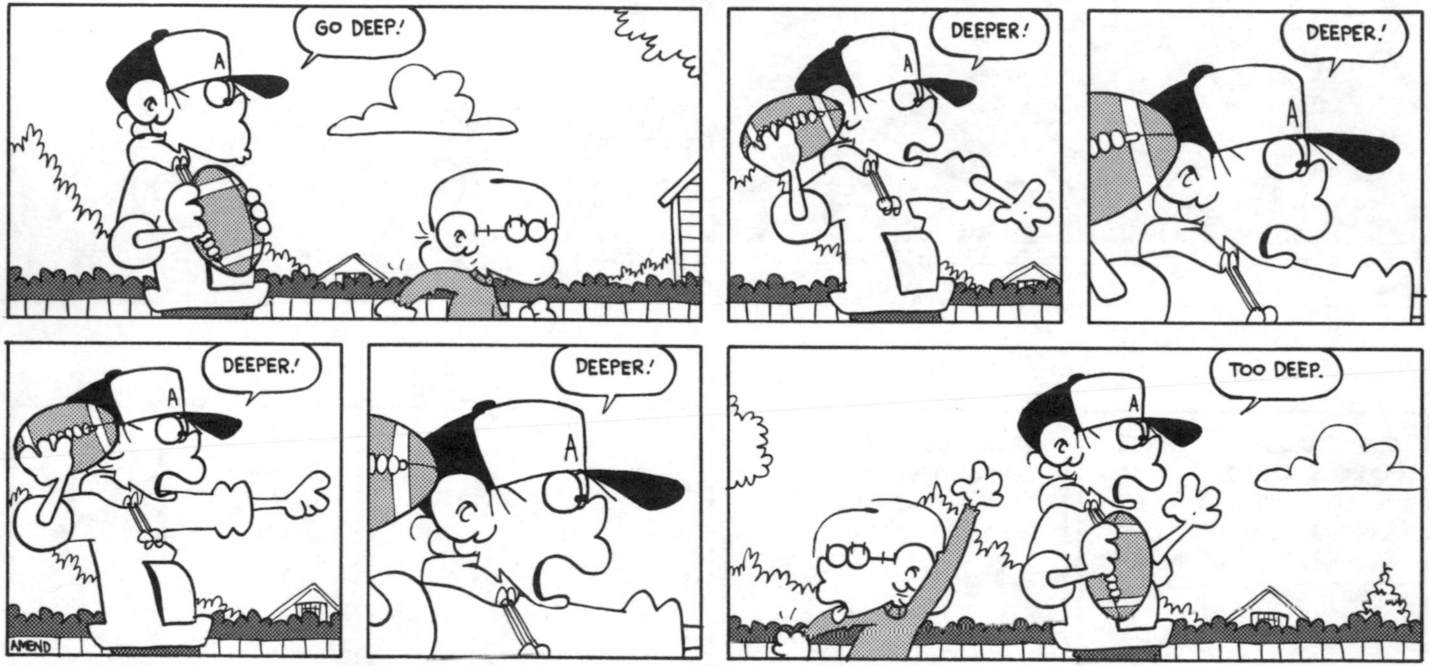
GO DEEP!
DEEPER!
DEEPER!
DEEPER!
DEEPER!
TOO DEEP.
AMEND

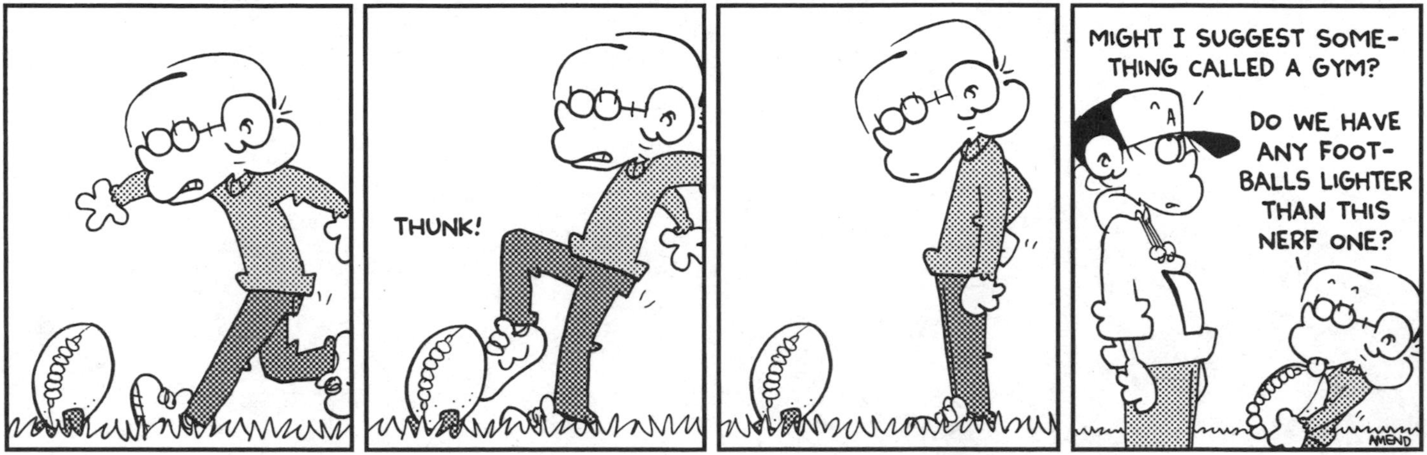
THUNK!
MIGHT I SUGGEST SOME-THING CALLED A GYM?
DO WE HAVE ANY FOOT-BALLS LIGHTER THAN THIS NERF ONE?
AMEND

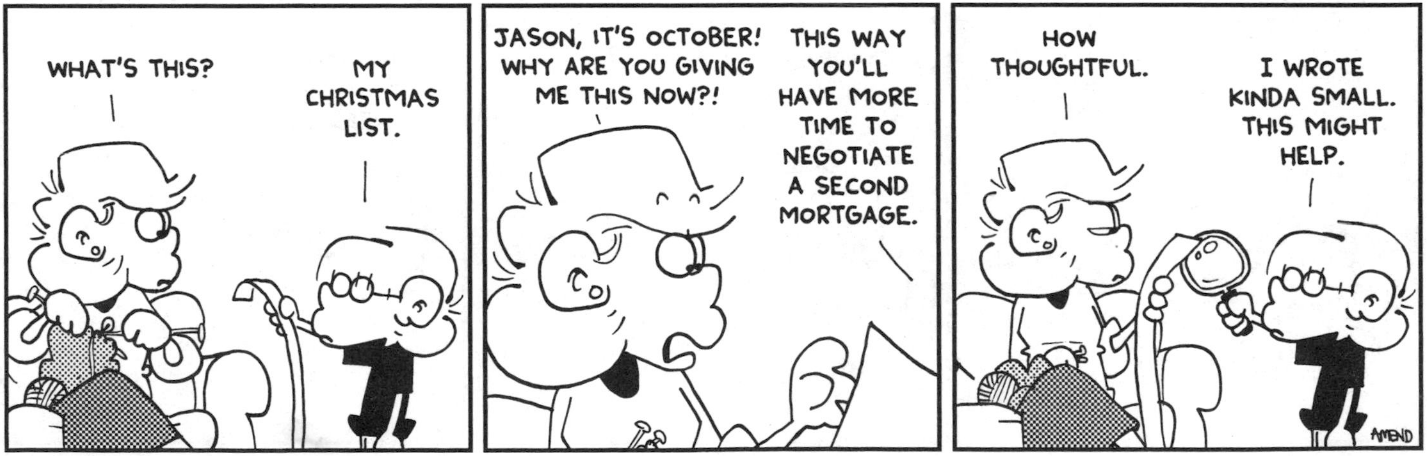
WHAT'S THIS?
MY CHRISTMAS LIST.
JASON, IT'S OCTOBER! WHY ARE YOU GIVING ME THIS NOW?!
THIS WAY YOU'LL HAVE MORE TIME TO NEGOTIATE A SECOND MORTGAGE.
HOW THOUGHTFUL.
I WROTE KINDA SMALL. THIS MIGHT HELP.
AMEND

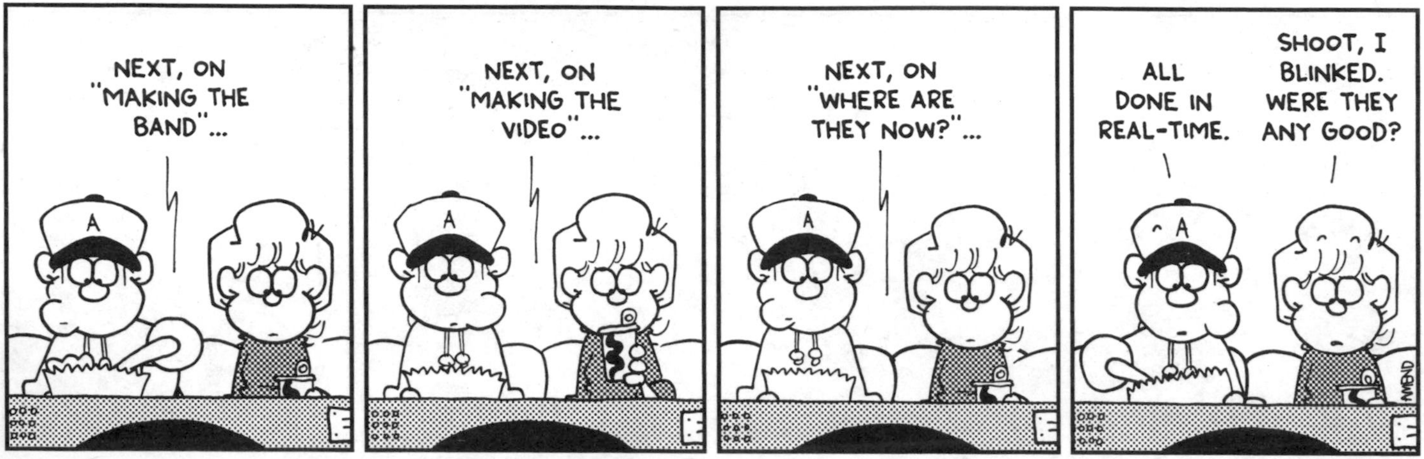
NEXT, ON "MAKING THE BAND"...
NEXT, ON "MAKING THE VIDEO"...
NEXT, ON "WHERE ARE THEY NOW?"...
ALL DONE IN REAL-TIME.
SHOOT, I BLINKED. WERE THEY ANY GOOD?
AMEND

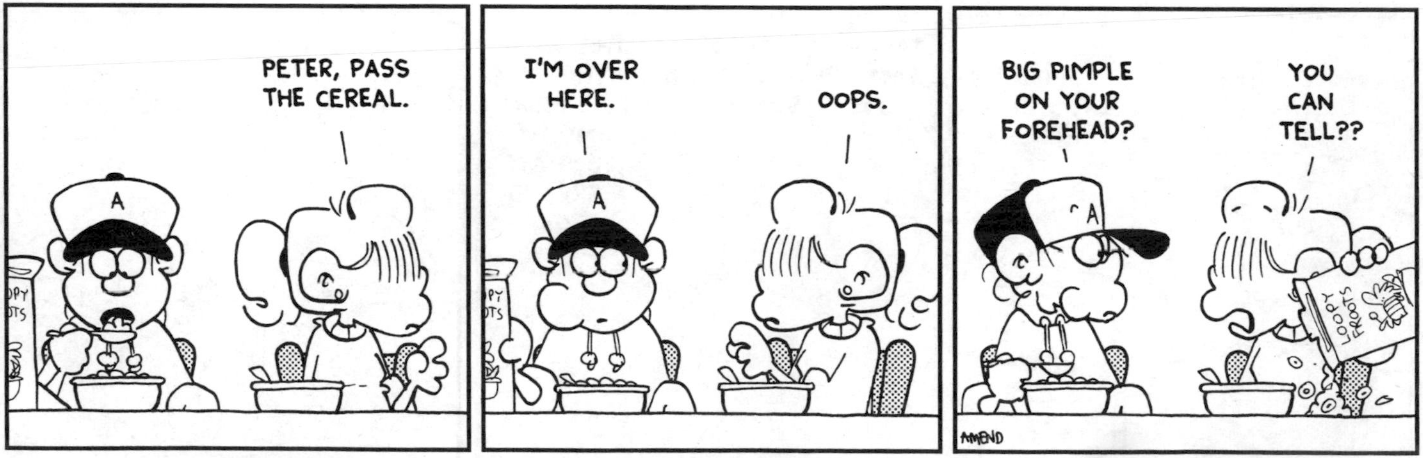
PETER, PASS THE CEREAL.
I'M OVER HERE.
OOPS.
BIG PIMPLE ON YOUR FOREHEAD?
YOU CAN TELL??
LOOPY FROOTS
AMEND

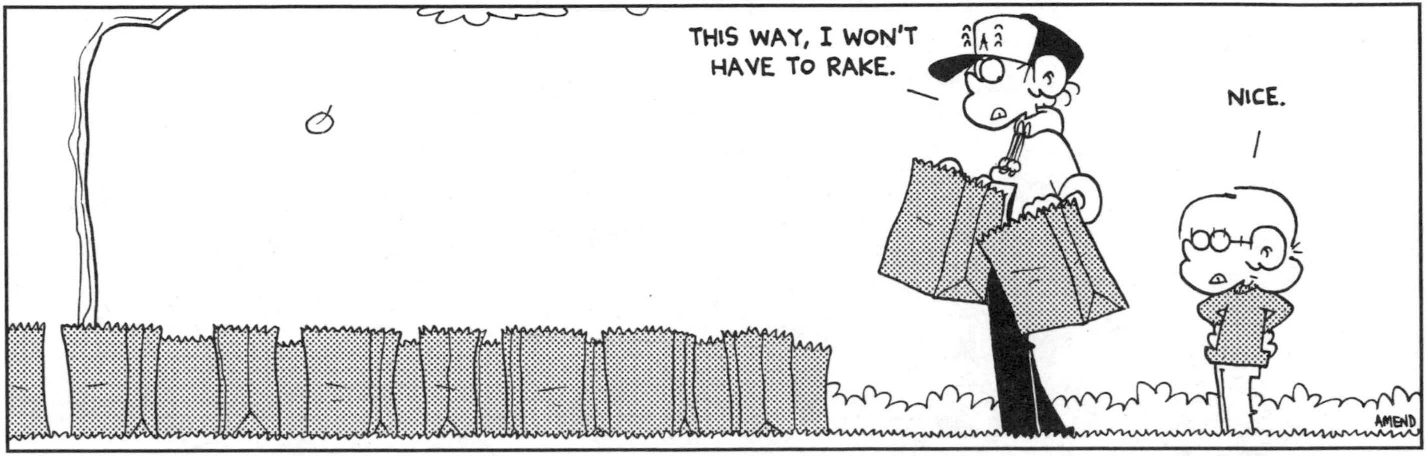
THIS WAY, I WON'T HAVE TO RAKE.
NICE.
AMEND

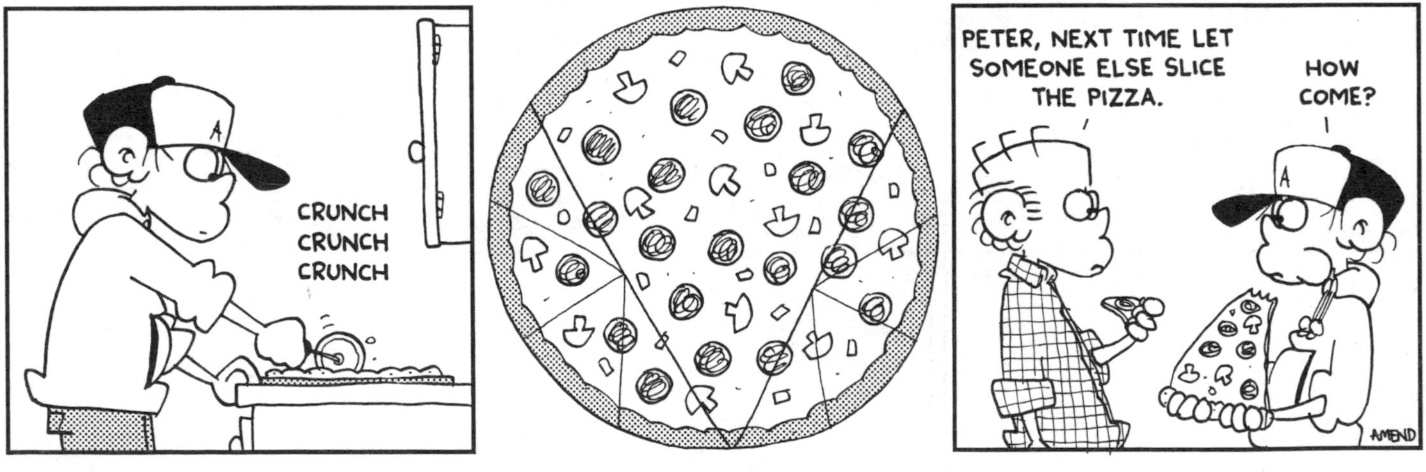
CRUNCH CRUNCH CRUNCH
PETER, NEXT TIME LET SOMEONE ELSE SLICE THE PIZZA.
HOW COME?
AMEND

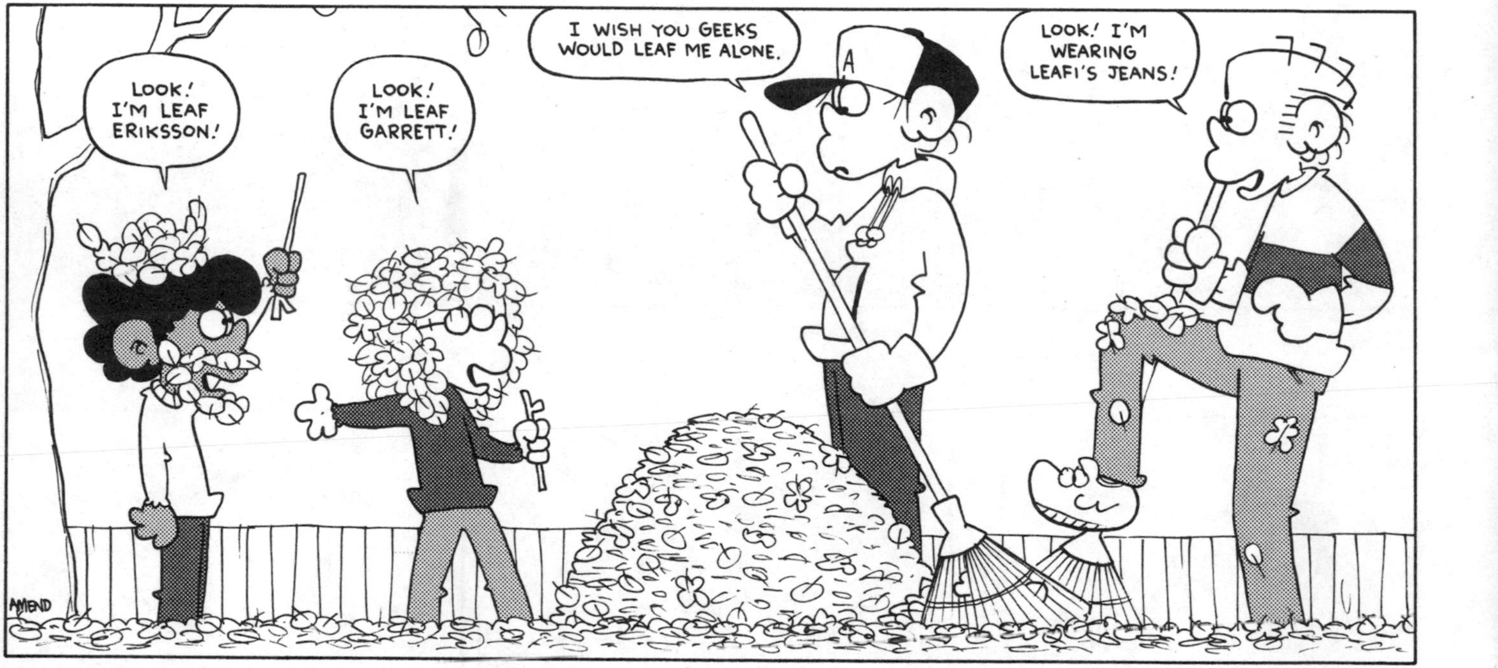
LOOK! I'M LEAF ERIKSSON!
LOOK! I'M LEAF GARRETT!
I WISH YOU GEEKS WOULD LEAF ME ALONE.
LOOK! I'M WEARING LEAFI'S JEANS!
AMEND

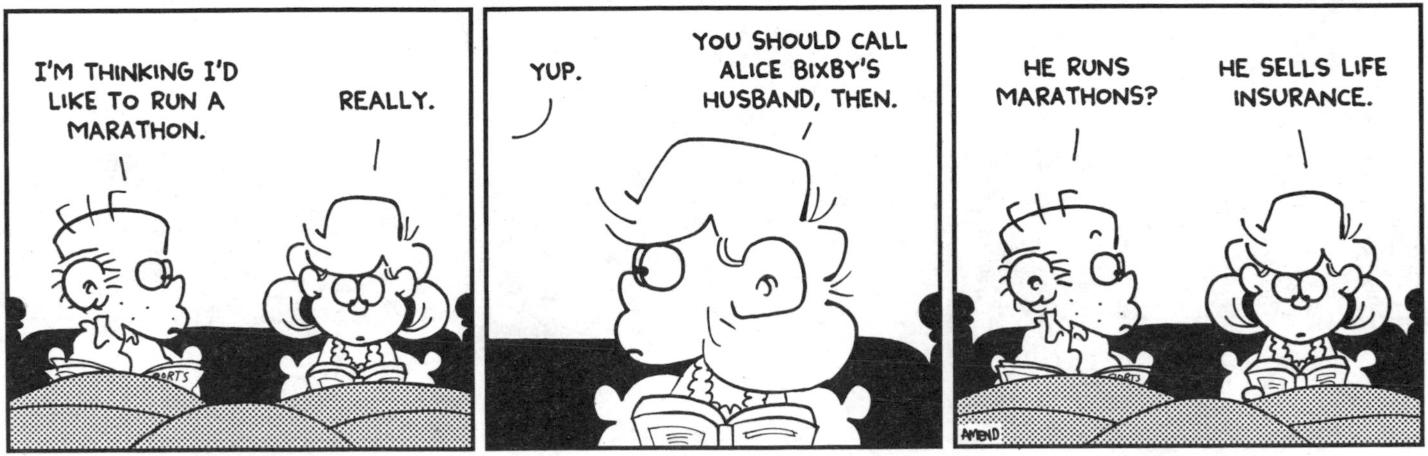
I'M THINKING I'D LIKE TO RUN A MARATHON.
REALLY.
YUP.
YOU SHOULD CALL ALICE BIXBY'S HUSBAND, THEN.
HE RUNS MARATHONS?
HE SELLS LIFE INSURANCE.
AMEND

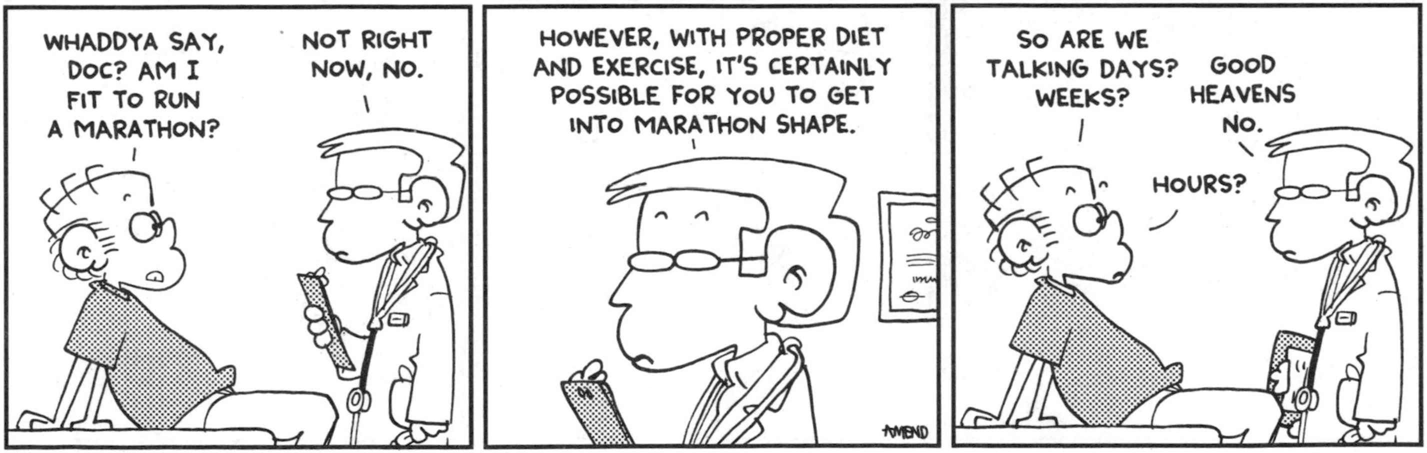
WHADDYA SAY, DOC? AM I FIT TO RUN A MARATHON?
NOT RIGHT NOW, NO.
HOWEVER, WITH PROPER DIET AND EXERCISE, IT'S CERTAINLY POSSIBLE FOR YOU TO GET INTO MARATHON SHAPE.
AMEND
SO ARE WE TALKING DAYS? WEEKS?
HOURS?
GOOD HEAVENS NO.

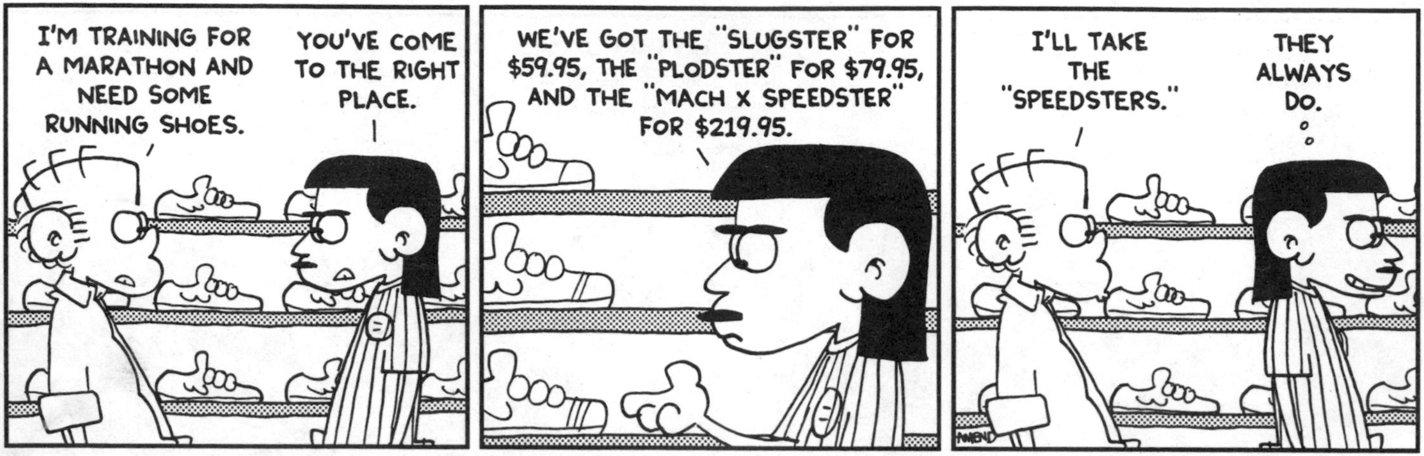
I'M TRAINING FOR A MARATHON AND NEED SOME RUNNING SHOES.
YOU'VE COME TO THE RIGHT PLACE.
WE'VE GOT THE "SLUGSTER" FOR $59.95, THE "PLODSTER" FOR $79.95, AND THE "MACH X SPEEDSTER" FOR $219.95.
I'LL TAKE THE "SPEEDSTERS."
THEY ALWAYS DO.
AMEND

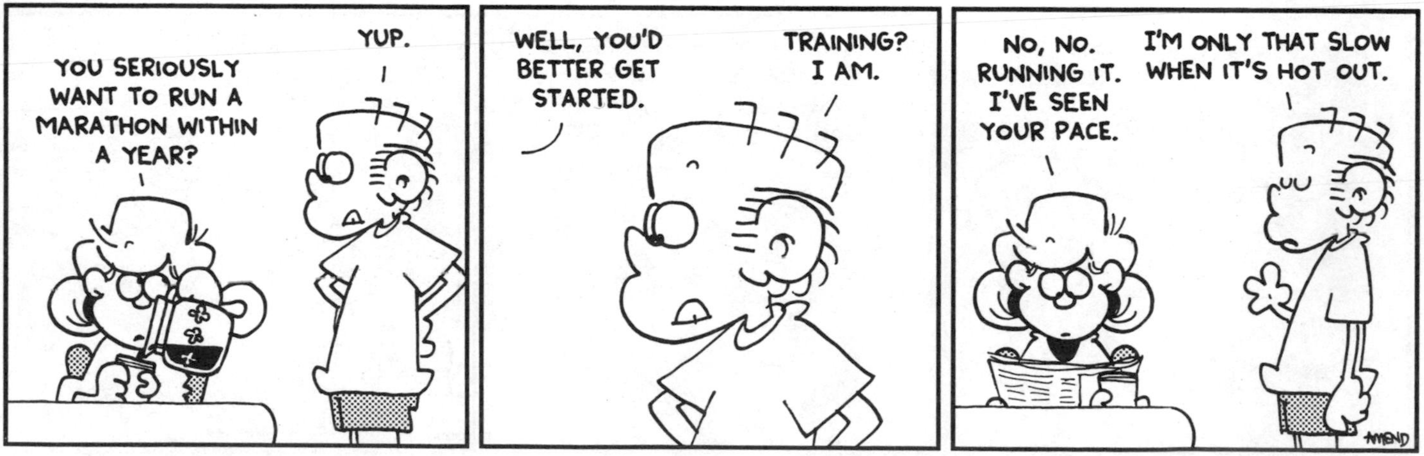
YOU SERIOUSLY WANT TO RUN A MARATHON WITHIN A YEAR?
YUP.
WELL, YOU'D BETTER GET STARTED.
TRAINING? I AM.
NO, NO. RUNNING IT. I'VE SEEN YOUR PACE.
I'M ONLY THAT SLOW WHEN IT'S HOT OUT.
AMEND

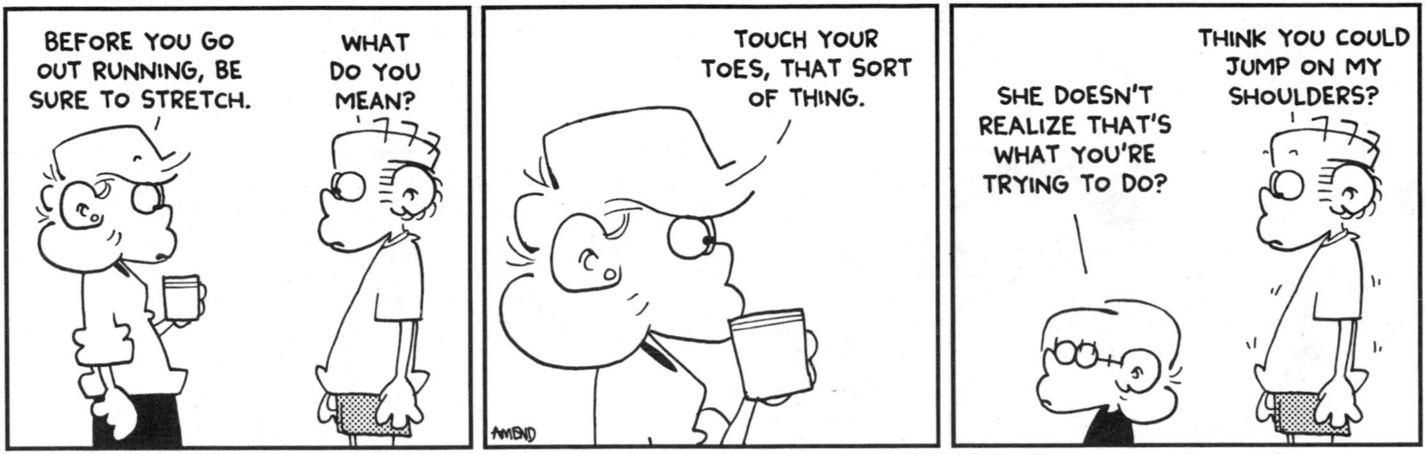
BEFORE YOU GO OUT RUNNING, BE SURE TO STRETCH.
WHAT DO YOU MEAN?
TOUCH YOUR TOES, THAT SORT OF THING.
THINK YOU COULD JUMP ON MY SHOULDERS?
SHE DOESN'T REALIZE THAT'S WHAT YOU'RE TRYING TO DO?
AMEND

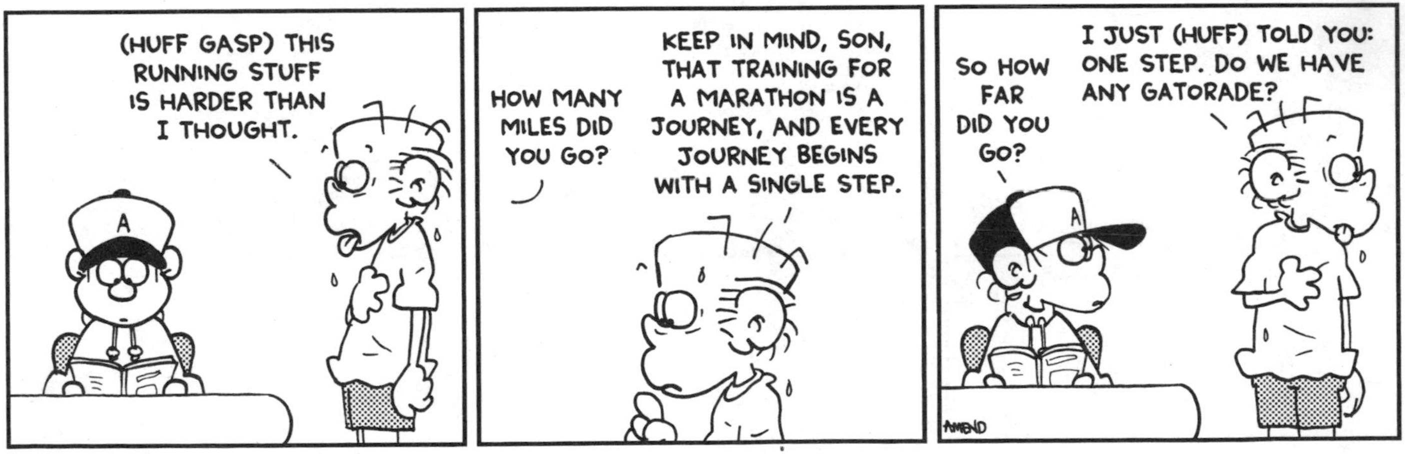
(HUFF GASP) THIS RUNNING STUFF IS HARDER THAN I THOUGHT.
A
HOW MANY MILES DID YOU GO?
KEEP IN MIND, SON, THAT TRAINING FOR A MARATHON IS A JOURNEY, AND EVERY JOURNEY BEGINS WITH A SINGLE STEP.
SO HOW FAR DID YOU GO?
I JUST (HUFF) TOLD YOU: ONE STEP. DO WE HAVE ANY GATORADE?
A
AMEND

AAAAAAAAAA!

AMEND

I MADE CREDIT CARDS WITH PAIGE'S NAME ON THEM.

THAT'S ALMOST **TOO** SCARY.

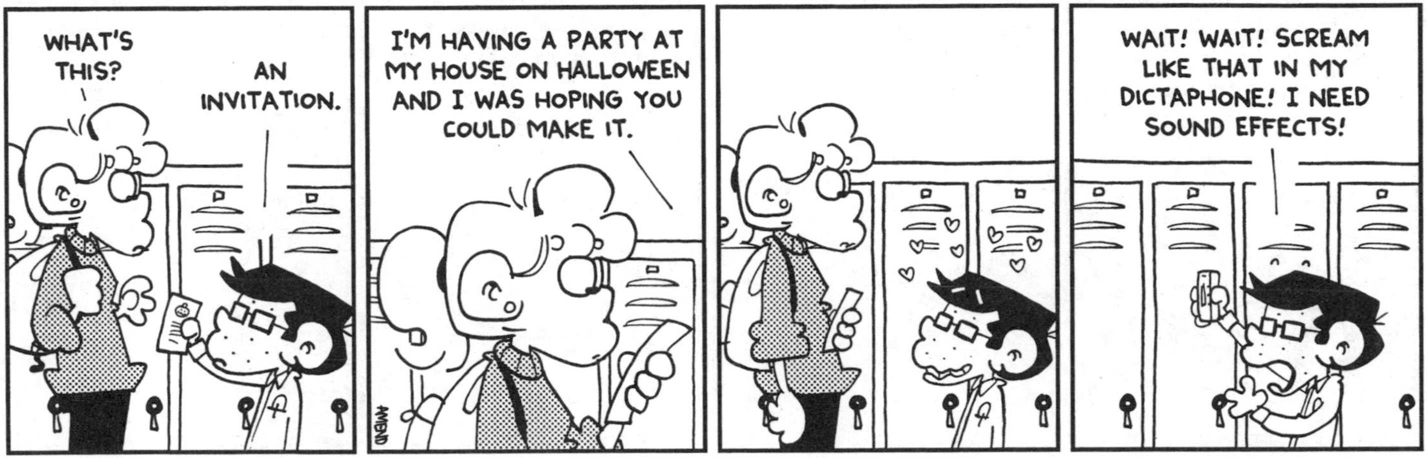
WHAT'S THIS?
AN INVITATION.
I'M HAVING A PARTY AT MY HOUSE ON HALLOWEEN AND I WAS HOPING YOU COULD MAKE IT.
WAIT! WAIT! SCREAM LIKE THAT IN MY DICTAPHONE! I NEED SOUND EFFECTS!
AMEND

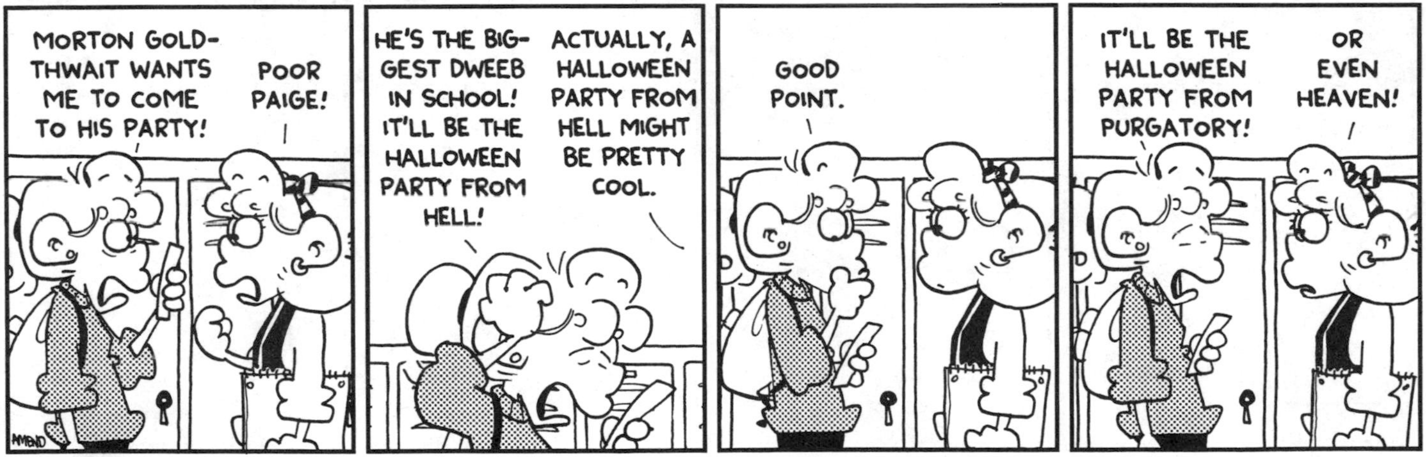
MORTON GOLD-THWAIT WANTS ME TO COME TO HIS PARTY!
POOR PAIGE!
AMEND
HE'S THE BIG-GEST DWEEB IN SCHOOL! IT'LL BE THE HALLOWEEN PARTY FROM HELL!
ACTUALLY, A HALLOWEEN PARTY FROM HELL MIGHT BE PRETTY COOL.
GOOD POINT.
IT'LL BE THE HALLOWEEN PARTY FROM PURGATORY!
OR EVEN HEAVEN!

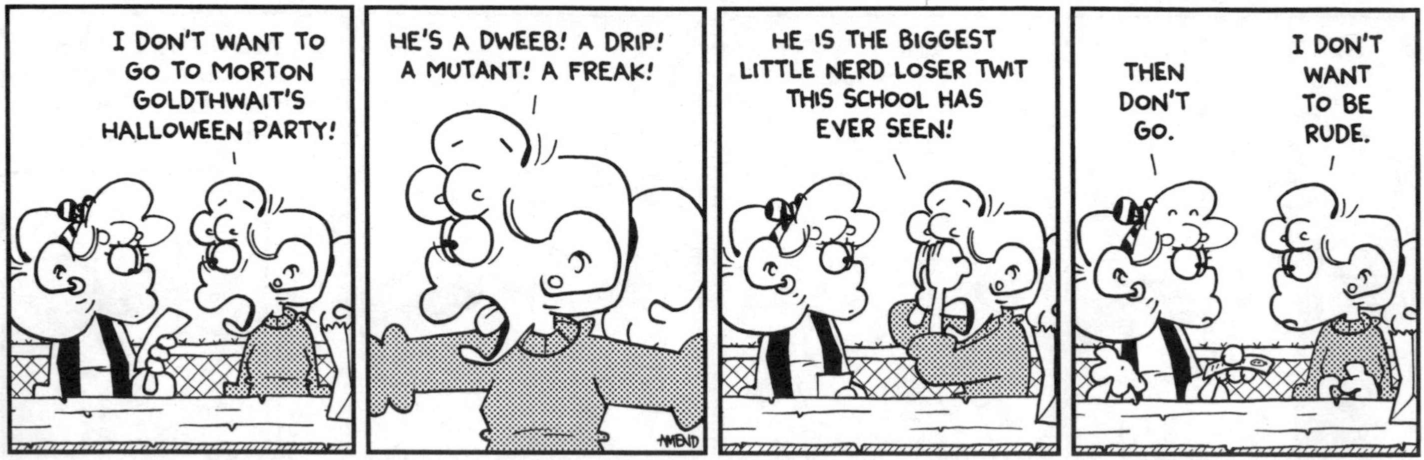
I DON'T WANT TO GO TO MORTON GOLDTHWAIT'S HALLOWEEN PARTY!
HE'S A DWEEB! A DRIP! A MUTANT! A FREAK!
AMEND
HE IS THE BIGGEST LITTLE NERD LOSER TWIT THIS SCHOOL HAS EVER SEEN!
THEN DON'T GO.
I DON'T WANT TO BE RUDE.

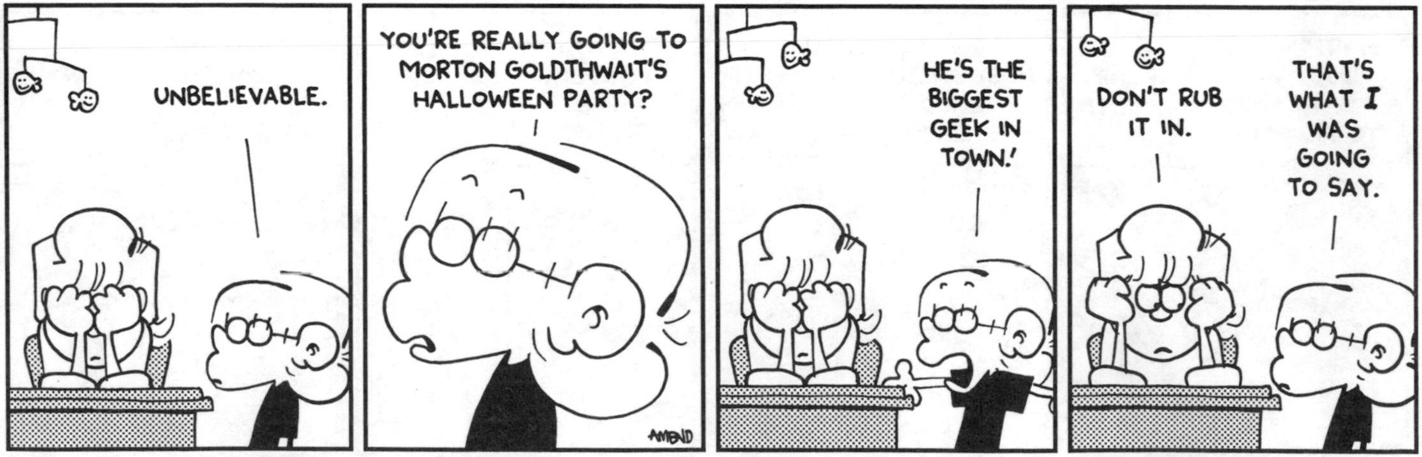
UNBELIEVABLE.
YOU'RE REALLY GOING TO MORTON GOLDTHWAIT'S HALLOWEEN PARTY?
AMEND
HE'S THE BIGGEST GEEK IN TOWN.'
DON'T RUB IT IN.
THAT'S WHAT I WAS GOING TO SAY.

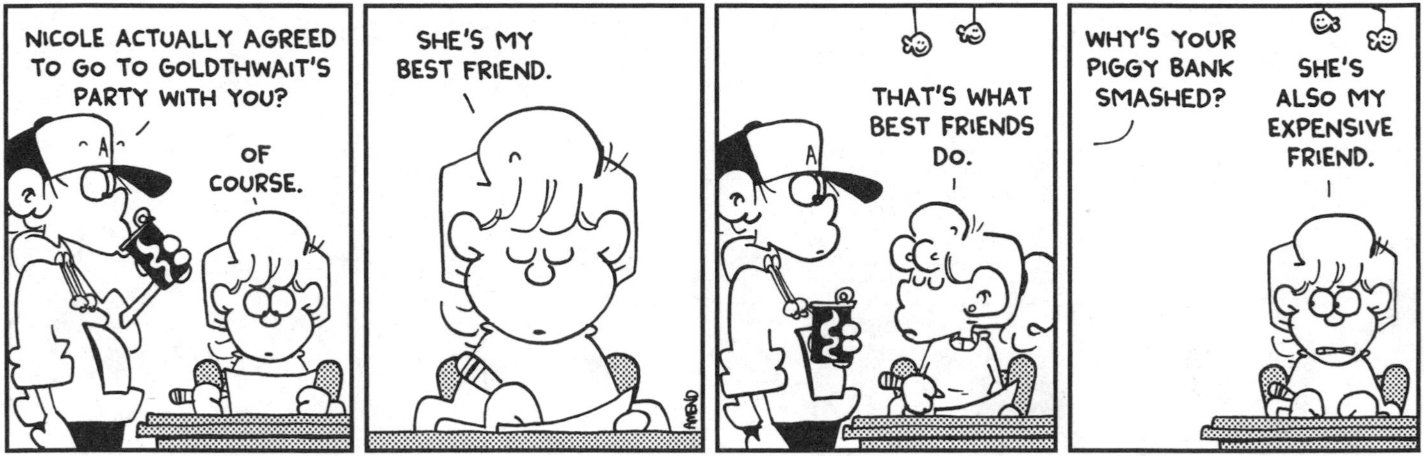
NICOLE ACTUALLY AGREED TO GO TO GOLDTHWAIT'S PARTY WITH YOU?
OF COURSE.
SHE'S MY BEST FRIEND.
THAT'S WHAT BEST FRIENDS DO.
WHY'S YOUR PIGGY BANK SMASHED?
SHE'S ALSO MY EXPENSIVE FRIEND.
AMEND

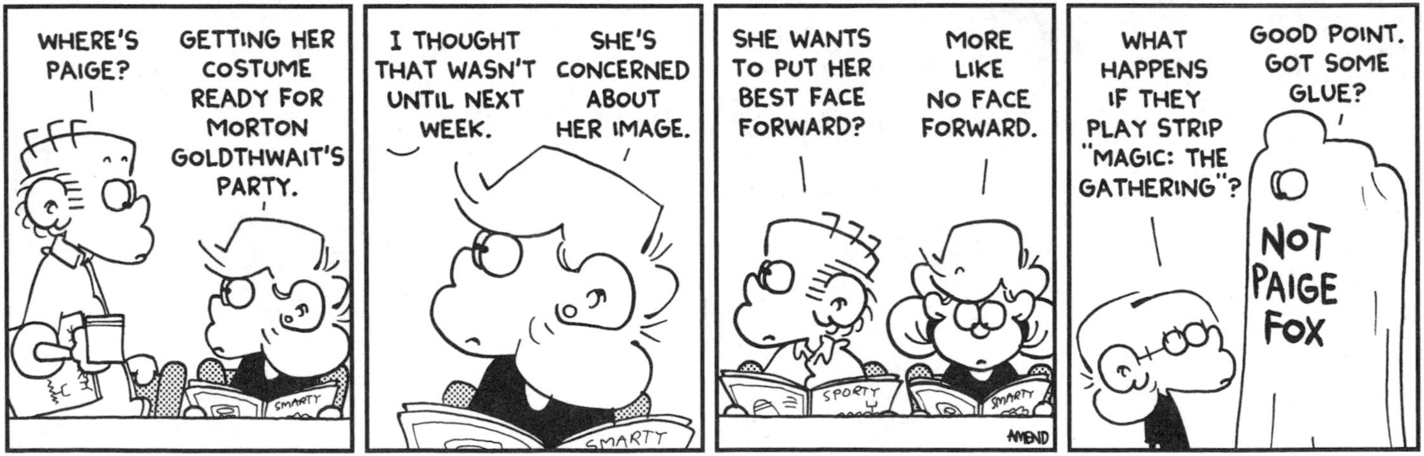
WHERE'S PAIGE?
GETTING HER COSTUME READY FOR MORTON GOLDTHWAIT'S PARTY.
SMARTY
I THOUGHT THAT WASN'T UNTIL NEXT WEEK.
SHE'S CONCERNED ABOUT HER IMAGE.
SMARTY
SHE WANTS TO PUT HER BEST FACE FORWARD?
MORE LIKE NO FACE FORWARD.
SPORTY
SMARTY
AMEND
WHAT HAPPENS IF THEY PLAY STRIP "MAGIC: THE GATHERING"?
GOOD POINT. GOT SOME GLUE?
NOT PAIGE FOX

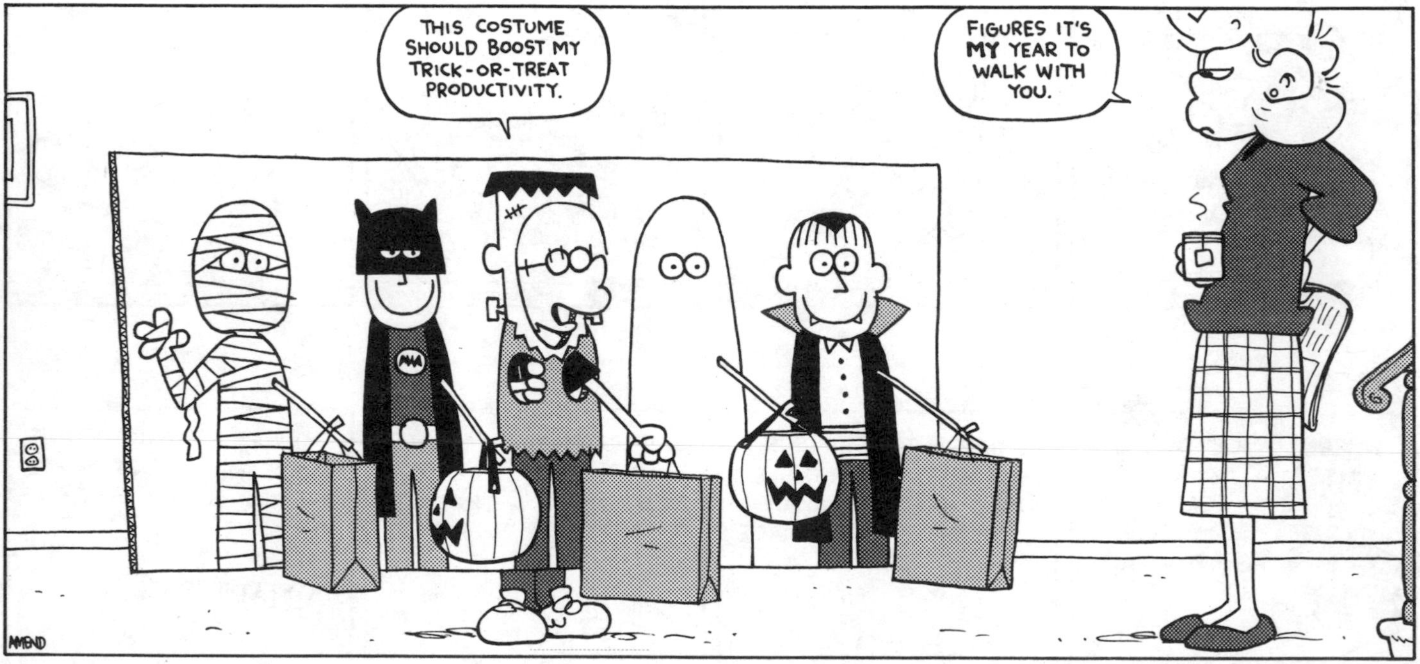
THIS COSTUME SHOULD BOOST MY TRICK-OR-TREAT PRODUCTIVITY.
FIGURES IT'S MY YEAR TO WALK WITH YOU.
AMEND

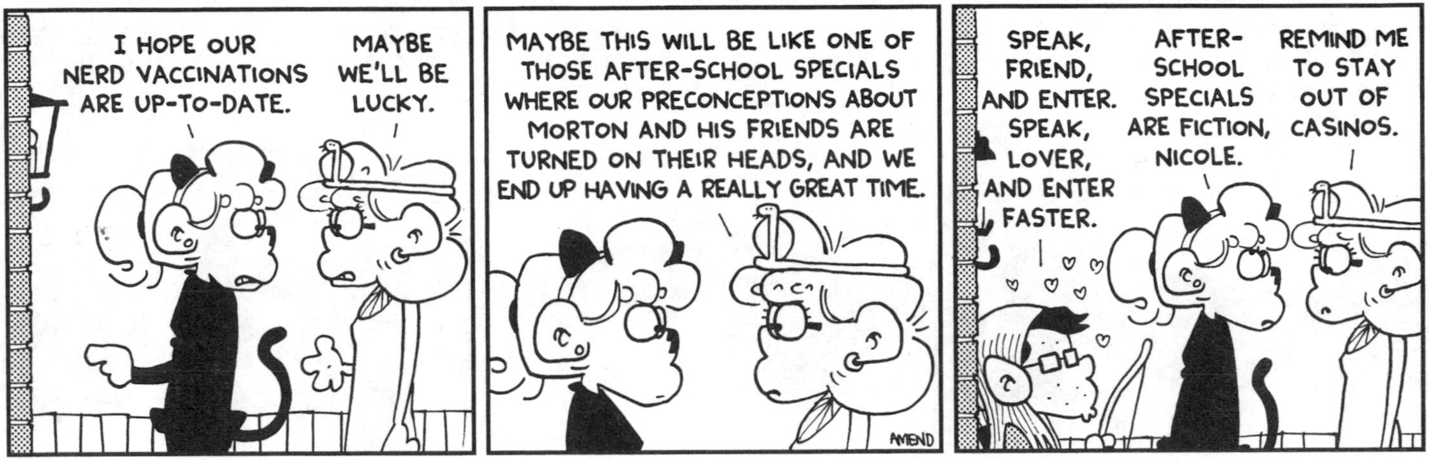
I HOPE OUR NERD VACCINATIONS ARE UP-TO-DATE.
MAYBE WE'LL BE LUCKY.
MAYBE THIS WILL BE LIKE ONE OF THOSE AFTER-SCHOOL SPECIALS WHERE OUR PRECONCEPTIONS ABOUT MORTON AND HIS FRIENDS ARE TURNED ON THEIR HEADS, AND WE END UP HAVING A REALLY GREAT TIME.
AMEND
SPEAK, FRIEND, AND ENTER. SPEAK, LOVER, AND ENTER FASTER.
AFTER-SCHOOL SPECIALS ARE FICTION, NICOLE.
REMIND ME TO STAY OUT OF CASINOS.

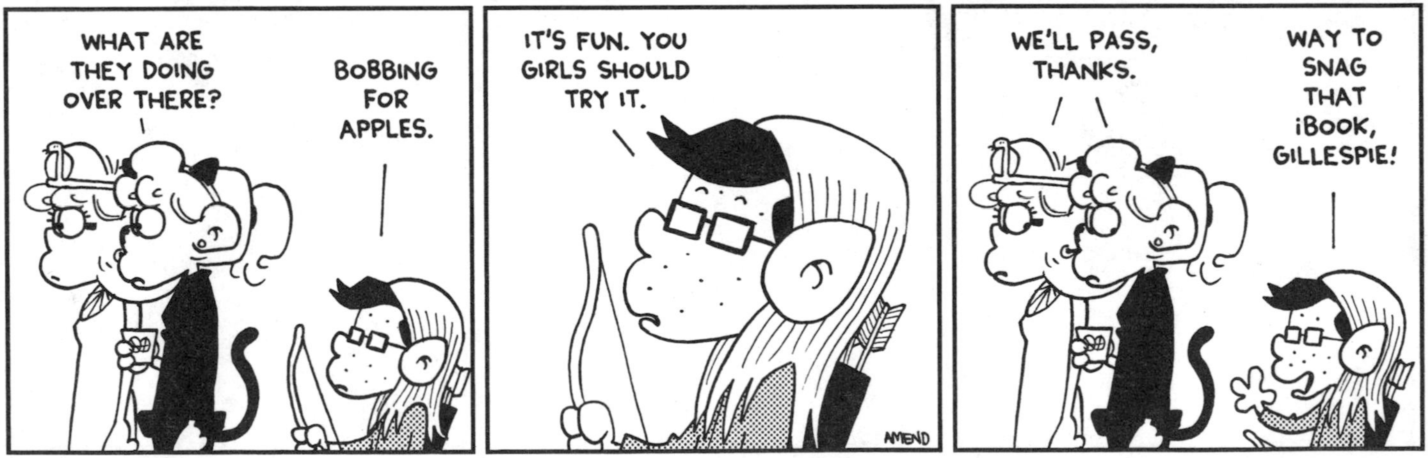
WHAT ARE THEY DOING OVER THERE?
BOBBING FOR APPLES.
IT'S FUN. YOU GIRLS SHOULD TRY IT.
AMEND
WE'LL PASS, THANKS.
WAY TO SNAG THAT iBOOK, GILLESPIE!

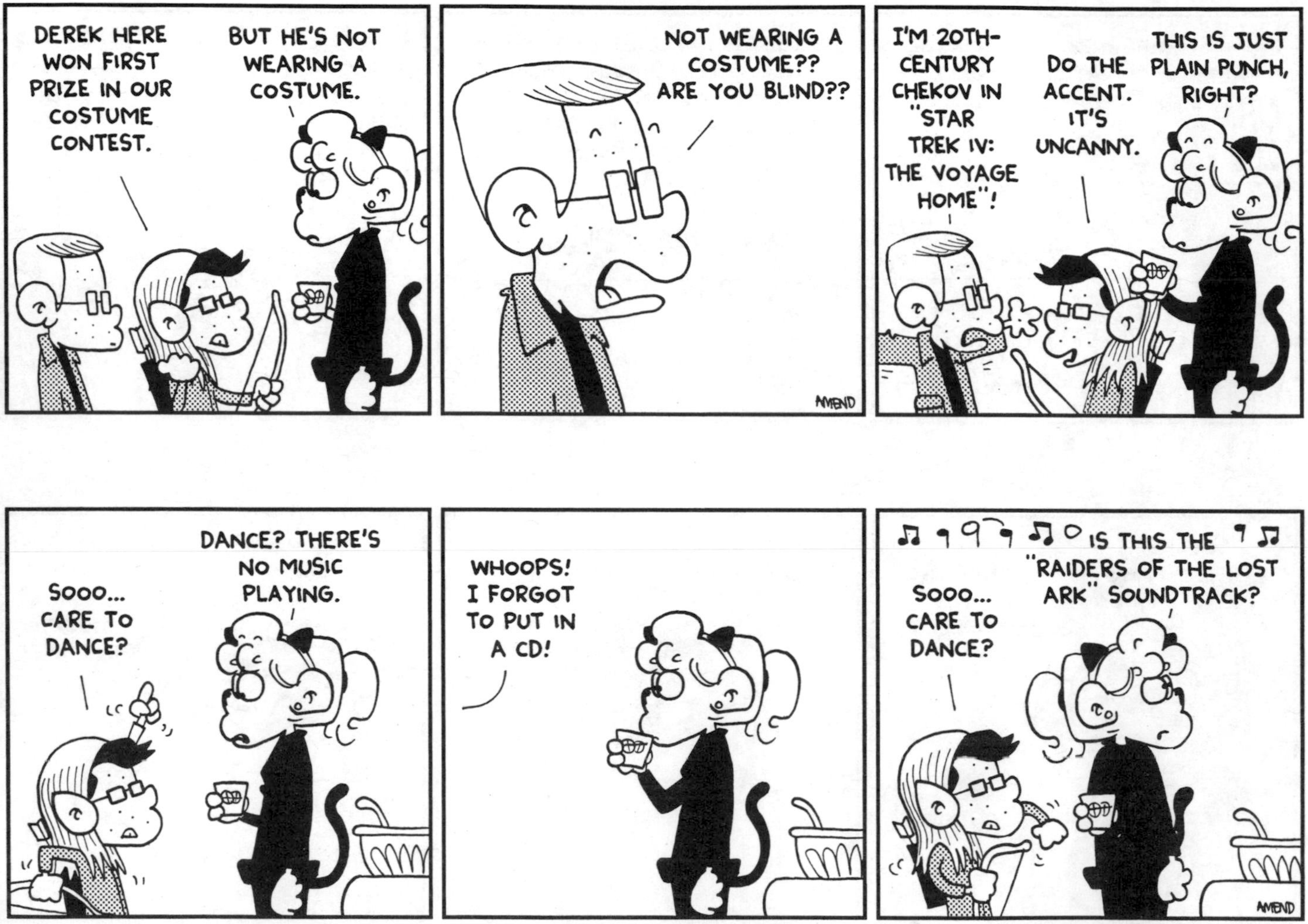
DEREK HERE WON FIRST PRIZE IN OUR COSTUME CONTEST.
BUT HE'S NOT WEARING A COSTUME.
NOT WEARING A COSTUME?? ARE YOU BLIND??
AMEND
I'M 20TH-CENTURY CHEKOV IN "STAR TREK IV: THE VOYAGE HOME"!
DO THE ACCENT. IT'S UNCANNY.
THIS IS JUST PLAIN PUNCH, RIGHT?
SOOO... CARE TO DANCE?
DANCE? THERE'S NO MUSIC PLAYING.
WHOOPS! I FORGOT TO PUT IN A CD!
IS THIS THE "RAIDERS OF THE LOST ARK" SOUNDTRACK?
SOOO... CARE TO DANCE?
AMEND

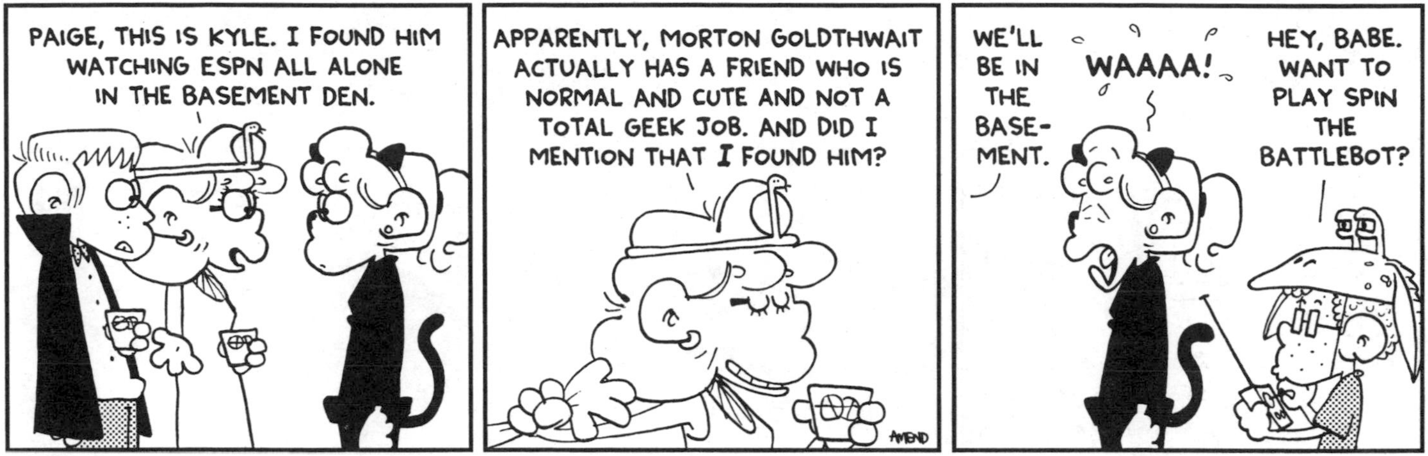
PAIGE, THIS IS KYLE. I FOUND HIM WATCHING ESPN ALL ALONE IN THE BASEMENT DEN.
APPARENTLY, MORTON GOLDTHWAIT ACTUALLY HAS A FRIEND WHO IS NORMAL AND CUTE AND NOT A TOTAL GEEK JOB. AND DID I MENTION THAT I FOUND HIM?
AMEND
WE'LL BE IN THE BASE-MENT.
WAAAA!
HEY, BABE. WANT TO PLAY SPIN THE BATTLEBOT?

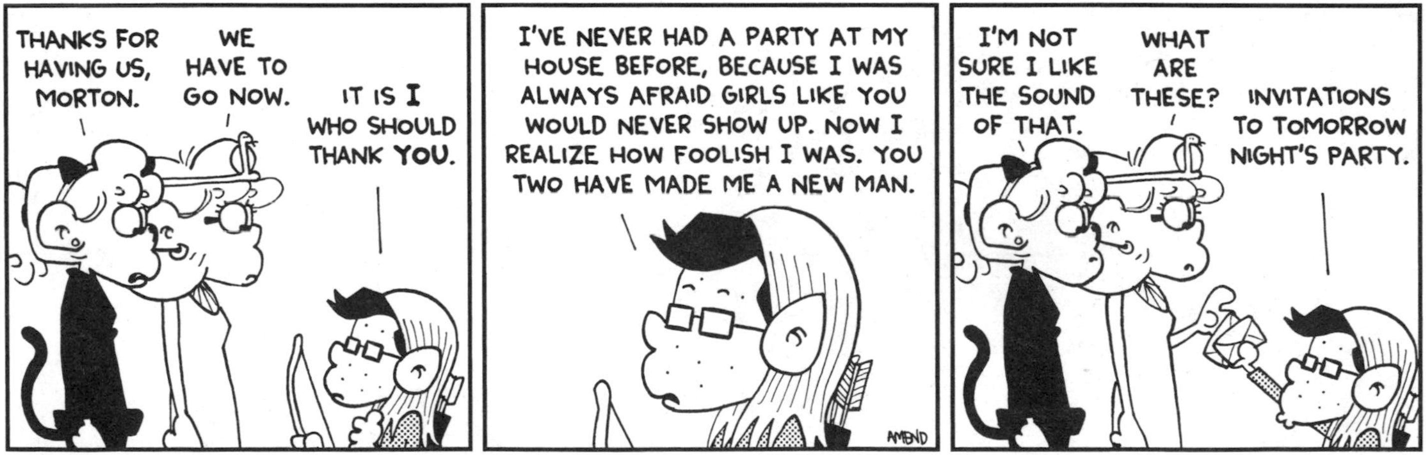
THANKS FOR HAVING US, MORTON.
WE HAVE TO GO NOW.
IT IS I WHO SHOULD THANK YOU.
I'VE NEVER HAD A PARTY AT MY HOUSE BEFORE, BECAUSE I WAS ALWAYS AFRAID GIRLS LIKE YOU WOULD NEVER SHOW UP. NOW I REALIZE HOW FOOLISH I WAS. YOU TWO HAVE MADE ME A NEW MAN.
AMEND
I'M NOT SURE I LIKE THE SOUND OF THAT.
WHAT ARE THESE?
INVITATIONS TO TOMORROW NIGHT'S PARTY.

$CH_3O + C_2 \rightarrow C_2H_3O + C$
$\frac{[CHO][C]}{[CH_1P]}$
$CO_3 + CO_2 \rightarrow$
CHO_4C
$C_2HO + CH + P \rightarrow$
$CH + O + K \rightarrow$
KH_1P CO
AMEND
WILL YOU STOP BAKING?! I'M TRYING TO STUDY!
I'LL TAKE THAT AS A COMPLIMENT.

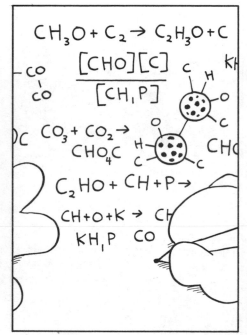

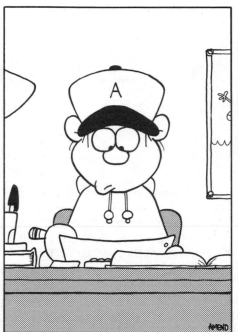

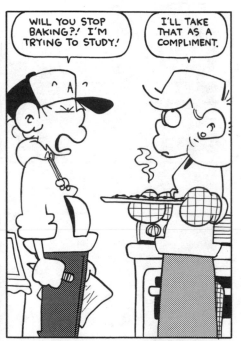

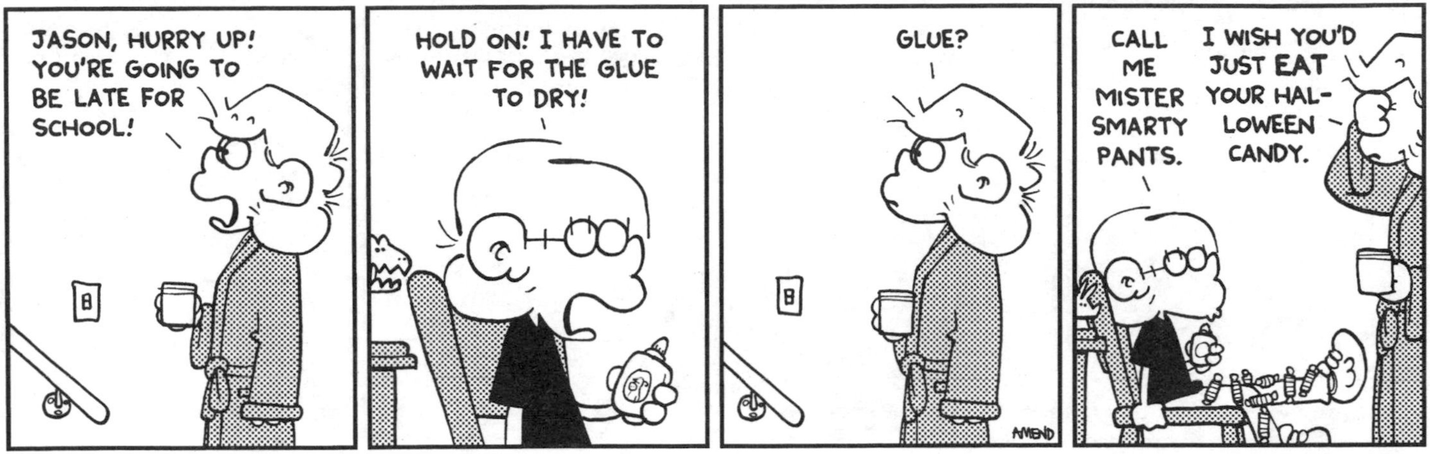
JASON, HURRY UP! YOU'RE GOING TO BE LATE FOR SCHOOL!
HOLD ON! I HAVE TO WAIT FOR THE GLUE TO DRY!
GLUE?
CALL ME MISTER SMARTY PANTS.
I WISH YOU'D JUST EAT YOUR HALLOWEEN CANDY.
AMEND

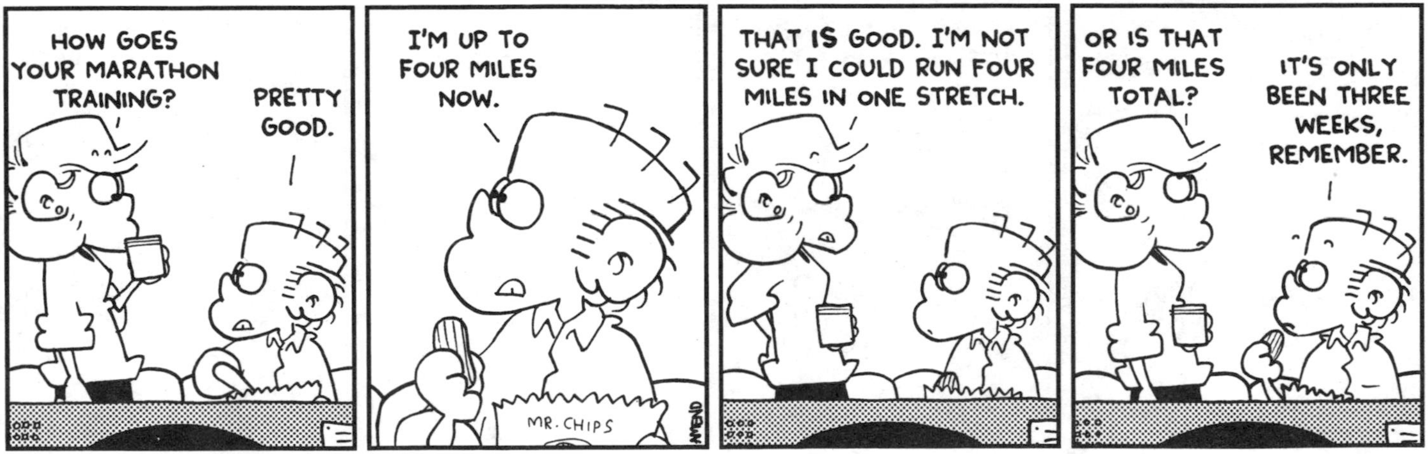
HOW GOES YOUR MARATHON TRAINING?
PRETTY GOOD.
I'M UP TO FOUR MILES NOW.
MR. CHIPS
AMEND
THAT IS GOOD. I'M NOT SURE I COULD RUN FOUR MILES IN ONE STRETCH.
OR IS THAT FOUR MILES TOTAL?
IT'S ONLY BEEN THREE WEEKS, REMEMBER.

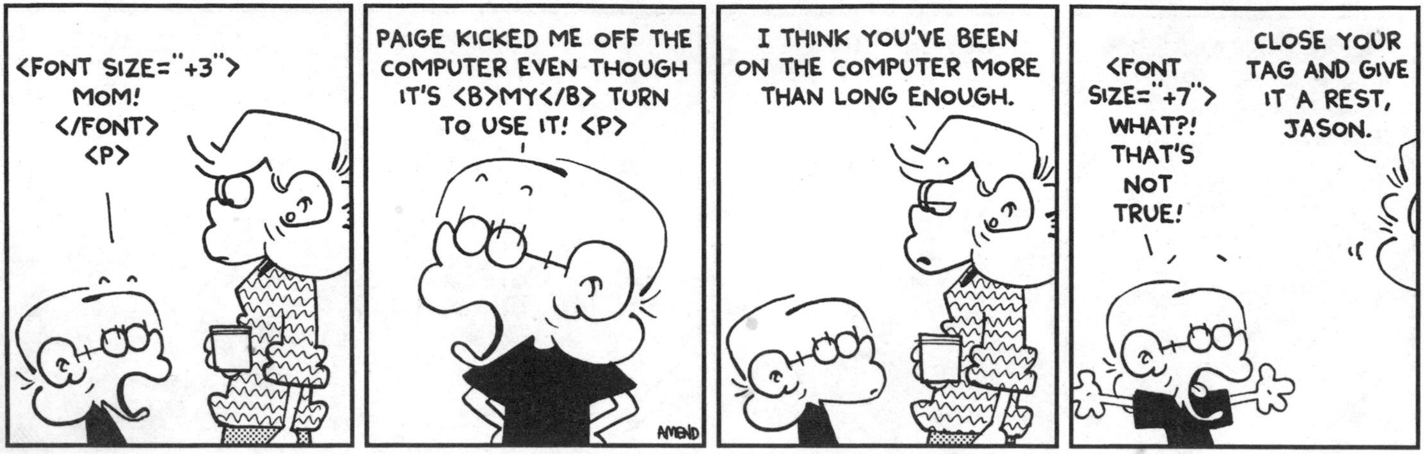
<FONT SIZE="+3"> MOM! </FONT> <P>
PAIGE KICKED ME OFF THE COMPUTER EVEN THOUGH IT'S <B>MY</B> TURN TO USE IT! <P>
AMEND
I THINK YOU'VE BEEN ON THE COMPUTER MORE THAN LONG ENOUGH.
<FONT SIZE="+7"> WHAT?! THAT'S NOT TRUE!
CLOSE YOUR TAG AND GIVE IT A REST, JASON.

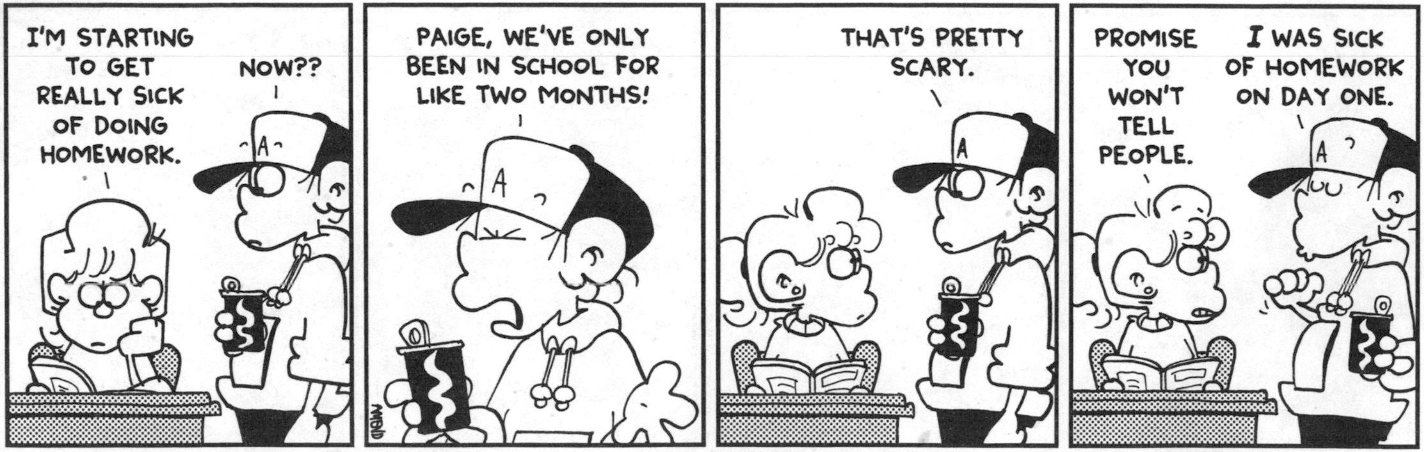
I'M STARTING TO GET REALLY SICK OF DOING HOMEWORK.
NOW??
PAIGE, WE'VE ONLY BEEN IN SCHOOL FOR LIKE TWO MONTHS!
AMEND
THAT'S PRETTY SCARY.
PROMISE YOU WON'T TELL PEOPLE.
I WAS SICK OF HOMEWORK ON DAY ONE.

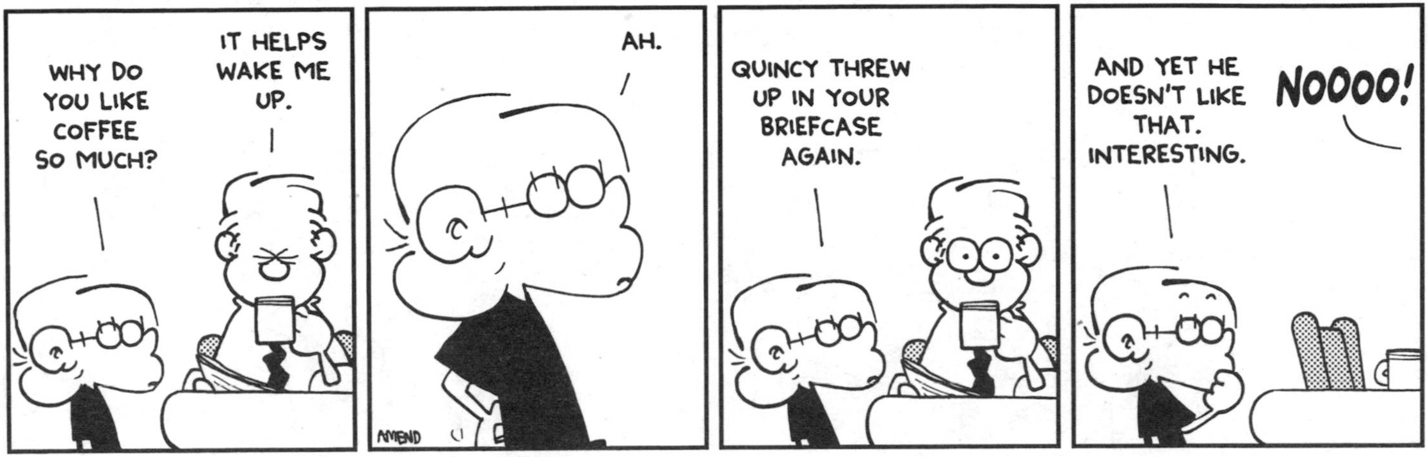
WHY DO YOU LIKE COFFEE SO MUCH?
IT HELPS WAKE ME UP.
AH.
AMEND
QUINCY THREW UP IN YOUR BRIEFCASE AGAIN.
AND YET HE DOESN'T LIKE THAT. INTERESTING.
NOOOO!

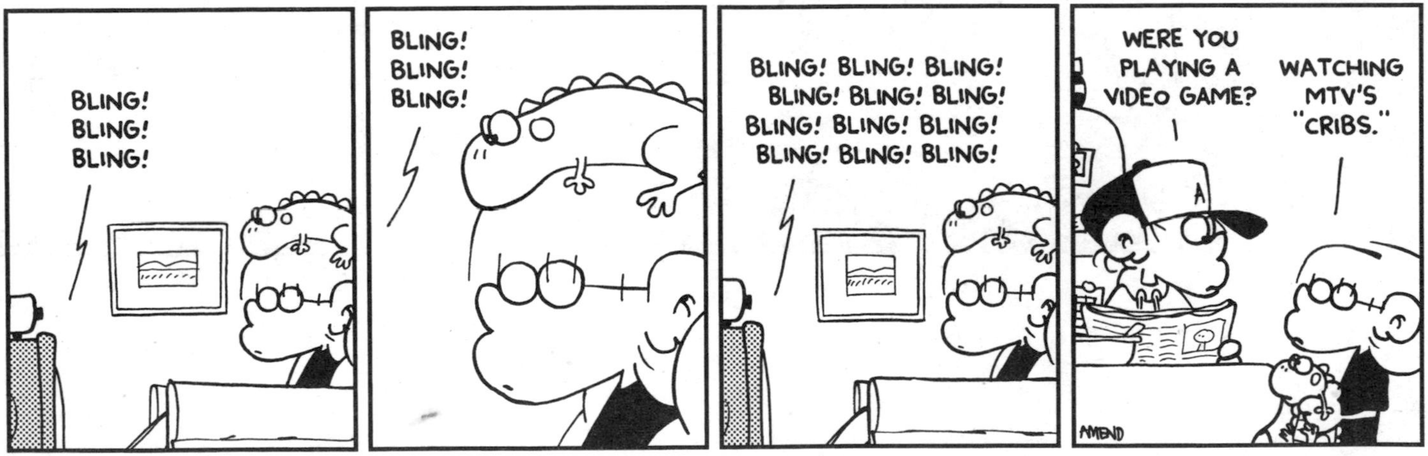
BLING! BLING! BLING!
BLING! BLING! BLING!
BLING! BLING! BLING! BLING! BLING! BLING! BLING! BLING! BLING! BLING! BLING! BLING!
WERE YOU PLAYING A VIDEO GAME?
WATCHING MTV'S "CRIBS."
AMEND

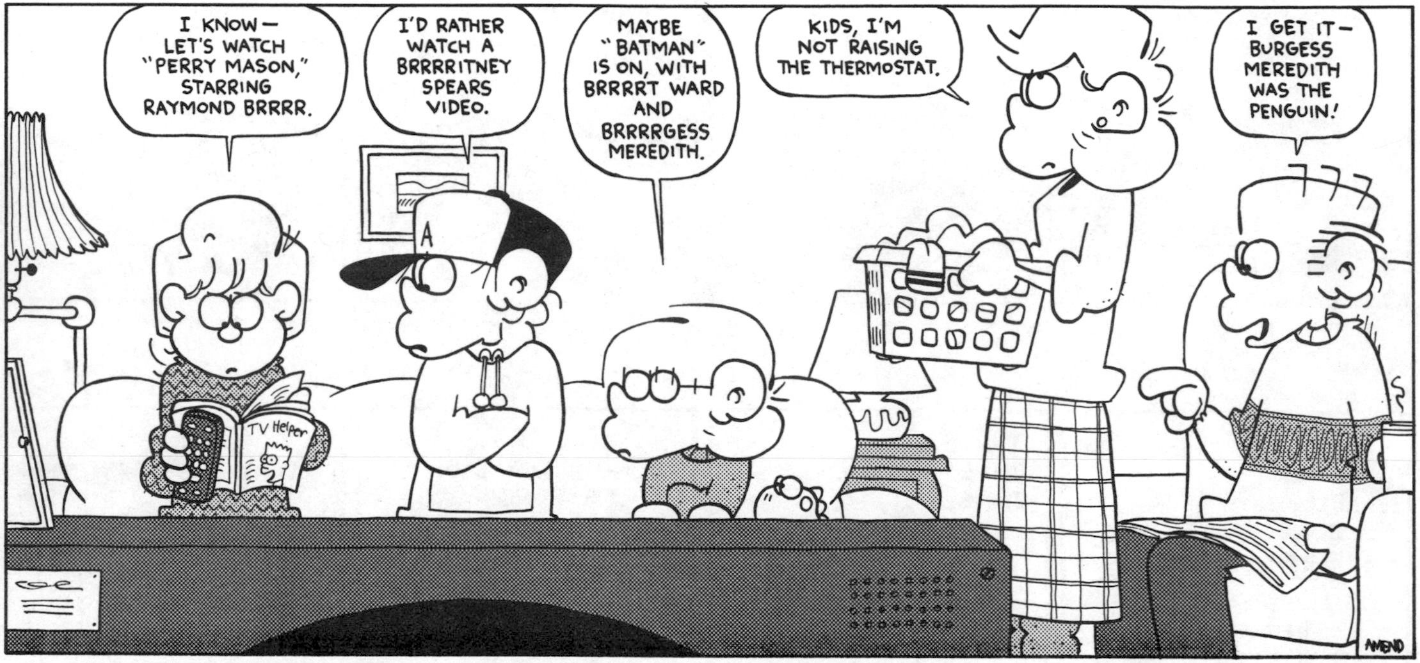
I KNOW—
LET'S WATCH
"PERRY MASON,"
STARRING
RAYMOND BRRRR.
I'D RATHER
WATCH A
BRRRRITNEY
SPEARS
VIDEO.
MAYBE
"BATMAN"
IS ON, WITH
BRRRRT WARD
AND
BRRRRGESS
MEREDITH.
KIDS, I'M
NOT RAISING
THE THERMOSTAT.
I GET IT—
BURGESS
MEREDITH
WAS THE
PENGUIN!
TV Helper
AMEND

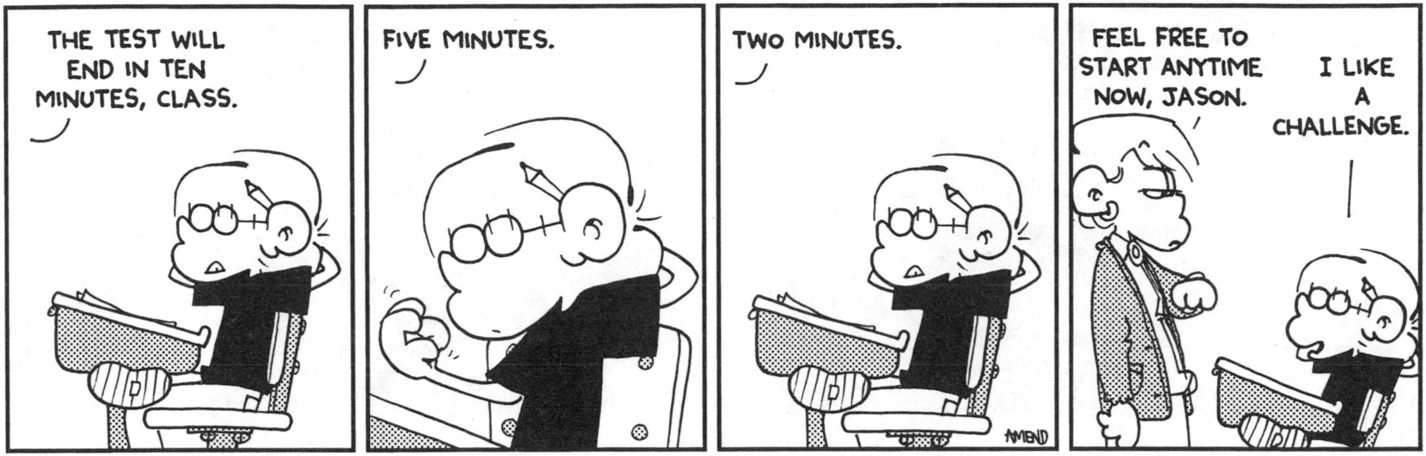
THE TEST WILL END IN TEN MINUTES, CLASS.
FIVE MINUTES.
TWO MINUTES.
AMEND
FEEL FREE TO START ANYTIME NOW, JASON.
I LIKE A CHALLENGE.

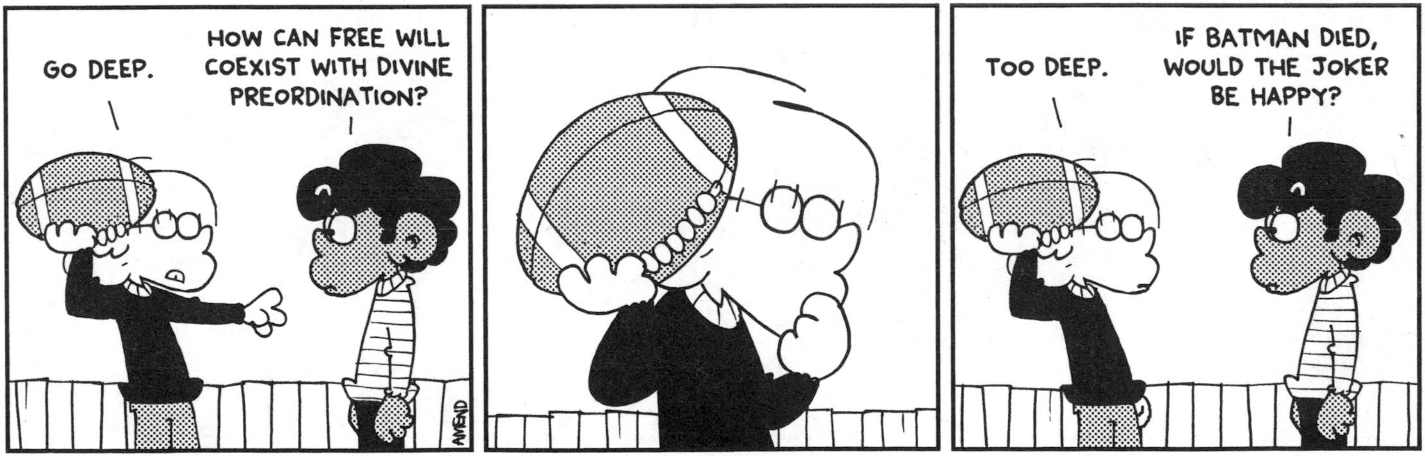
GO DEEP.
HOW CAN FREE WILL COEXIST WITH DIVINE PREORDINATION?
AMEND
TOO DEEP.
IF BATMAN DIED, WOULD THE JOKER BE HAPPY?

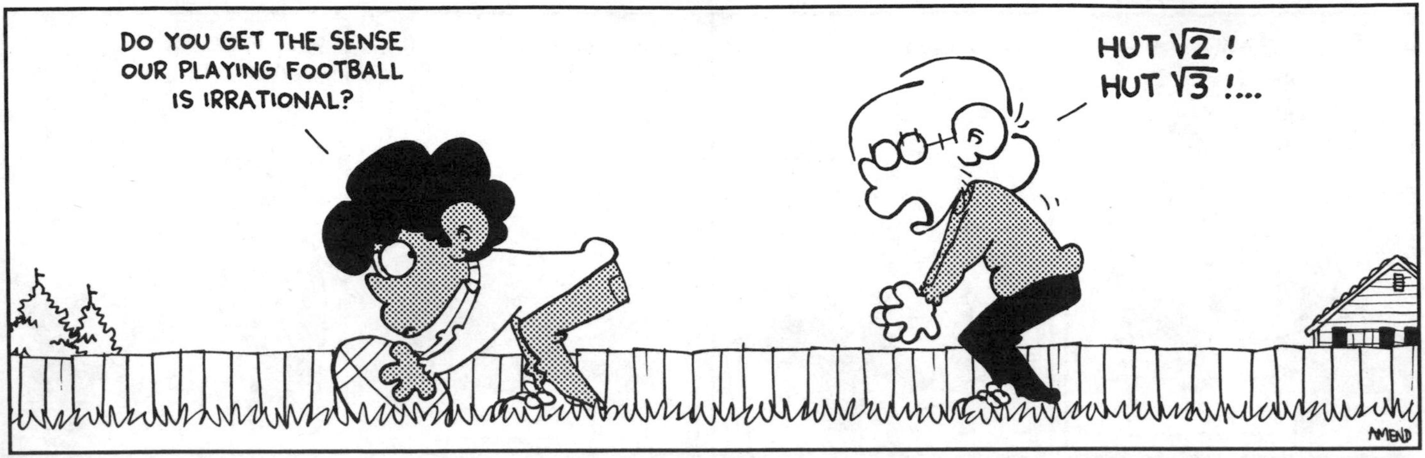
DO YOU GET THE SENSE OUR PLAYING FOOTBALL IS IRRATIONAL?
HUT √2 ! HUT √3 !...
AMEND

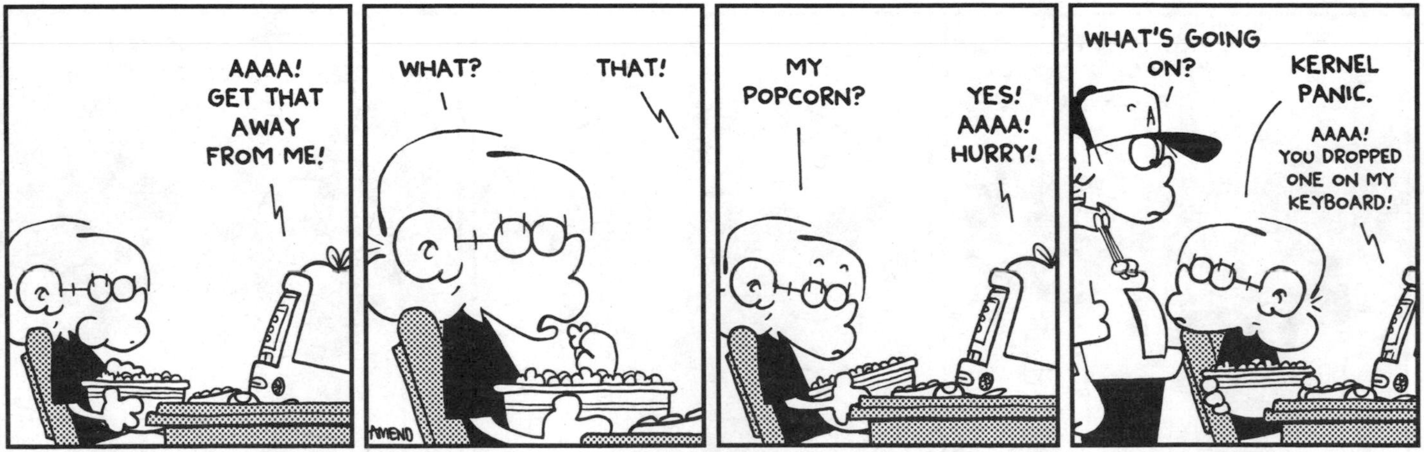
AAAA! GET THAT AWAY FROM ME!
WHAT?
THAT!
AMEND
MY POPCORN?
YES! AAAA! HURRY!
WHAT'S GOING ON?
KERNEL PANIC.
AAAA! YOU DROPPED ONE ON MY KEYBOARD!

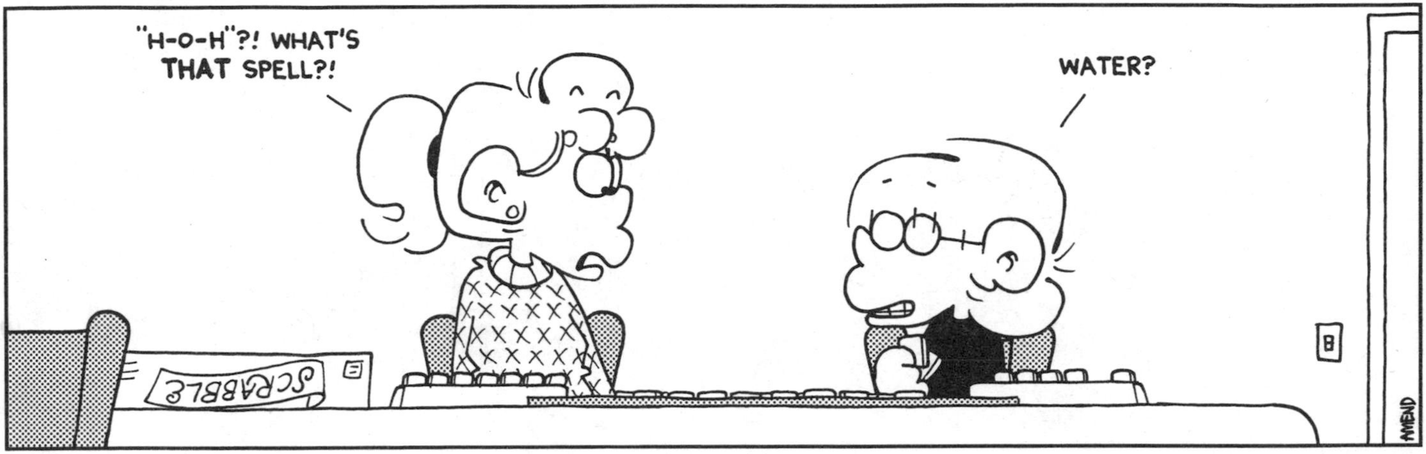
"H-O-H"?! WHAT'S THAT SPELL?!
WATER?
SCRABBLE
AMEND

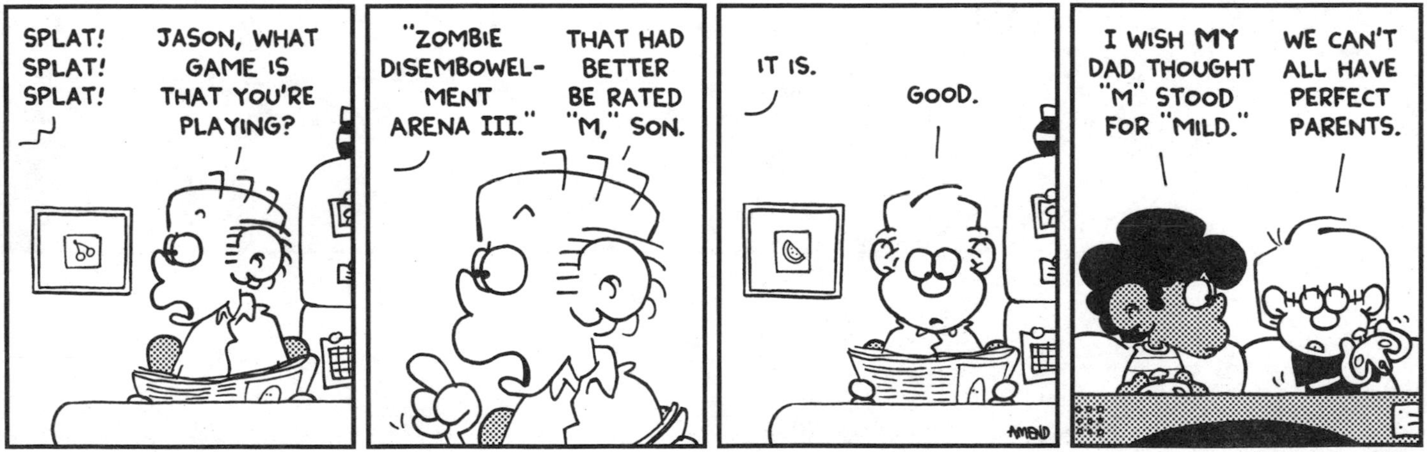
SPLAT! SPLAT! SPLAT!
JASON, WHAT GAME IS THAT YOU'RE PLAYING?
"ZOMBIE DISEMBOWEL-MENT ARENA III."
THAT HAD BETTER BE RATED "M," SON.
IT IS.
GOOD.
AMEND
I WISH MY DAD THOUGHT "M" STOOD FOR "MILD."
WE CAN'T ALL HAVE PERFECT PARENTS.

IT'S THE EYE OF THE TIGER, IT'S THE THRILL OF THE FIGHT...
MY EYES ADORED YOU...
SHE'S GOT BETTY DAVIS EYES...
YOU, MY BROWN-EYED GIRL...
EYETUNES?
I'M NOT SO SURE ABOUT THIS NEW MUSIC SERVICE.
AMEND

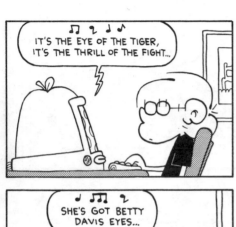

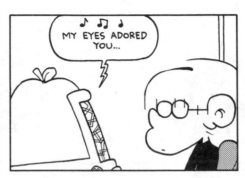

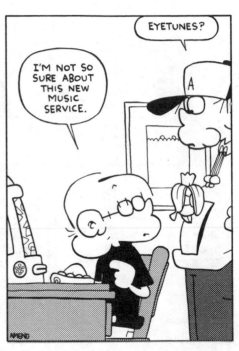

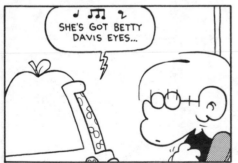

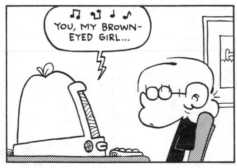

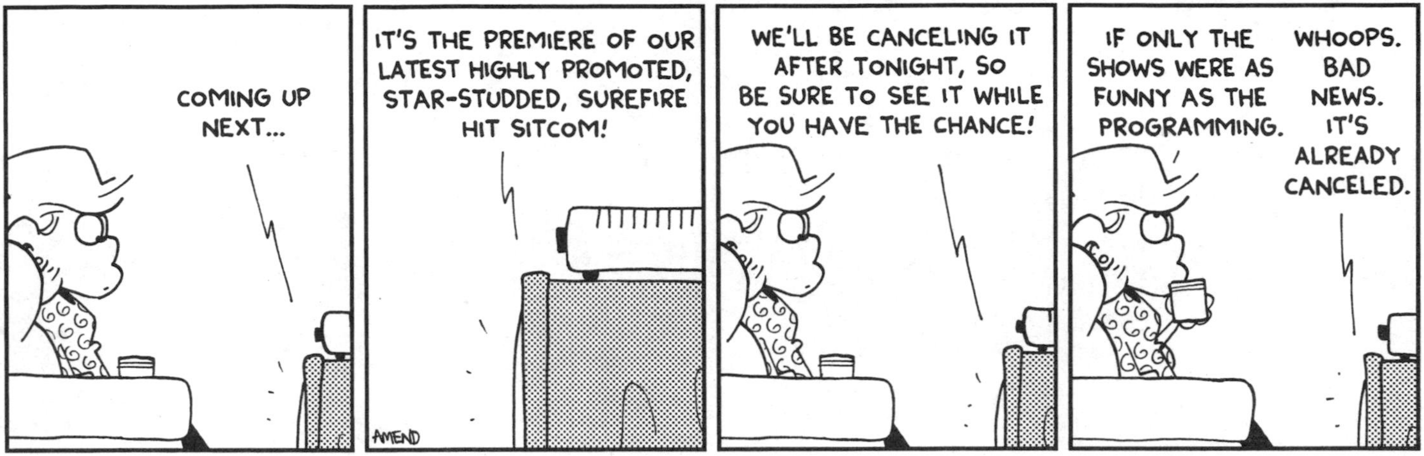
COMING UP NEXT...
IT'S THE PREMIERE OF OUR LATEST HIGHLY PROMOTED, STAR-STUDDED, SUREFIRE HIT SITCOM!
AMEND
WE'LL BE CANCELING IT AFTER TONIGHT, SO BE SURE TO SEE IT WHILE YOU HAVE THE CHANCE!
IF ONLY THE SHOWS WERE AS FUNNY AS THE PROGRAMMING.
WHOOPS. BAD NEWS. IT'S ALREADY CANCELED.

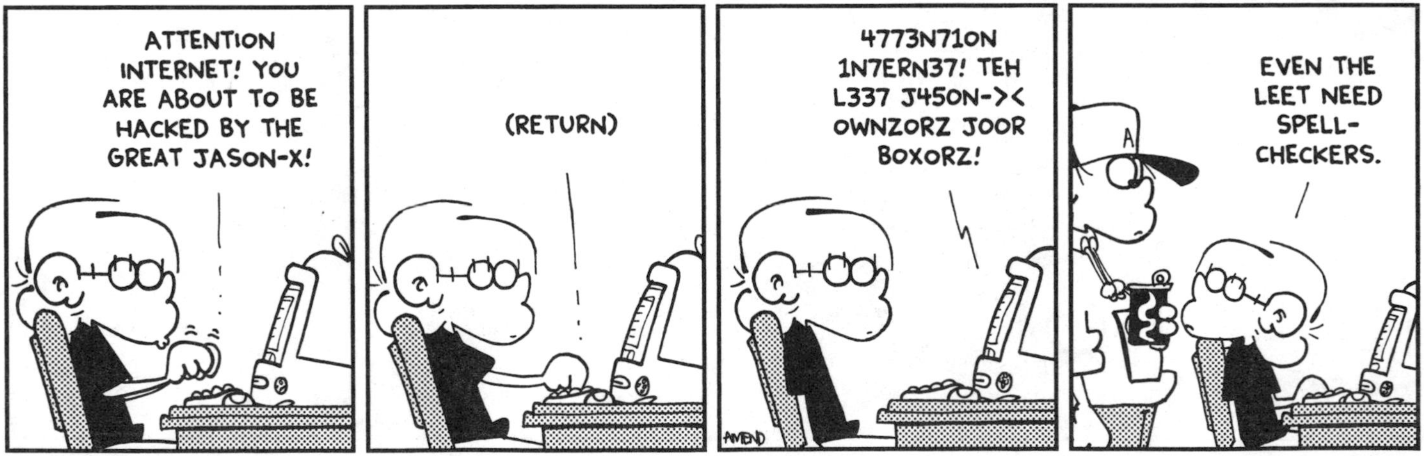
ATTENTION INTERNET! YOU ARE ABOUT TO BE HACKED BY THE GREAT JASON-X!
(RETURN)
4773N71ON 1N7ERN37! TEH L337 J450N->< OWNZORZ JOOR BOXORZ!
AMEND
EVEN THE LEET NEED SPELL-CHECKERS.

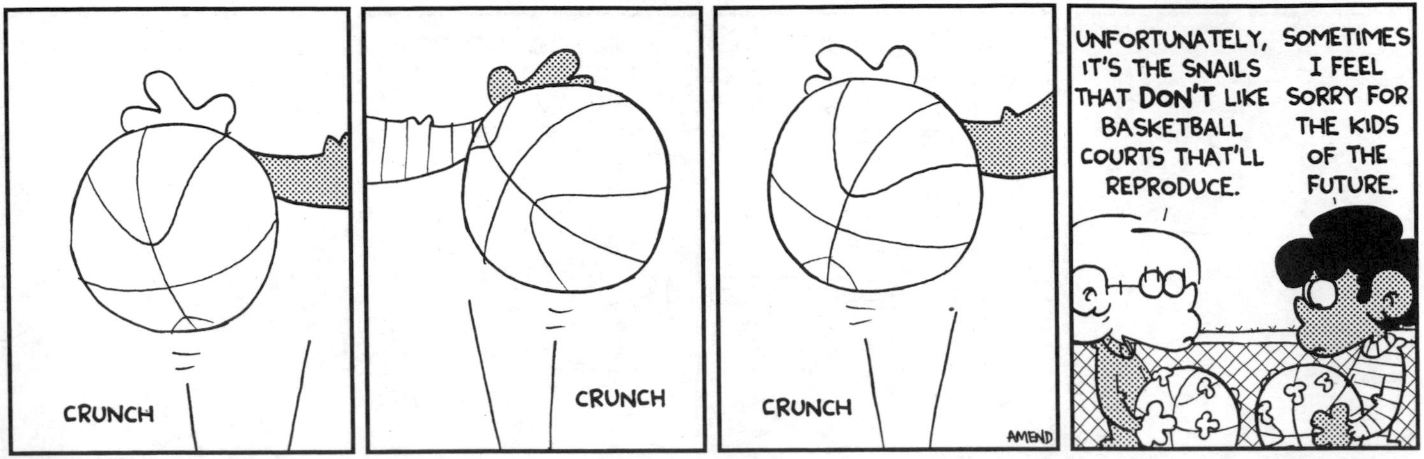
CRUNCH
CRUNCH
CRUNCH
UNFORTUNATELY, IT'S THE SNAILS THAT **DON'T** LIKE BASKETBALL COURTS THAT'LL REPRODUCE.
SOMETIMES I FEEL SORRY FOR THE KIDS OF THE FUTURE.
AMEND

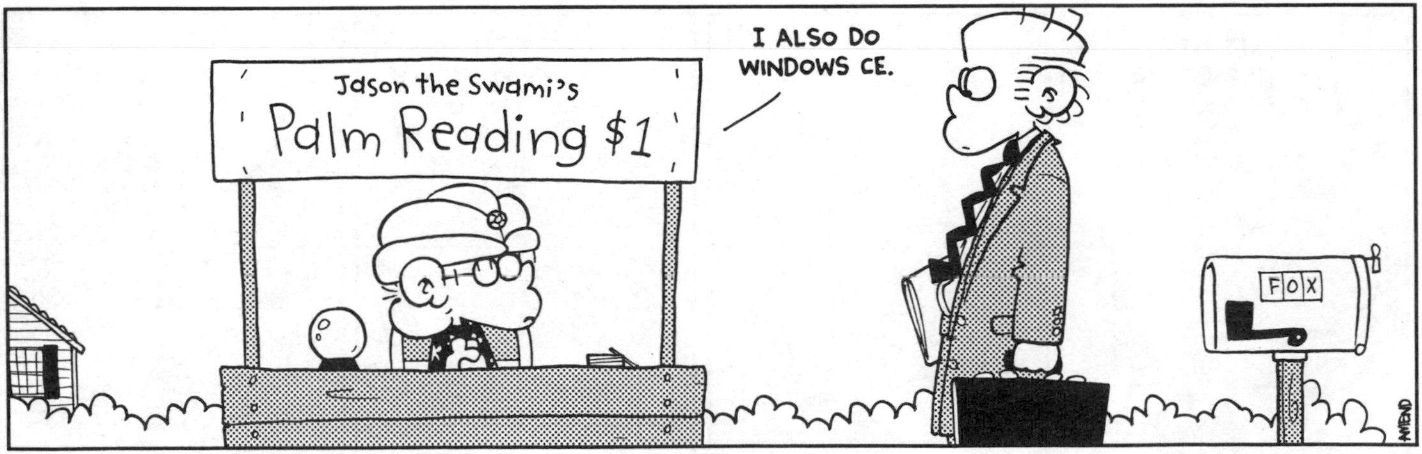
Jason the Swami's
Palm Reading $1
I ALSO DO WINDOWS CE.
FOX
AMEND

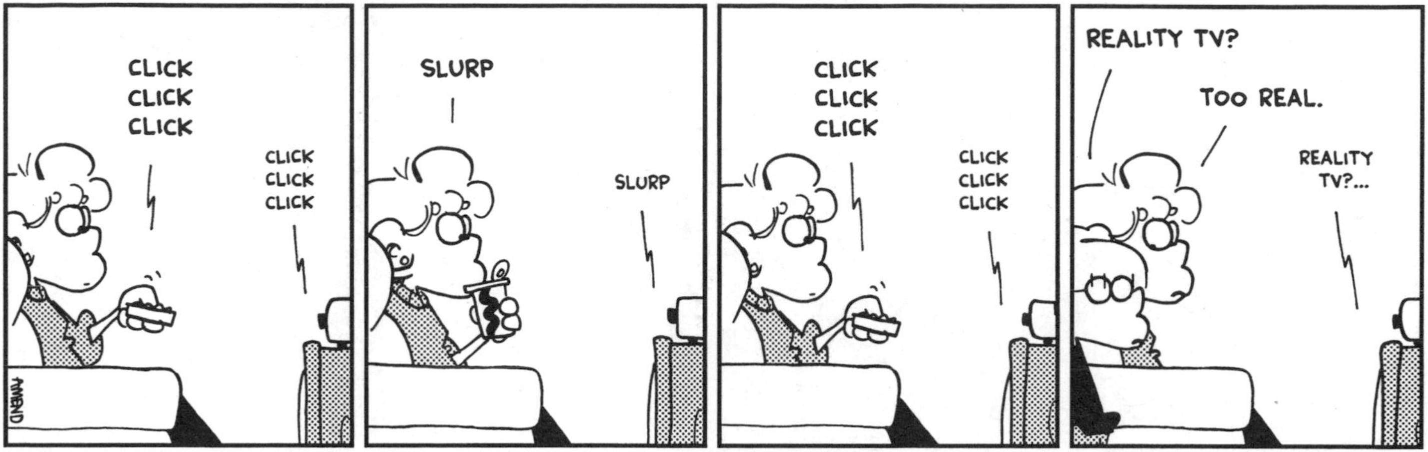
CLICK CLICK CLICK
CLICK CLICK CLICK
AMEND
SLURP
SLURP
CLICK CLICK CLICK
CLICK CLICK CLICK
REALITY TV?
TOO REAL.
REALITY TV?...

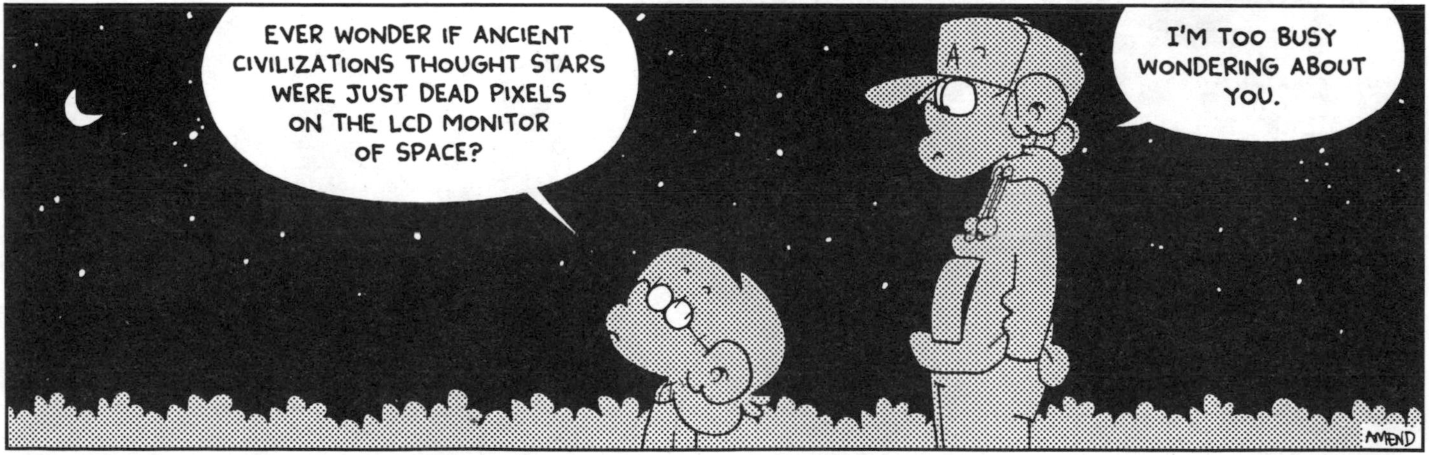
EVER WONDER IF ANCIENT CIVILIZATIONS THOUGHT STARS WERE JUST DEAD PIXELS ON THE LCD MONITOR OF SPACE?
I'M TOO BUSY WONDERING ABOUT YOU.
AMEND

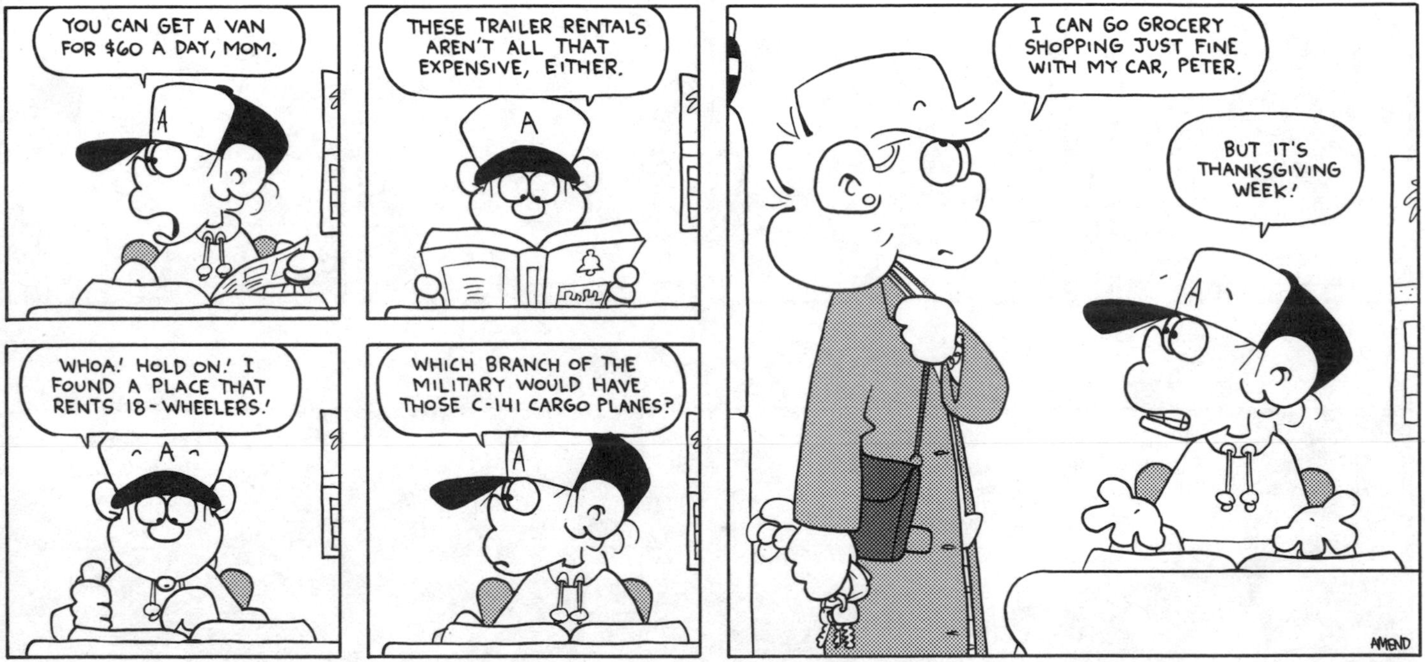
YOU CAN GET A VAN FOR $60 A DAY, MOM.
THESE TRAILER RENTALS AREN'T ALL THAT EXPENSIVE, EITHER.
WHOA! HOLD ON! I FOUND A PLACE THAT RENTS 18-WHEELERS!
WHICH BRANCH OF THE MILITARY WOULD HAVE THOSE C-141 CARGO PLANES?
I CAN GO GROCERY SHOPPING JUST FINE WITH MY CAR, PETER.
BUT IT'S THANKSGIVING WEEK!
AMEND

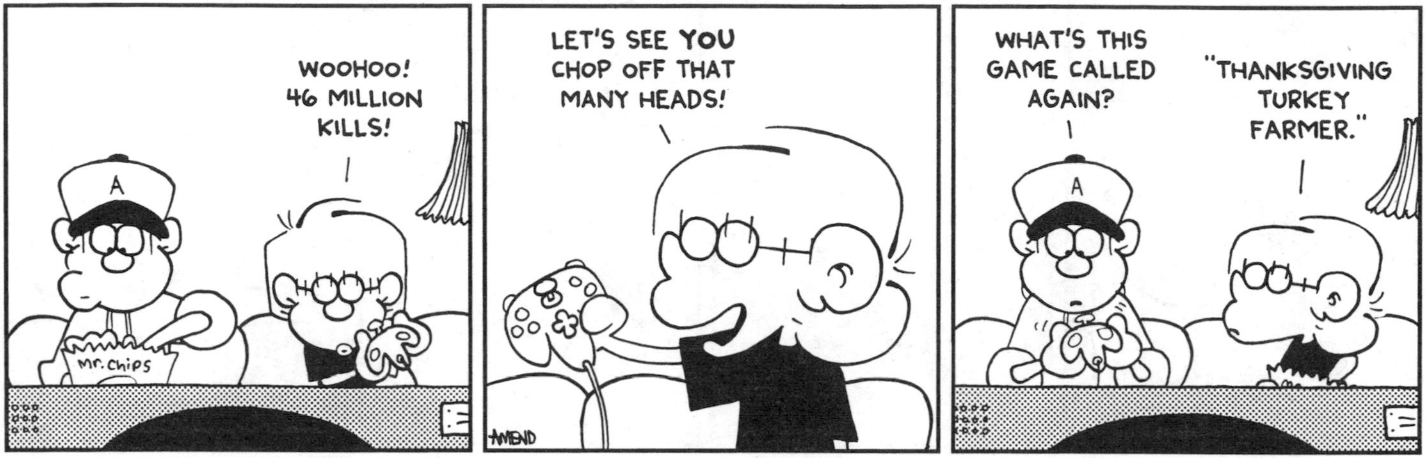
WOOHOO! 46 MILLION KILLS!
Mr. Chips
LET'S SEE YOU CHOP OFF THAT MANY HEADS!
AMEND
WHAT'S THIS GAME CALLED AGAIN?
"THANKSGIVING TURKEY FARMER."

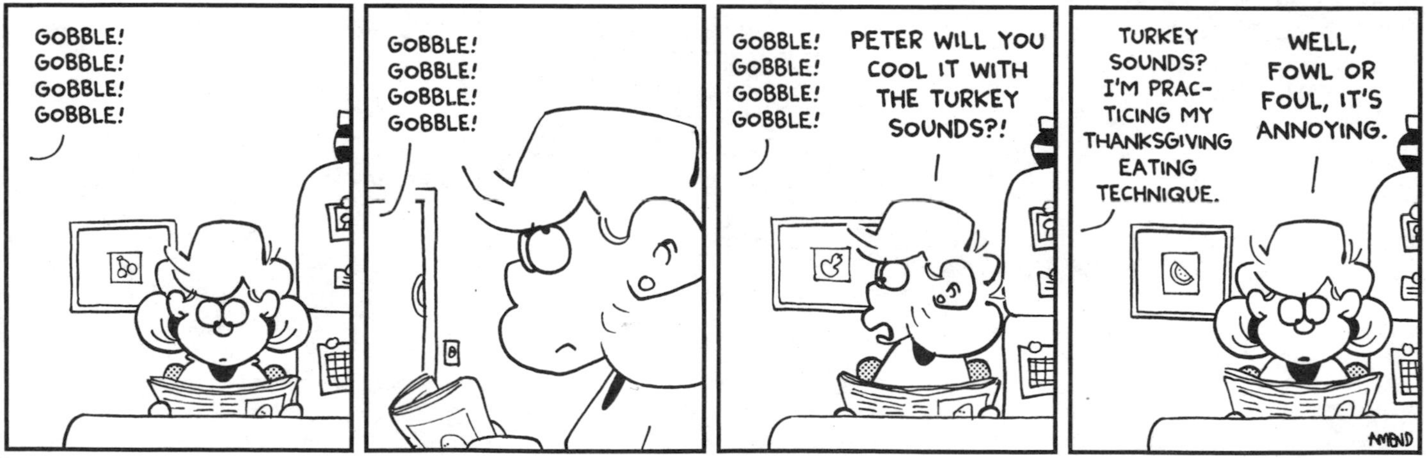
GOBBLE! GOBBLE! GOBBLE! GOBBLE!
GOBBLE! GOBBLE! GOBBLE! GOBBLE!
GOBBLE! GOBBLE! GOBBLE! GOBBLE!
PETER WILL YOU COOL IT WITH THE TURKEY SOUNDS?!
TURKEY SOUNDS? I'M PRACTICING MY THANKSGIVING EATING TECHNIQUE.
WELL, FOWL OR FOUL, IT'S ANNOYING.
AMEND

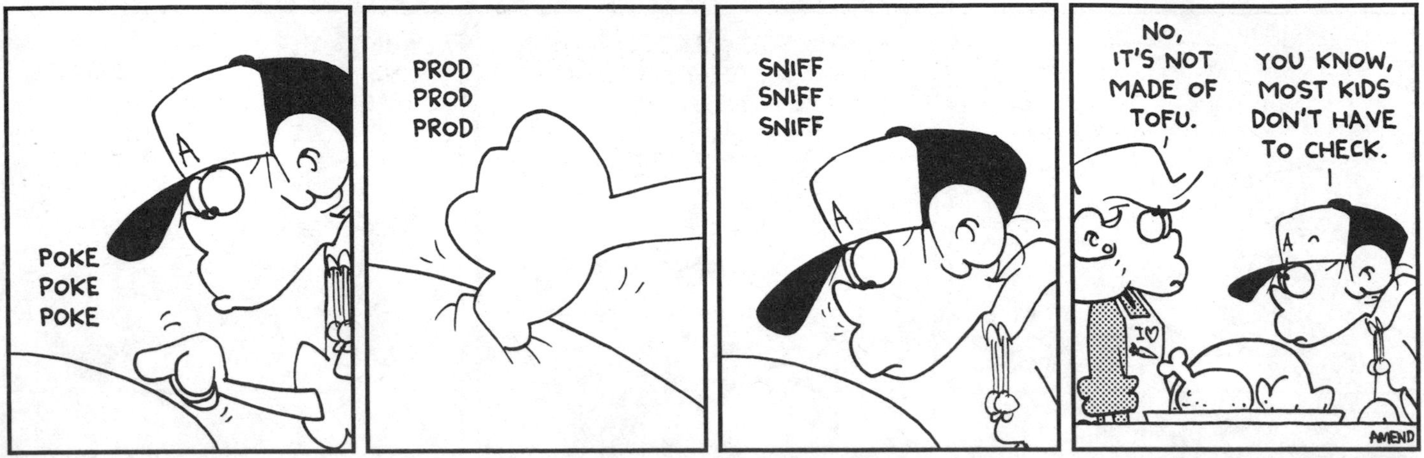
POKE
POKE
POKE
PROD
PROD
PROD
SNIFF
SNIFF
SNIFF
NO, IT'S NOT MADE OF TOFU.
YOU KNOW, MOST KIDS DON'T HAVE TO CHECK.
AMEND

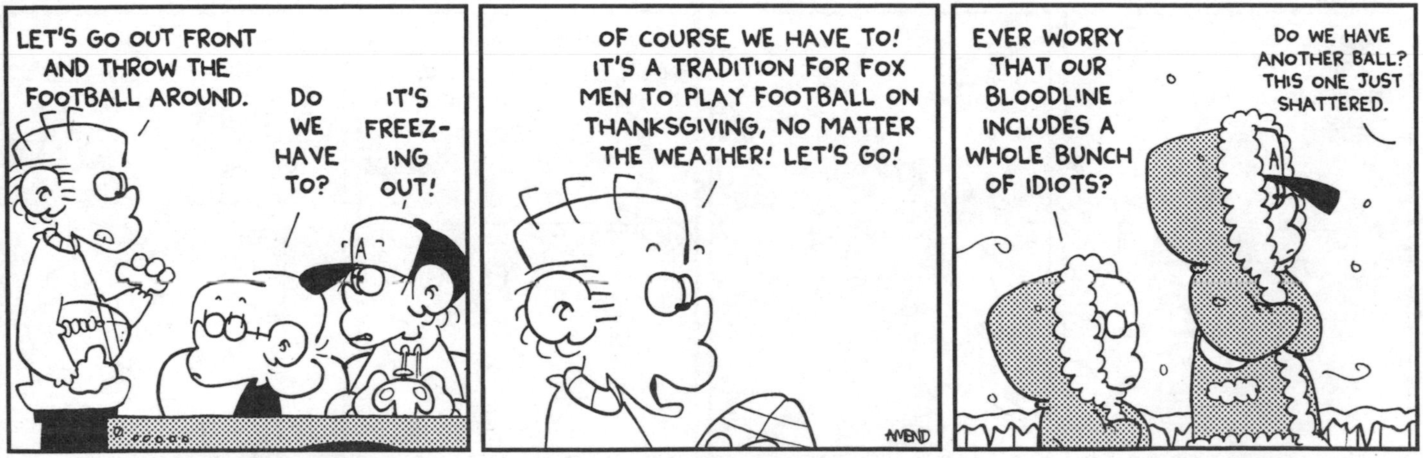
LET'S GO OUT FRONT AND THROW THE FOOTBALL AROUND.
DO WE HAVE TO?
IT'S FREEZ-ING OUT!
OF COURSE WE HAVE TO! IT'S A TRADITION FOR FOX MEN TO PLAY FOOTBALL ON THANKSGIVING, NO MATTER THE WEATHER! LET'S GO!
AMEND
EVER WORRY THAT OUR BLOODLINE INCLUDES A WHOLE BUNCH OF IDIOTS?
DO WE HAVE ANOTHER BALL? THIS ONE JUST SHATTERED.

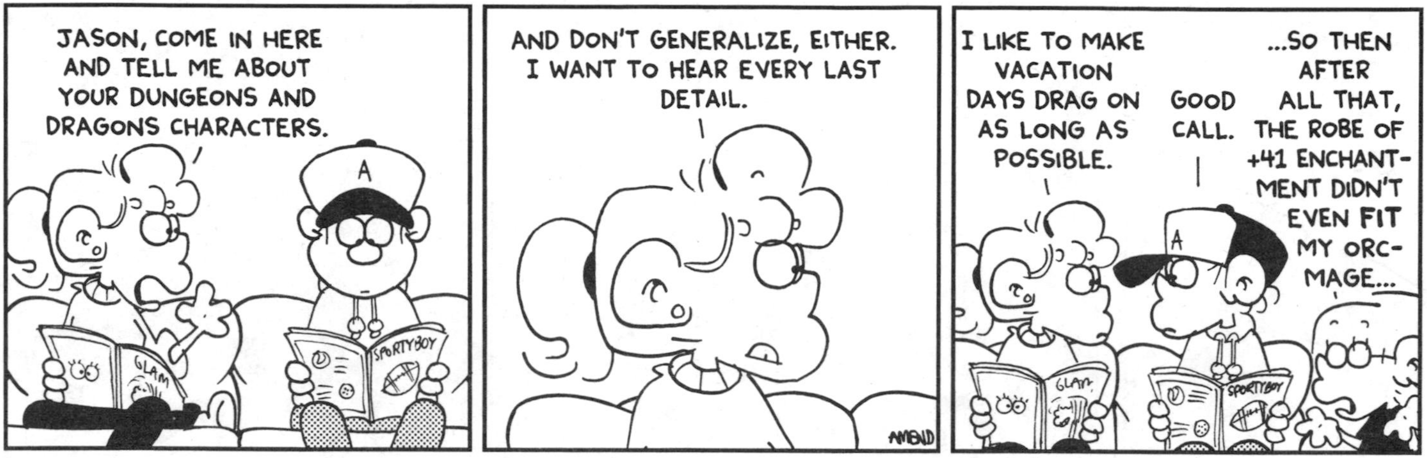
JASON, COME IN HERE AND TELL ME ABOUT YOUR DUNGEONS AND DRAGONS CHARACTERS.
AND DON'T GENERALIZE, EITHER. I WANT TO HEAR EVERY LAST DETAIL.
AMEND
I LIKE TO MAKE VACATION DAYS DRAG ON AS LONG AS POSSIBLE.
GOOD CALL.
...SO THEN AFTER ALL THAT, THE ROBE OF +41 ENCHANTMENT DIDN'T EVEN FIT MY ORC-MAGE...

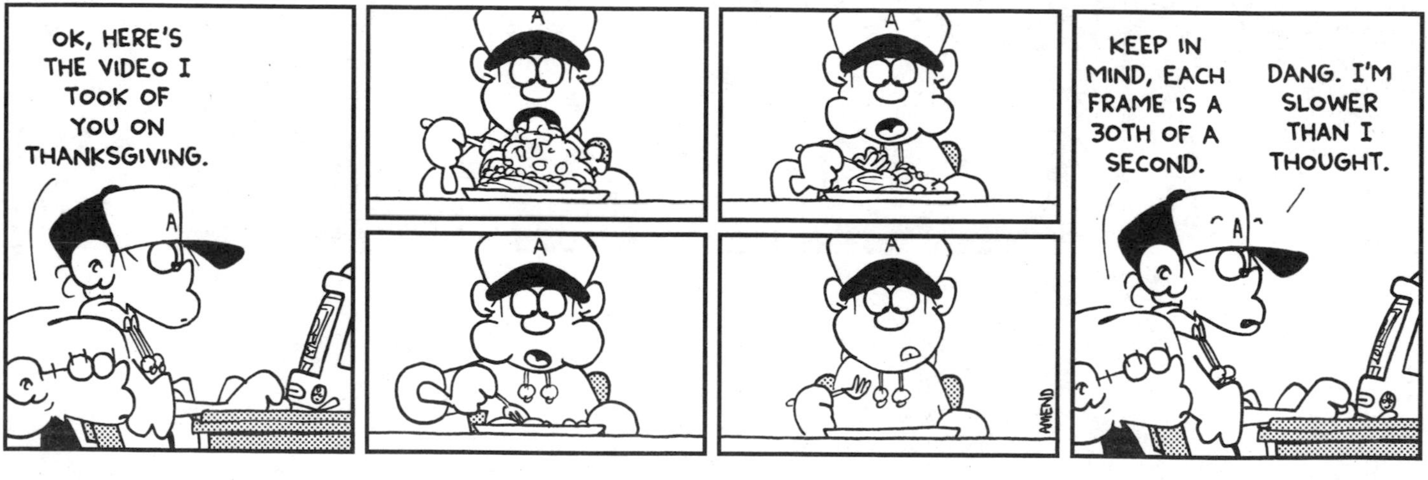
OK, HERE'S THE VIDEO I TOOK OF YOU ON THANKSGIVING.
AMEND
KEEP IN MIND, EACH FRAME IS A 30TH OF A SECOND.
DANG. I'M SLOWER THAN I THOUGHT.

MOM, WILL YOU TURN OFF THAT VIVALDI !?
IF YOU'RE COLD, I CAN REWIND IT.

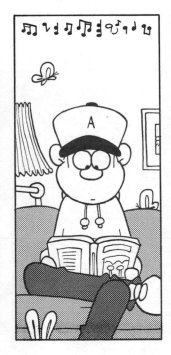

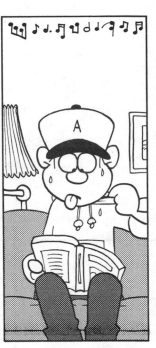

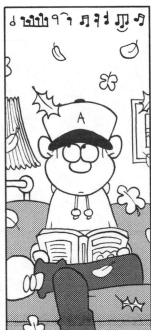

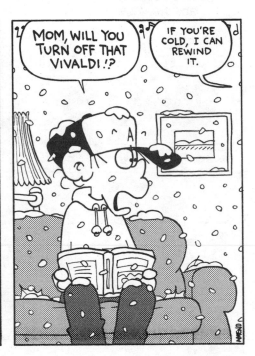

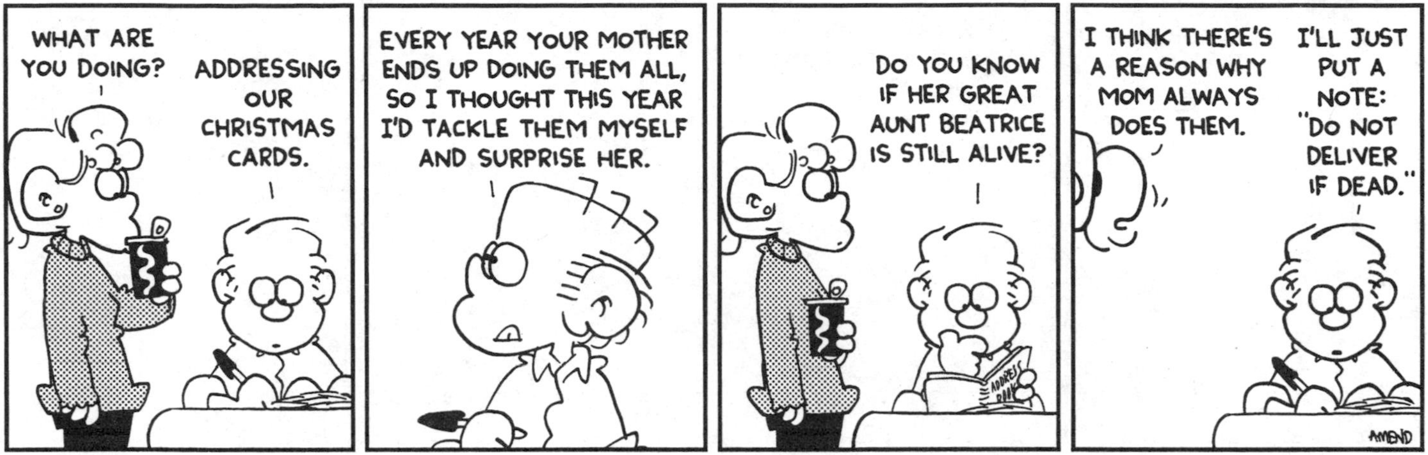
WHAT ARE YOU DOING?
ADDRESSING OUR CHRISTMAS CARDS.
EVERY YEAR YOUR MOTHER ENDS UP DOING THEM ALL, SO I THOUGHT THIS YEAR I'D TACKLE THEM MYSELF AND SURPRISE HER.
DO YOU KNOW IF HER GREAT AUNT BEATRICE IS STILL ALIVE?
ADDRESS BOOK
I THINK THERE'S A REASON WHY MOM ALWAYS DOES THEM.
I'LL JUST PUT A NOTE: "DO NOT DELIVER IF DEAD."
AMEND

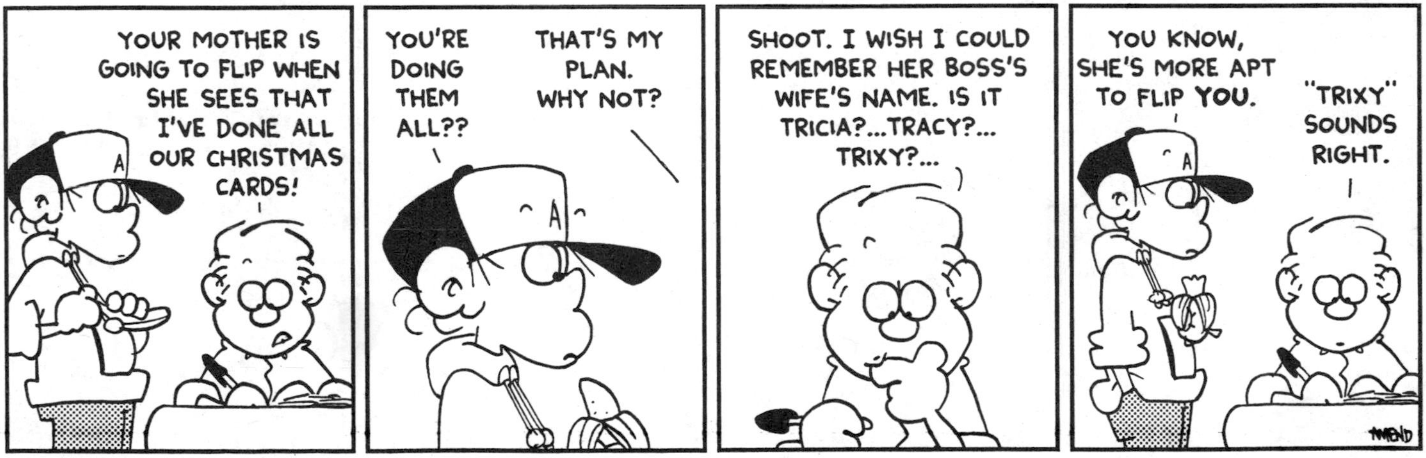
YOUR MOTHER IS GOING TO FLIP WHEN SHE SEES THAT I'VE DONE ALL OUR CHRISTMAS CARDS!
YOU'RE DOING THEM ALL??
THAT'S MY PLAN. WHY NOT?
SHOOT. I WISH I COULD REMEMBER HER BOSS'S WIFE'S NAME. IS IT TRICIA?...TRACY?... TRIXY?...
YOU KNOW, SHE'S MORE APT TO FLIP YOU.
"TRIXY" SOUNDS RIGHT.
AMEND

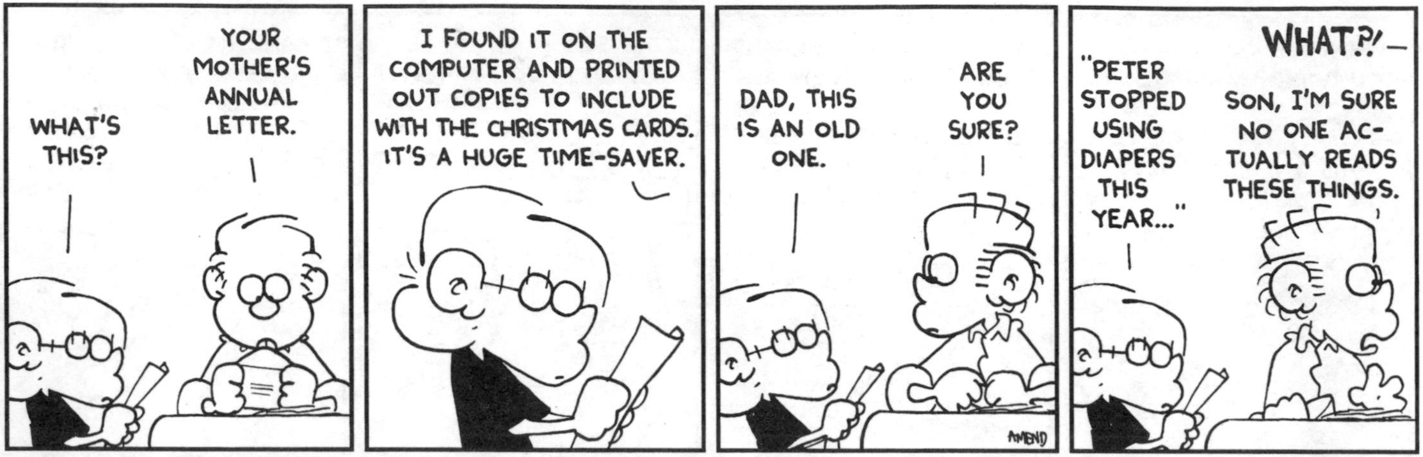
WHAT'S THIS?
YOUR MOTHER'S ANNUAL LETTER.
I FOUND IT ON THE COMPUTER AND PRINTED OUT COPIES TO INCLUDE WITH THE CHRISTMAS CARDS. IT'S A HUGE TIME-SAVER.
DAD, THIS IS AN OLD ONE.
ARE YOU SURE?
"PETER STOPPED USING DIAPERS THIS YEAR..."
WHAT?!
SON, I'M SURE NO ONE ACTUALLY READS THESE THINGS.
AMEND

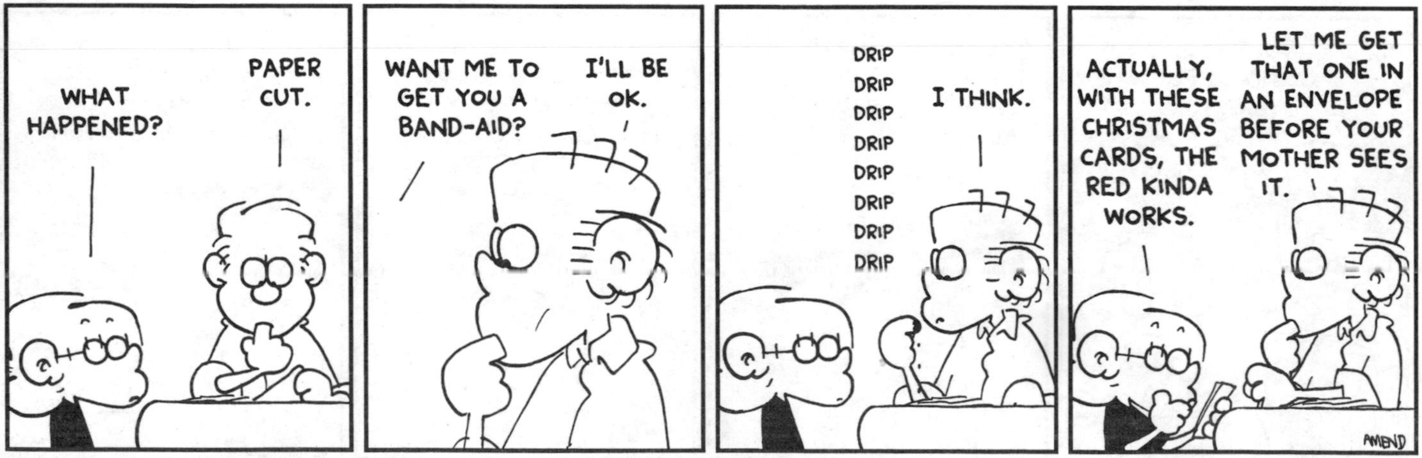
WHAT HAPPENED?
PAPER CUT.
WANT ME TO GET YOU A BAND-AID?
I'LL BE OK.
DRIP DRIP DRIP DRIP DRIP DRIP DRIP DRIP
I THINK.
ACTUALLY, WITH THESE CHRISTMAS CARDS, THE RED KINDA WORKS.
LET ME GET THAT ONE IN AN ENVELOPE BEFORE YOUR MOTHER SEES IT.
AMEND

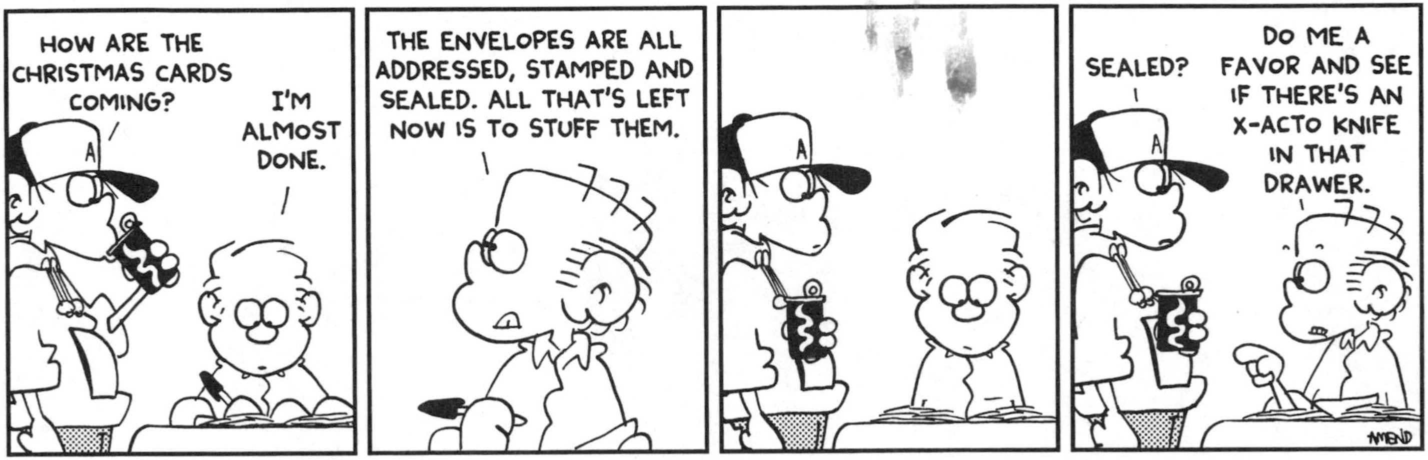
HOW ARE THE CHRISTMAS CARDS COMING?
I'M ALMOST DONE.
THE ENVELOPES ARE ALL ADDRESSED, STAMPED AND SEALED. ALL THAT'S LEFT NOW IS TO STUFF THEM.
SEALED?
DO ME A FAVOR AND SEE IF THERE'S AN X-ACTO KNIFE IN THAT DRAWER.
AMEND

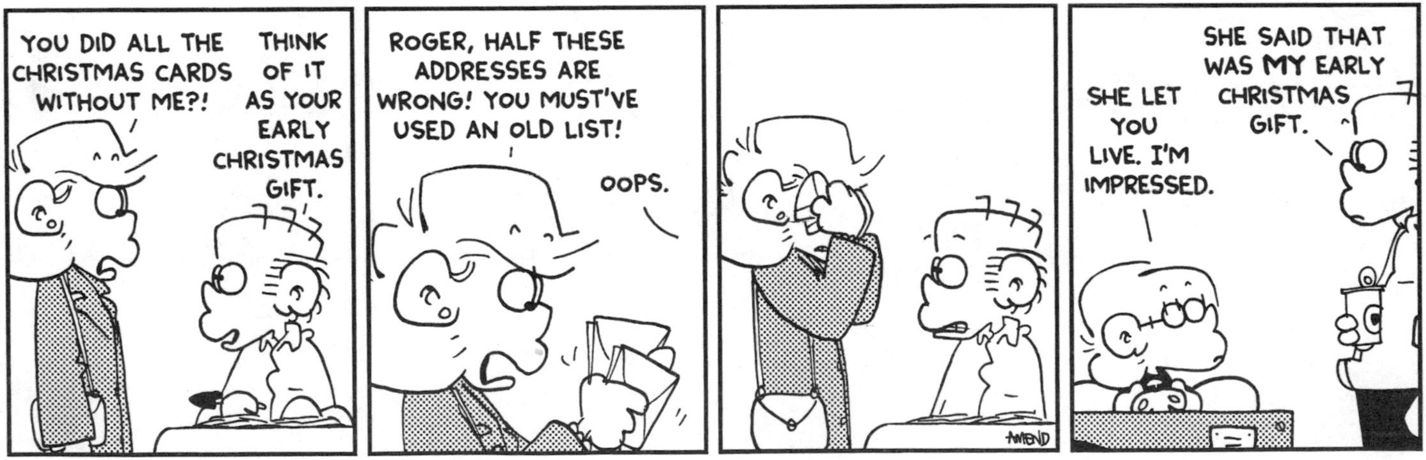
YOU DID ALL THE CHRISTMAS CARDS WITHOUT ME?!
THINK OF IT AS YOUR EARLY CHRISTMAS GIFT.
ROGER, HALF THESE ADDRESSES ARE WRONG! YOU MUST'VE USED AN OLD LIST!
OOPS.
AMEND
SHE LET YOU LIVE. I'M IMPRESSED.
SHE SAID THAT WAS MY EARLY CHRISTMAS GIFT.

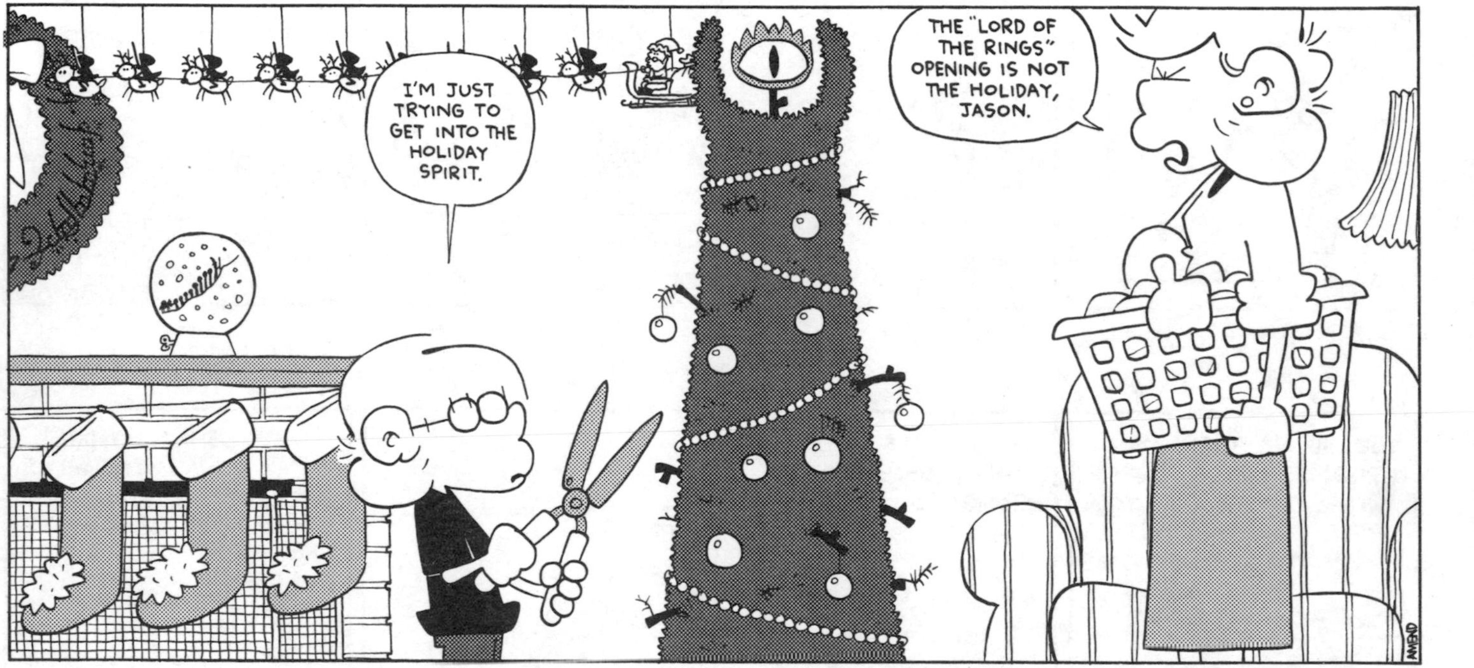
I'M JUST TRYING TO GET INTO THE HOLIDAY SPIRIT.
THE "LORD OF THE RINGS" OPENING IS NOT THE HOLIDAY, JASON.

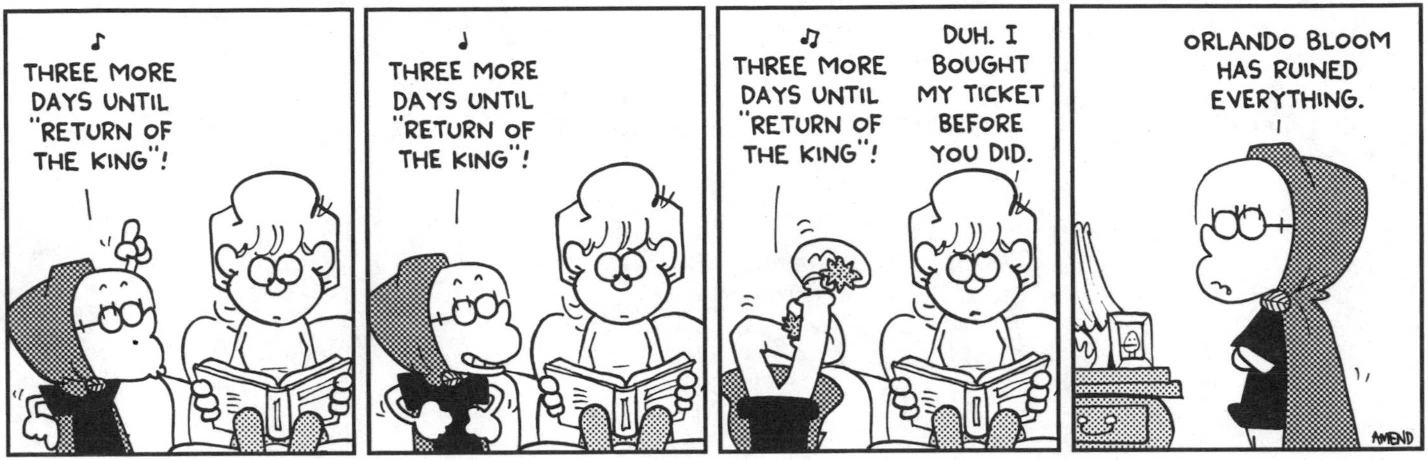
♪ THREE MORE DAYS UNTIL "RETURN OF THE KING"!
♩ THREE MORE DAYS UNTIL "RETURN OF THE KING"!
♫ THREE MORE DAYS UNTIL "RETURN OF THE KING"!
DUH. I BOUGHT MY TICKET BEFORE YOU DID.
ORLANDO BLOOM HAS RUINED EVERYTHING.
AMEND

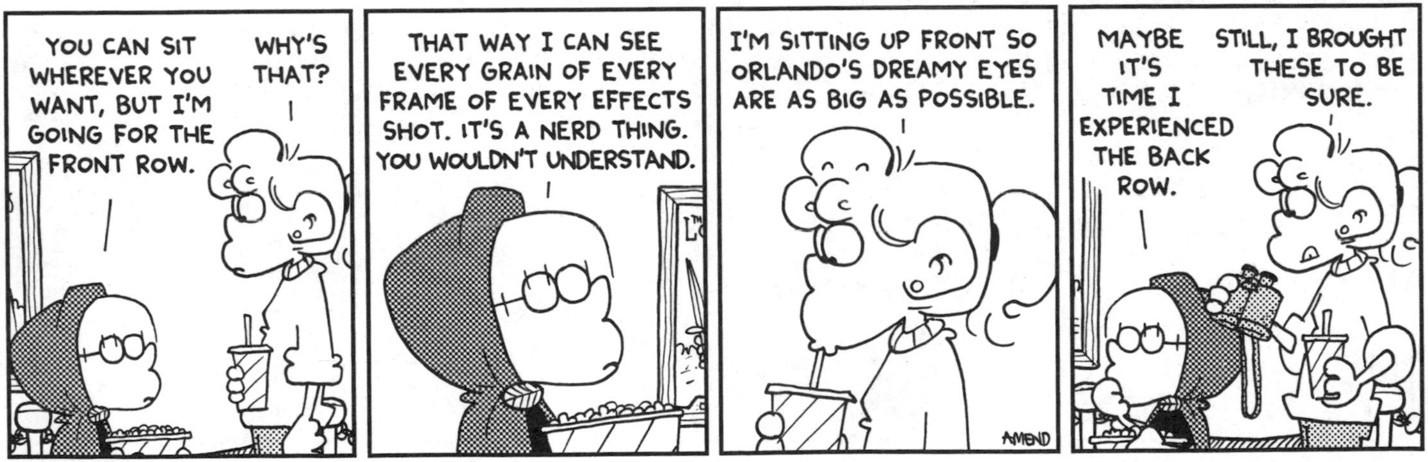
YOU CAN SIT WHEREVER YOU WANT, BUT I'M GOING FOR THE FRONT ROW.
WHY'S THAT?
THAT WAY I CAN SEE EVERY GRAIN OF EVERY FRAME OF EVERY EFFECTS SHOT. IT'S A NERD THING. YOU WOULDN'T UNDERSTAND.
I'M SITTING UP FRONT SO ORLANDO'S DREAMY EYES ARE AS BIG AS POSSIBLE.
AMEND
MAYBE IT'S TIME I EXPERIENCED THE BACK ROW.
STILL, I BROUGHT THESE TO BE SURE.

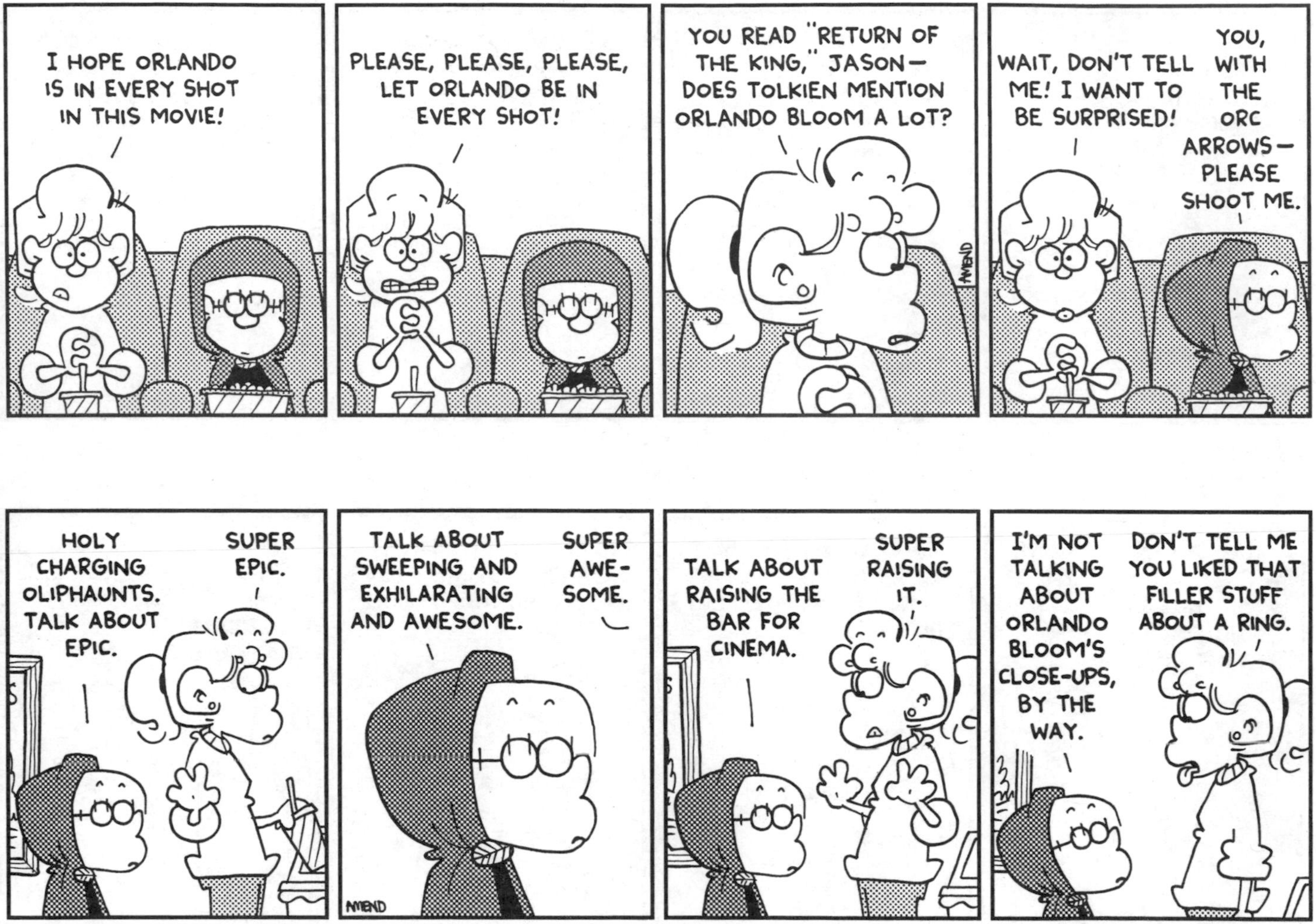
I HOPE ORLANDO IS IN EVERY SHOT IN THIS MOVIE!
PLEASE, PLEASE, PLEASE, LET ORLANDO BE IN EVERY SHOT!
YOU READ "RETURN OF THE KING," JASON— DOES TOLKIEN MENTION ORLANDO BLOOM A LOT?
AMEND
WAIT, DON'T TELL ME! I WANT TO BE SURPRISED!
YOU, WITH THE ORC ARROWS— PLEASE SHOOT ME.
HOLY CHARGING OLIPHAUNTS. TALK ABOUT EPIC.
SUPER EPIC.
TALK ABOUT SWEEPING AND EXHILARATING AND AWESOME.
SUPER AWE-SOME.
AMEND
TALK ABOUT RAISING THE BAR FOR CINEMA.
SUPER RAISING IT.
I'M NOT TALKING ABOUT ORLANDO BLOOM'S CLOSE-UPS, BY THE WAY.
DON'T TELL ME YOU LIKED THAT FILLER STUFF ABOUT A RING.

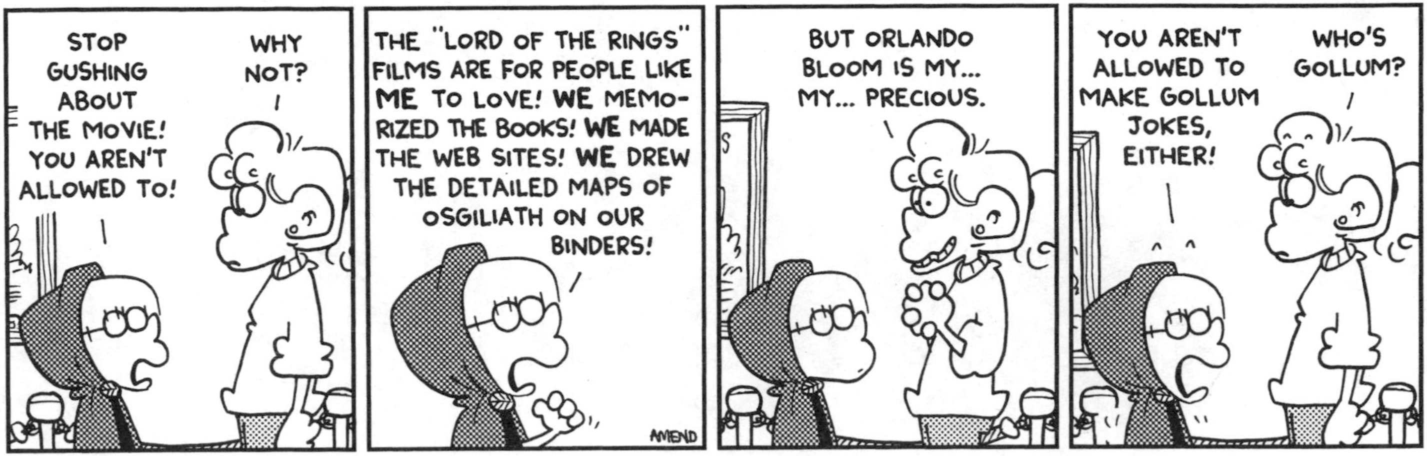
STOP GUSHING ABOUT THE MOVIE! YOU AREN'T ALLOWED TO!
WHY NOT?
THE "LORD OF THE RINGS" FILMS ARE FOR PEOPLE LIKE ME TO LOVE! WE MEMORIZED THE BOOKS! WE MADE THE WEB SITES! WE DREW THE DETAILED MAPS OF OSGILIATH ON OUR BINDERS!
AMEND
BUT ORLANDO BLOOM IS MY... MY... PRECIOUS.
YOU AREN'T ALLOWED TO MAKE GOLLUM JOKES, EITHER!
WHO'S GOLLUM?

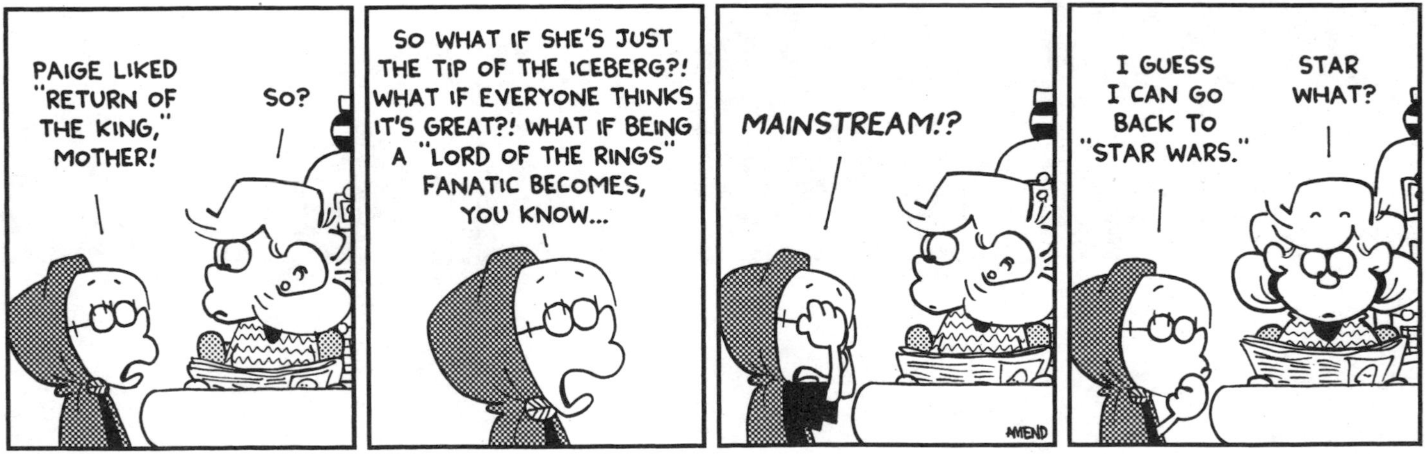
PAIGE LIKED "RETURN OF THE KING," MOTHER!
SO?
SO WHAT IF SHE'S JUST THE TIP OF THE ICEBERG?! WHAT IF EVERYONE THINKS IT'S GREAT?! WHAT IF BEING A "LORD OF THE RINGS" FANATIC BECOMES, YOU KNOW...
MAINSTREAM!?
AMEND
I GUESS I CAN GO BACK TO "STAR WARS."
STAR WHAT?

BEHOLD THE NINJABREAD MAN!
NEXT CHRISTMAS WE'RE **BUYING** COOKIES.
AMEND

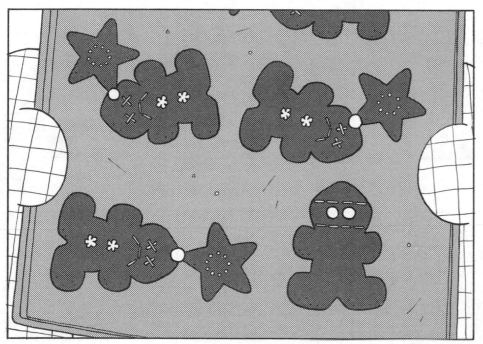

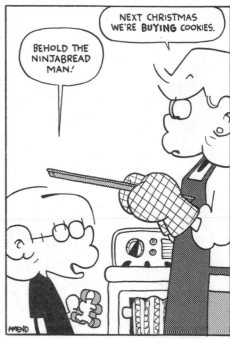

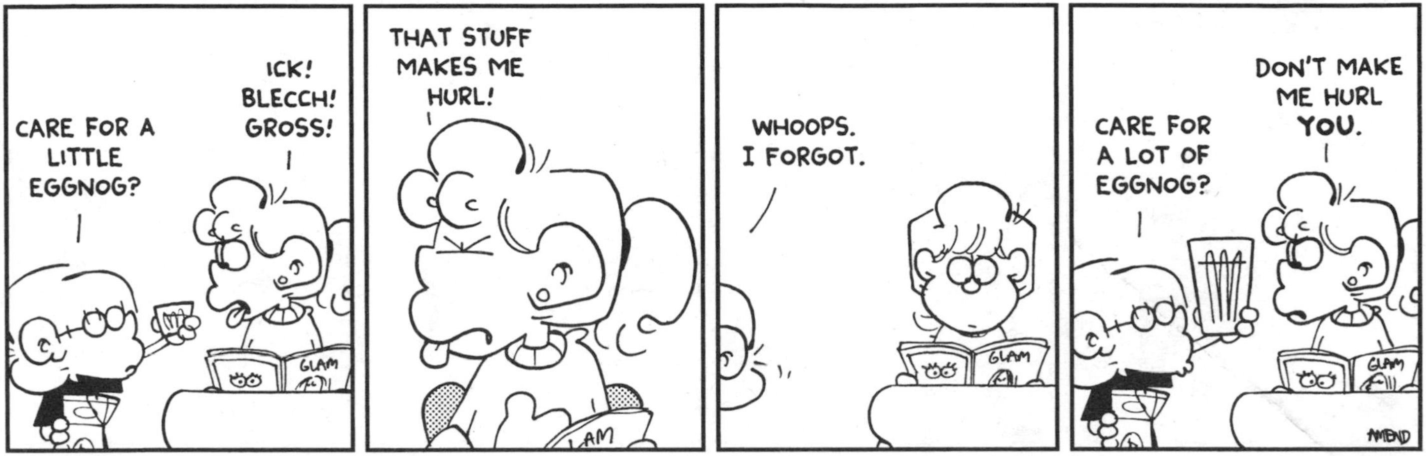
CARE FOR A LITTLE EGGNOG?
ICK! BLECCH! GROSS!
GLAM
THAT STUFF MAKES ME HURL!
WHOOPS. I FORGOT.
CARE FOR A LOT OF EGGNOG?
DON'T MAKE ME HURL **YOU**.
AMEND

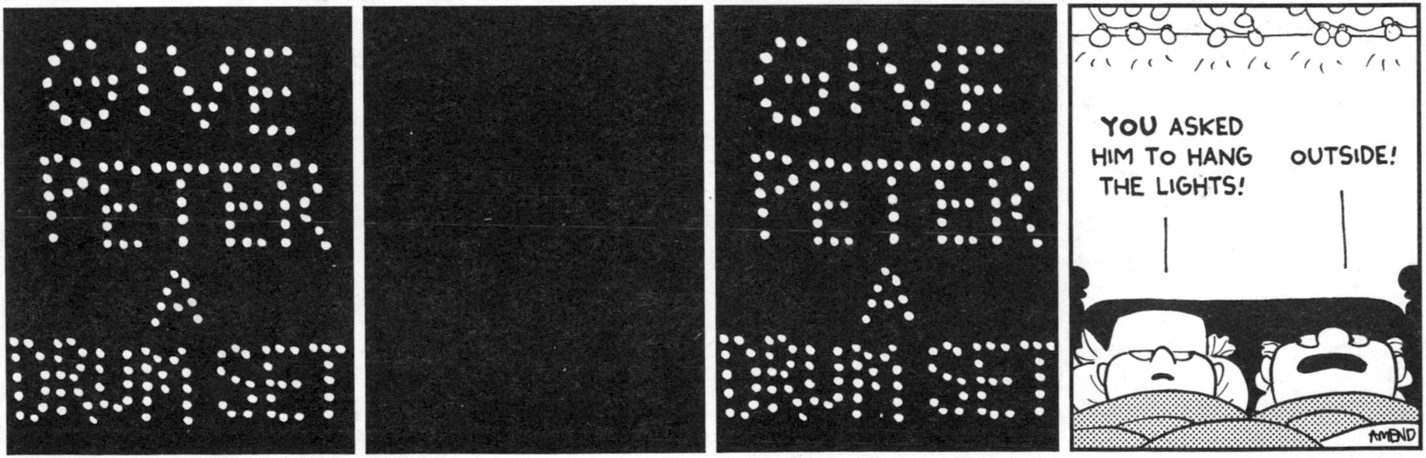
GIVE PETER A DRUM SET
GIVE PETER A DRUM SET
YOU ASKED HIM TO HANG THE LIGHTS!
OUTSIDE!
AMEND

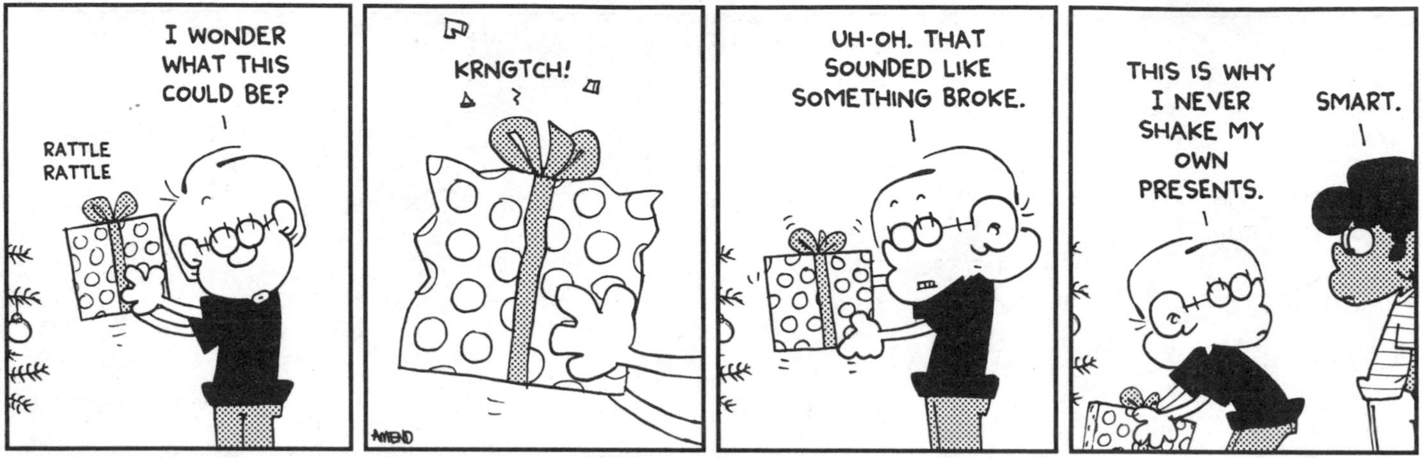
I WONDER WHAT THIS COULD BE?
RATTLE RATTLE
KRNGTCH!
AMEND
UH-OH. THAT SOUNDED LIKE SOMETHING BROKE.
THIS IS WHY I NEVER SHAKE MY OWN PRESENTS.
SMART.

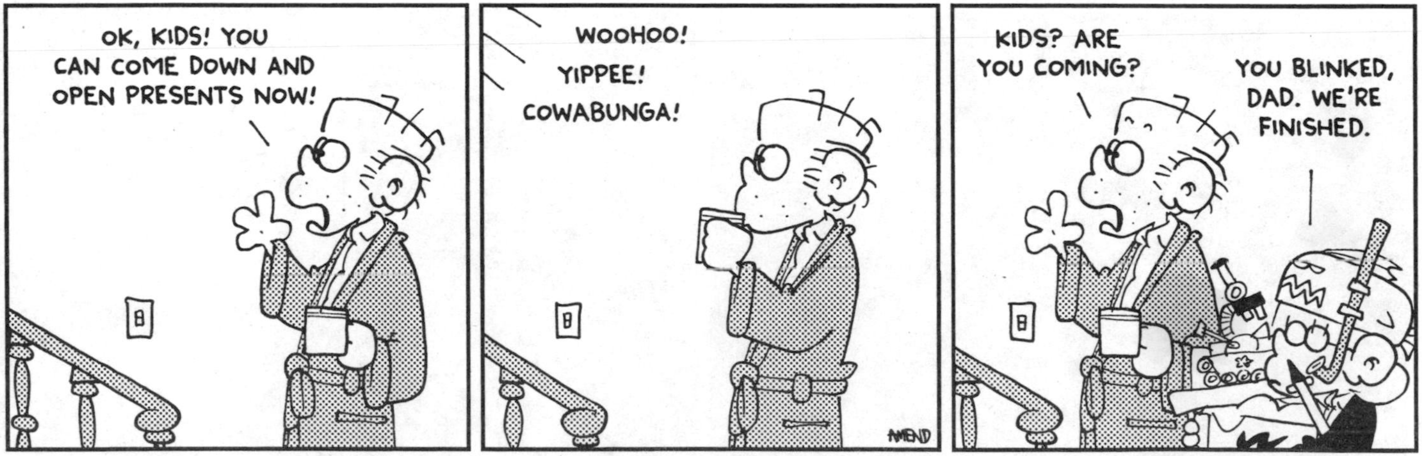
OK, KIDS! YOU CAN COME DOWN AND OPEN PRESENTS NOW!
WOOHOO!
YIPPEE!
COWABUNGA!
AMEND
KIDS? ARE YOU COMING?
YOU BLINKED, DAD. WE'RE FINISHED.

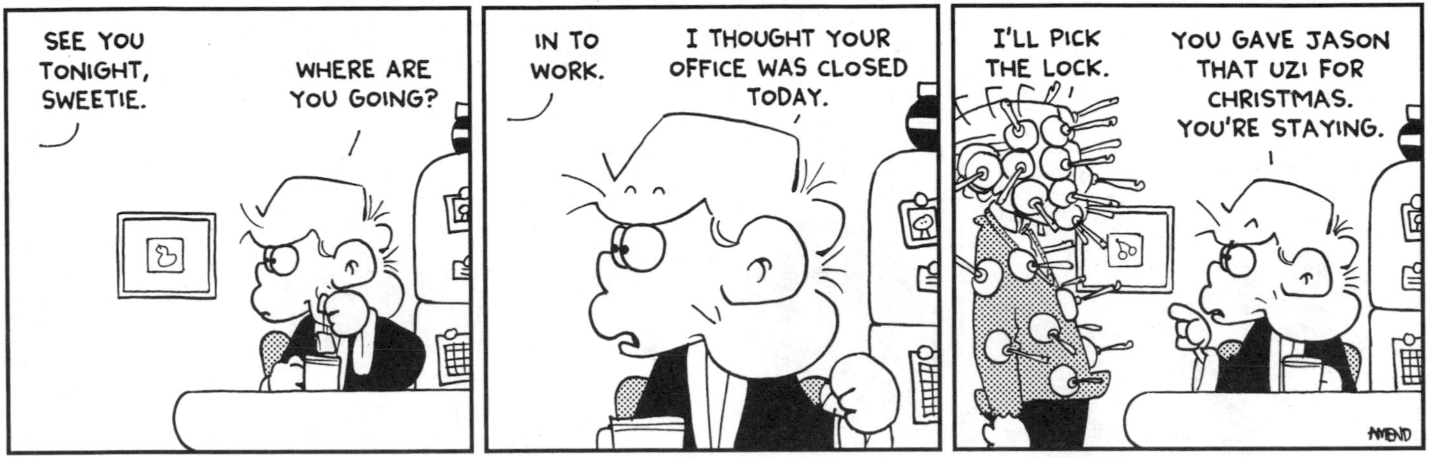
SEE YOU TONIGHT, SWEETIE.
WHERE ARE YOU GOING?
IN TO WORK.
I THOUGHT YOUR OFFICE WAS CLOSED TODAY.
I'LL PICK THE LOCK.
YOU GAVE JASON THAT UZI FOR CHRISTMAS. YOU'RE STAYING.
AMEND

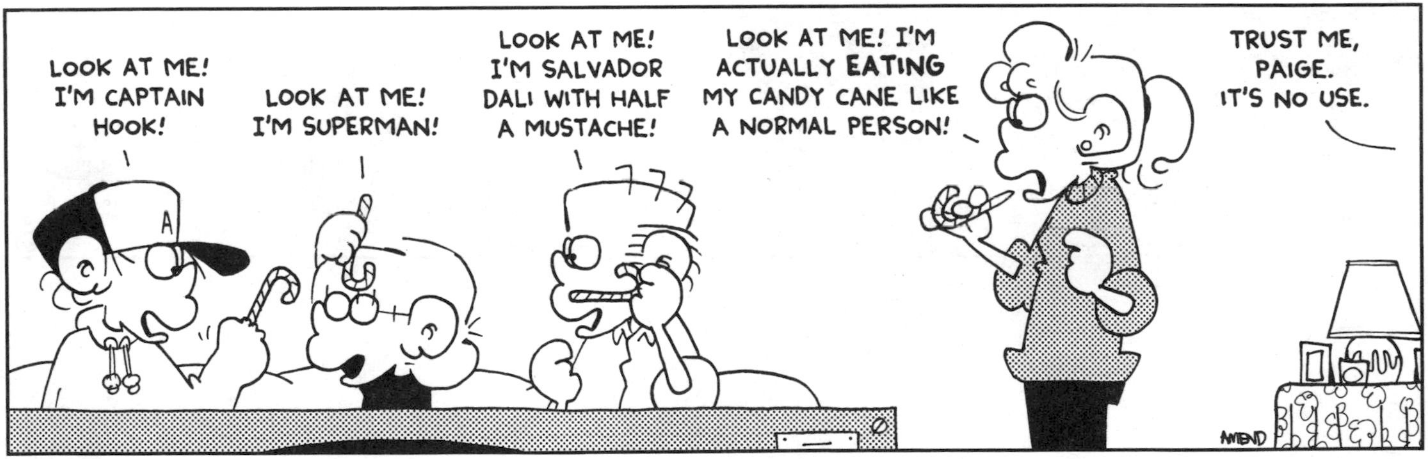
LOOK AT ME! I'M CAPTAIN HOOK!
LOOK AT ME! I'M SUPERMAN!
LOOK AT ME! I'M SALVADOR DALI WITH HALF A MUSTACHE!
LOOK AT ME! I'M ACTUALLY **EATING** MY CANDY CANE LIKE A NORMAL PERSON!
TRUST ME, PAIGE. IT'S NO USE.
AMEND

GET ANYTHING GOOD FOR CHRISTMAS?
I GOT A G.I. JIM M-1 TANK.
COOL.
AND A G.I. JIM F-16 FIGHTER JET.
VERY COOL.
AND THIS G.I. JIM NIMITZ-CLASS AIRCRAFT CARRIER.
WHY'S IT HAVE THIS RED, WHITE AND BLUE "MISSION ACCOMPLISHED" BANNER?
YOU GOT THE G.I. JIM PRESIDENTIAL FLIGHT-DECK PHOTO-OP SET?!?
I THOUGHT THOSE WERE ALL RECALLED.
I GUESS SANTA SHOPPED EARLY.
AMEND

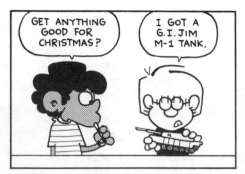

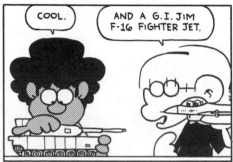

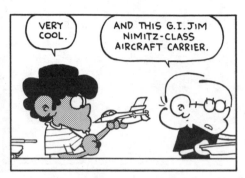

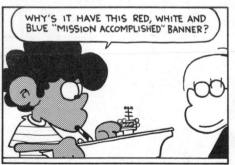

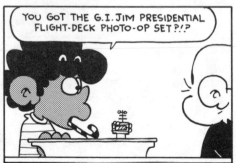

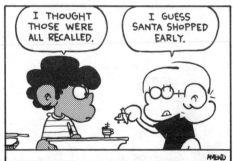

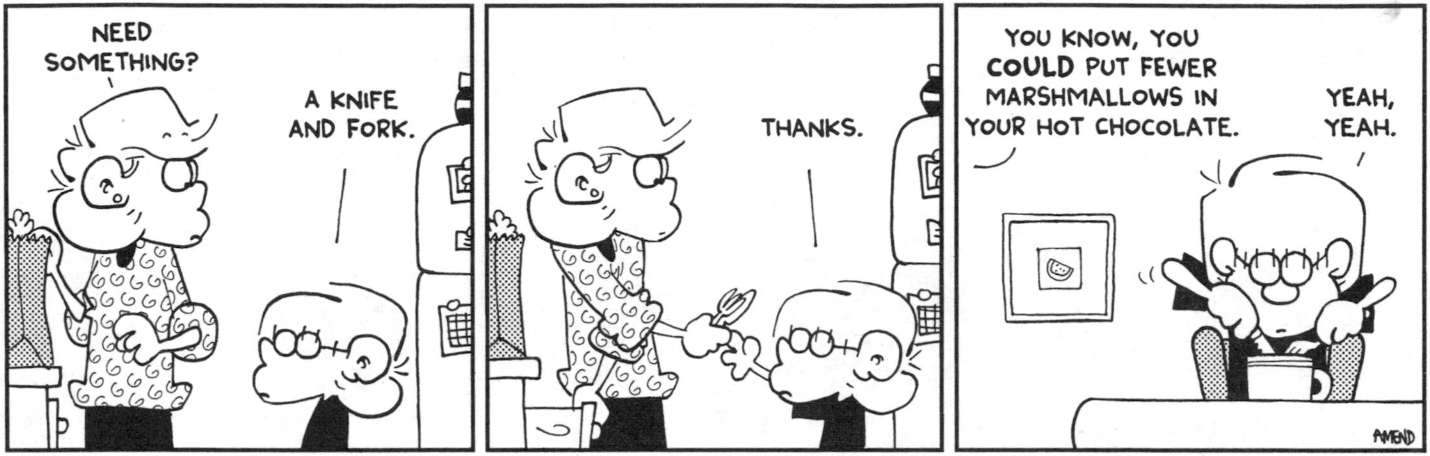
NEED SOMETHING?
A KNIFE AND FORK.
THANKS.
YOU KNOW, YOU COULD PUT FEWER MARSHMALLOWS IN YOUR HOT CHOCOLATE.
YEAH, YEAH.
AMEND

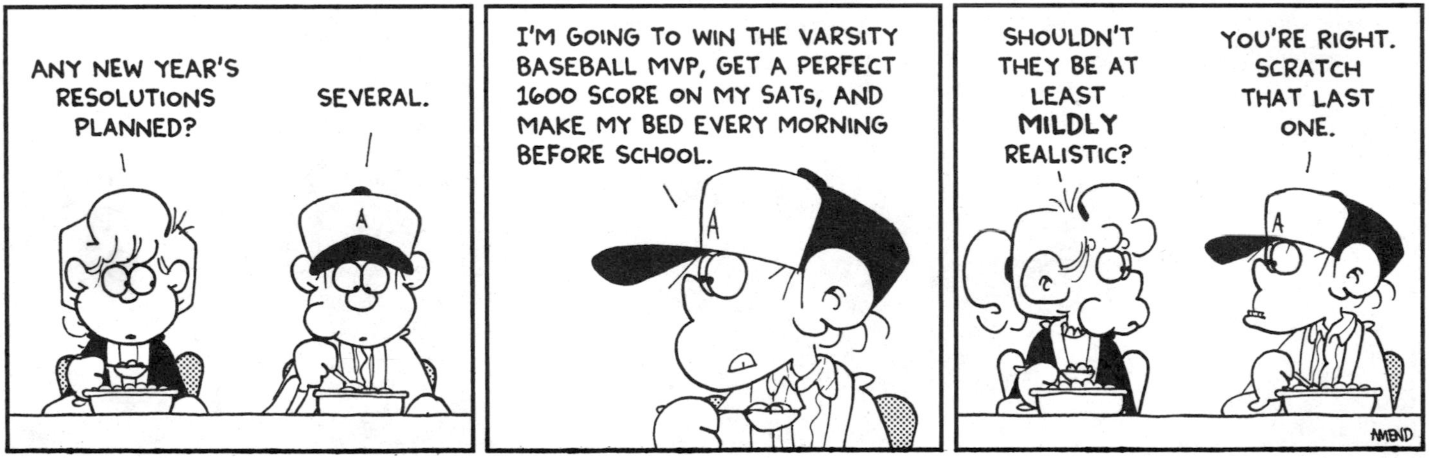
ANY NEW YEAR'S RESOLUTIONS PLANNED?
SEVERAL.
I'M GOING TO WIN THE VARSITY BASEBALL MVP, GET A PERFECT 1600 SCORE ON MY SATs, AND MAKE MY BED EVERY MORNING BEFORE SCHOOL.
SHOULDN'T THEY BE AT LEAST MILDLY REALISTIC?
YOU'RE RIGHT. SCRATCH THAT LAST ONE.
AMEND

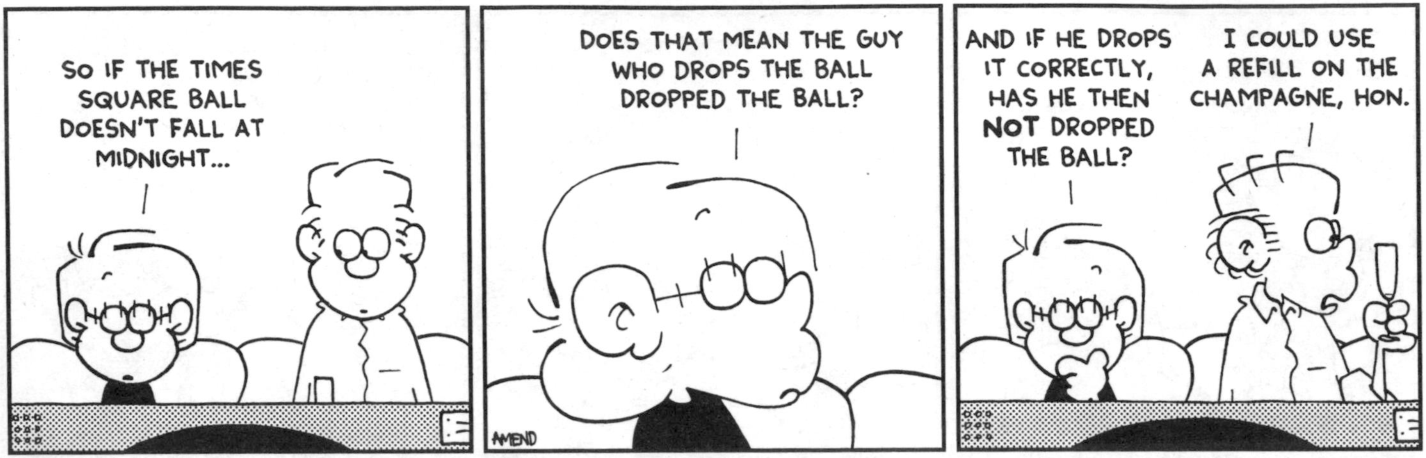
SO IF THE TIMES SQUARE BALL DOESN'T FALL AT MIDNIGHT...
DOES THAT MEAN THE GUY WHO DROPS THE BALL DROPPED THE BALL?
AMEND
AND IF HE DROPS IT CORRECTLY, HAS HE THEN **NOT** DROPPED THE BALL?
I COULD USE A REFILL ON THE CHAMPAGNE, HON.

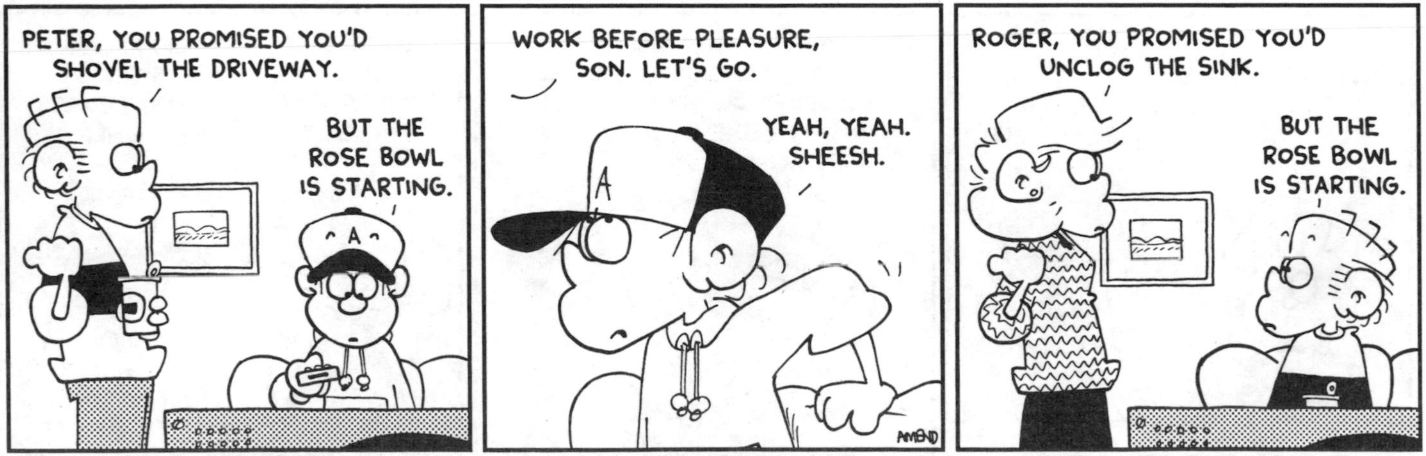
PETER, YOU PROMISED YOU'D SHOVEL THE DRIVEWAY.
BUT THE ROSE BOWL IS STARTING.
WORK BEFORE PLEASURE, SON. LET'S GO.
YEAH, YEAH. SHEESH.
AMEND
ROGER, YOU PROMISED YOU'D UNCLOG THE SINK.
BUT THE ROSE BOWL IS STARTING.

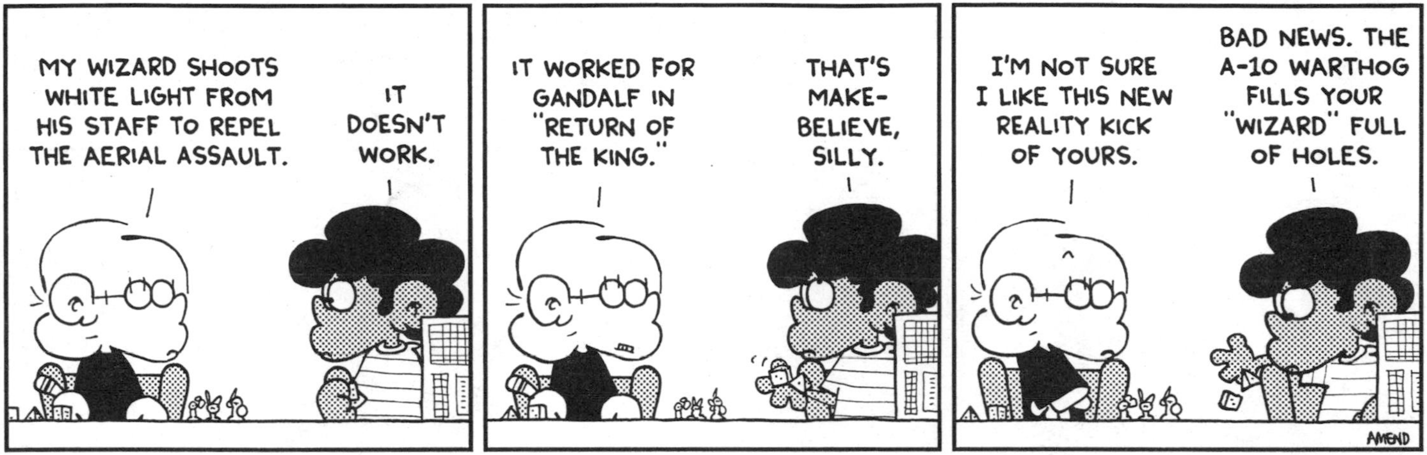
MY WIZARD SHOOTS WHITE LIGHT FROM HIS STAFF TO REPEL THE AERIAL ASSAULT.
IT DOESN'T WORK.
IT WORKED FOR GANDALF IN "RETURN OF THE KING."
THAT'S MAKE-BELIEVE, SILLY.
I'M NOT SURE I LIKE THIS NEW REALITY KICK OF YOURS.
BAD NEWS. THE A-10 WARTHOG FILLS YOUR "WIZARD" FULL OF HOLES.
AMEND

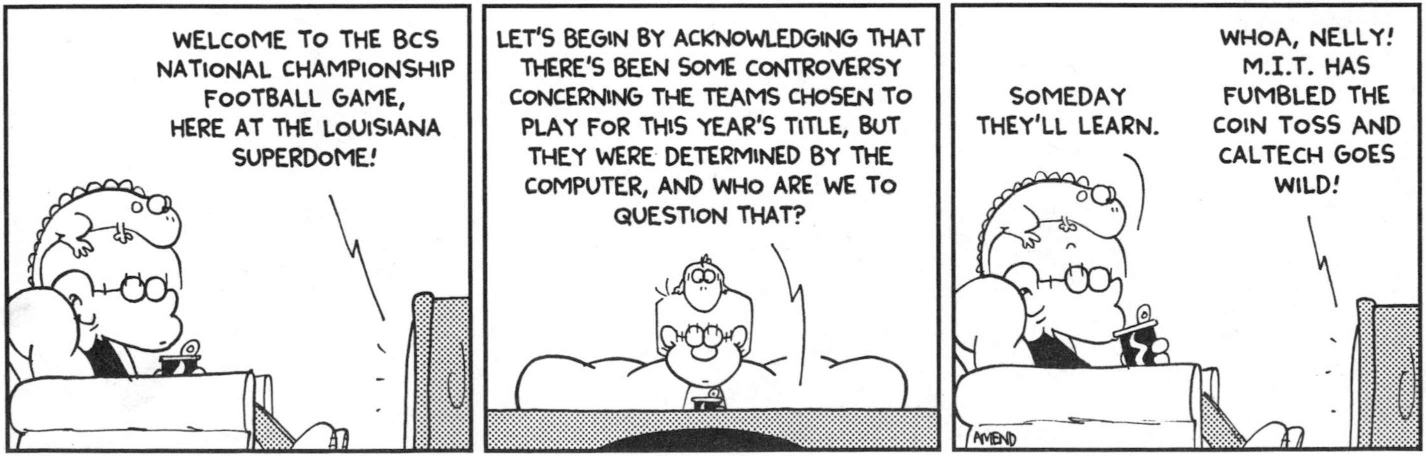
WELCOME TO THE BCS NATIONAL CHAMPIONSHIP FOOTBALL GAME, HERE AT THE LOUISIANA SUPERDOME!
LET'S BEGIN BY ACKNOWLEDGING THAT THERE'S BEEN SOME CONTROVERSY CONCERNING THE TEAMS CHOSEN TO PLAY FOR THIS YEAR'S TITLE, BUT THEY WERE DETERMINED BY THE COMPUTER, AND WHO ARE WE TO QUESTION THAT?
SOMEDAY THEY'LL LEARN.
WHOA, NELLY! M.I.T. HAS FUMBLED THE COIN TOSS AND CALTECH GOES WILD!
AMEND

Snow-
mantis
Snow-
mandible
Snow-
mandolin
Snow-
manatee
I GUESS BEING NORMAL IS JUST TOO HARD FOR SOME PEOPLE.
NO. TOO EASY.
AMEND

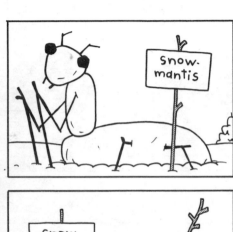

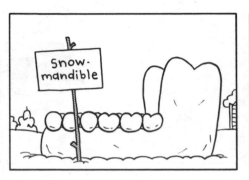

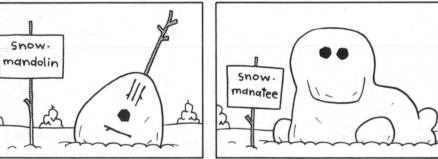

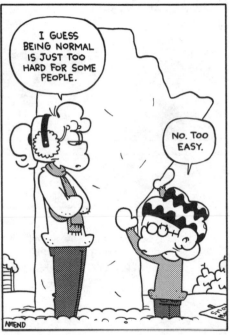

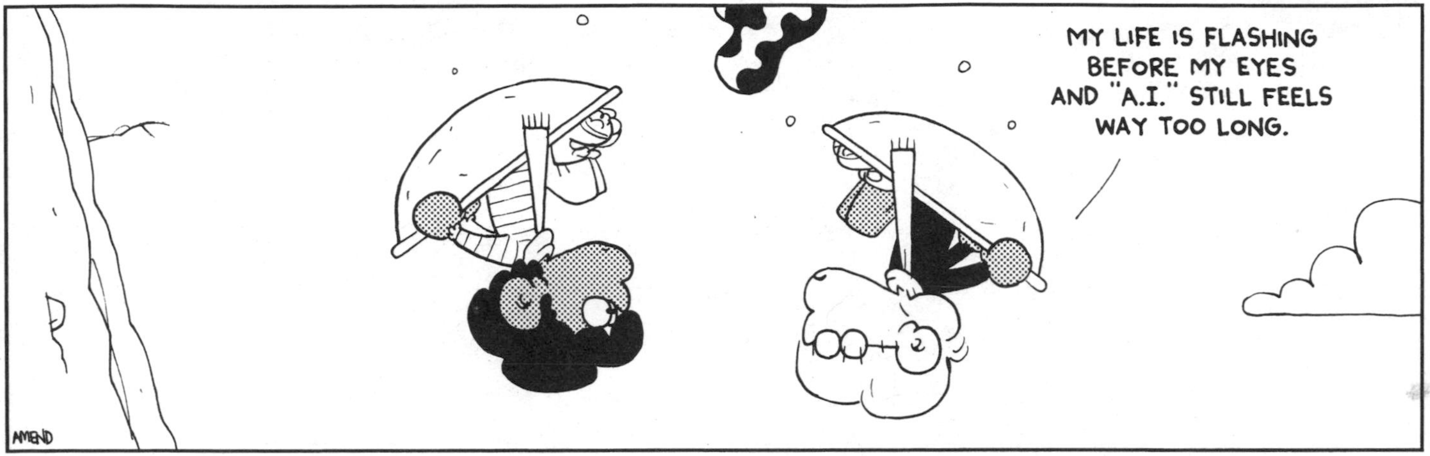
MY LIFE IS FLASHING BEFORE MY EYES AND "A.I." STILL FEELS WAY TOO LONG.
AMEND

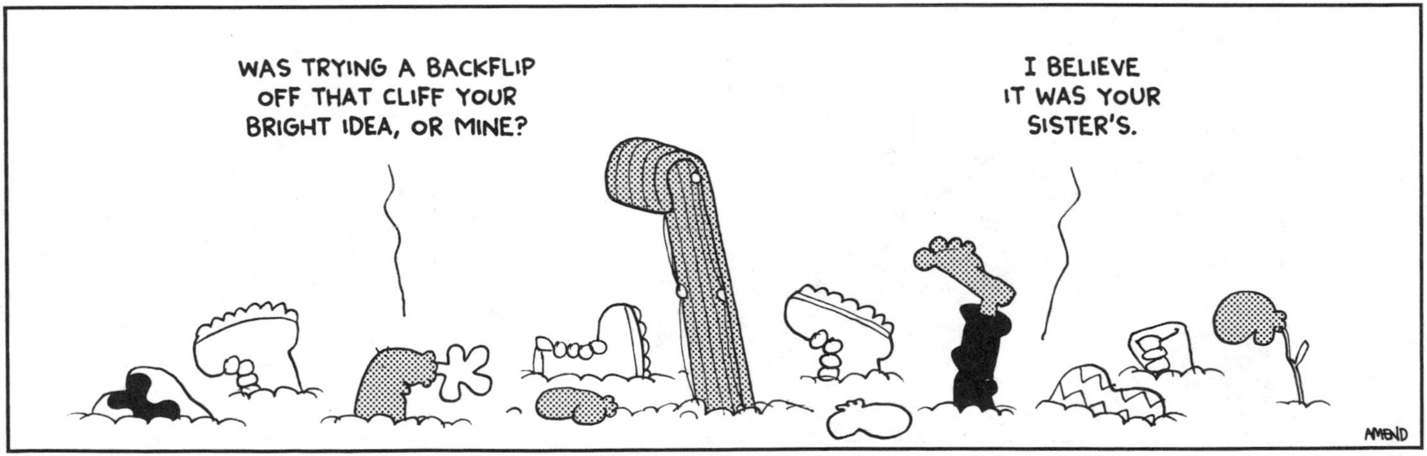
WAS TRYING A BACKFLIP OFF THAT CLIFF YOUR BRIGHT IDEA, OR MINE?
I BELIEVE IT WAS YOUR SISTER'S.
AMEND

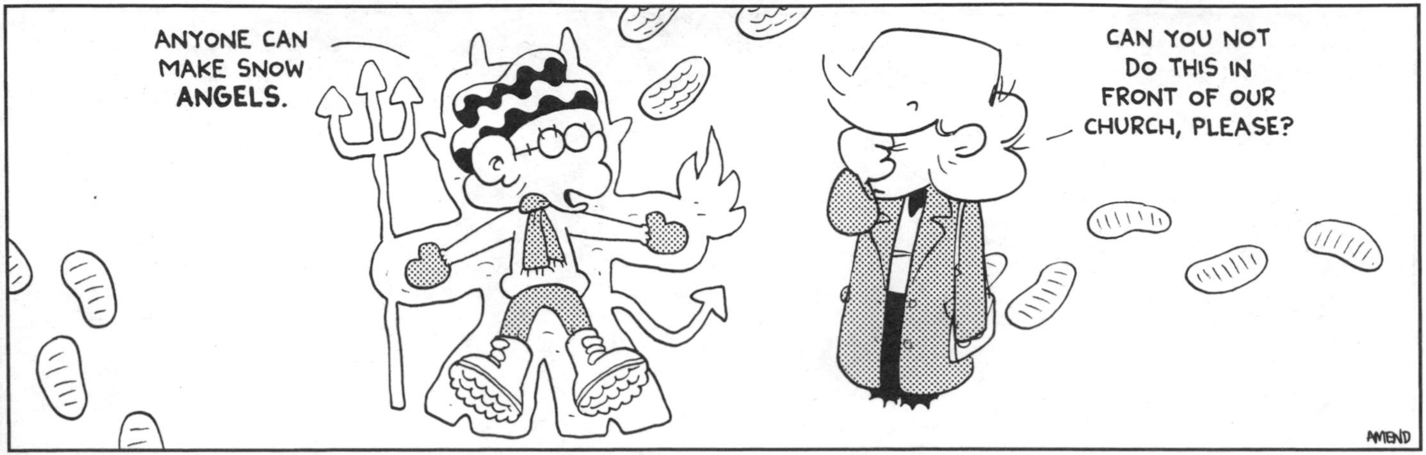
ANYONE CAN MAKE SNOW ANGELS.
CAN YOU NOT DO THIS IN FRONT OF OUR CHURCH, PLEASE?
AMEND

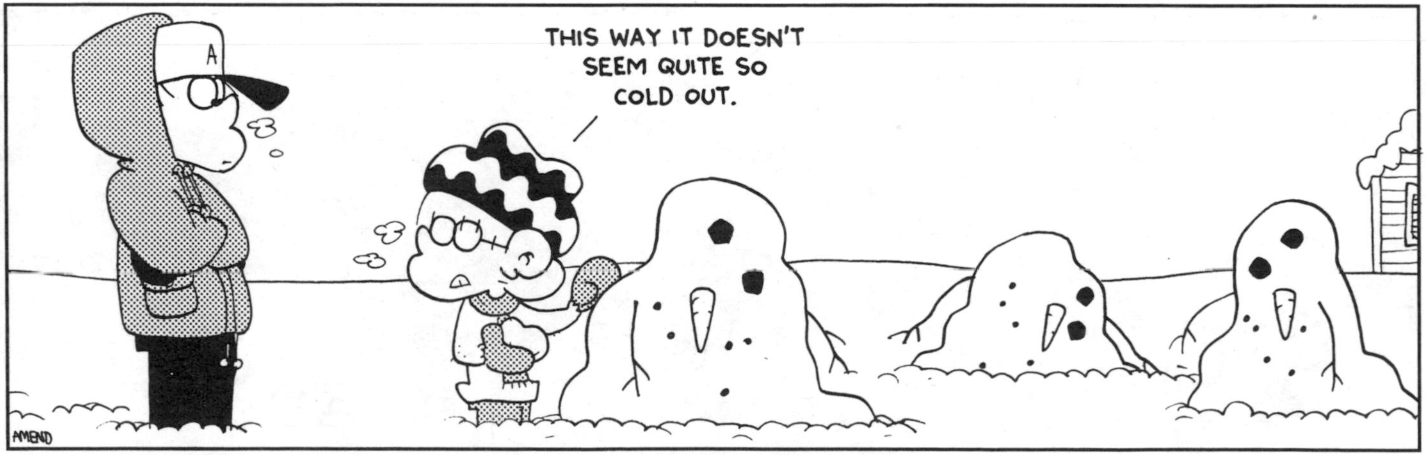
A
THIS WAY IT DOESN'T SEEM QUITE SO COLD OUT.
AMEND

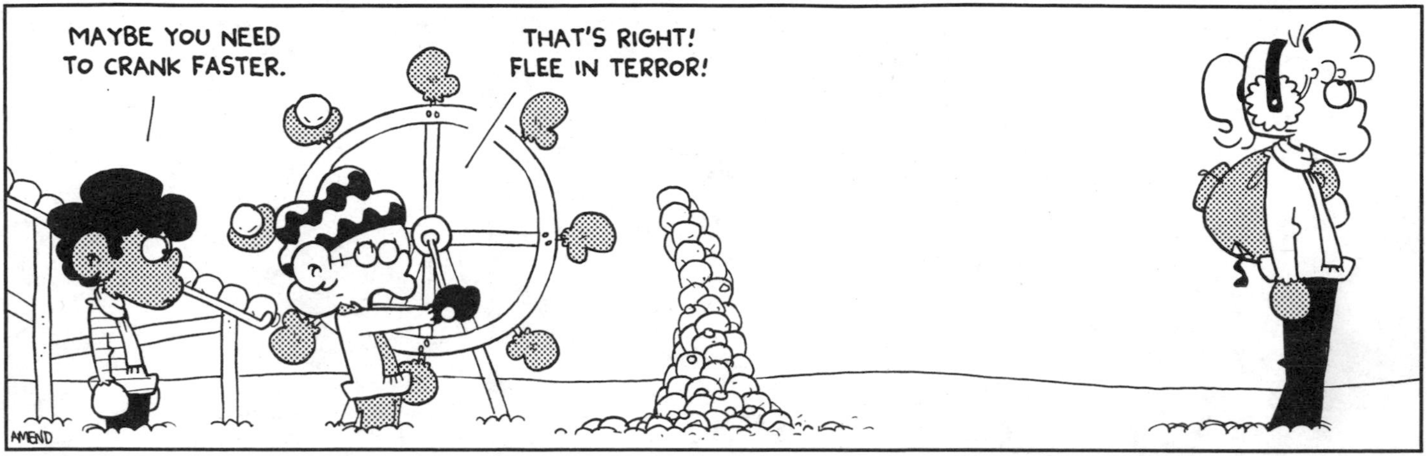
MAYBE YOU NEED TO CRANK FASTER.
THAT'S RIGHT! FLEE IN TERROR!
AMEND

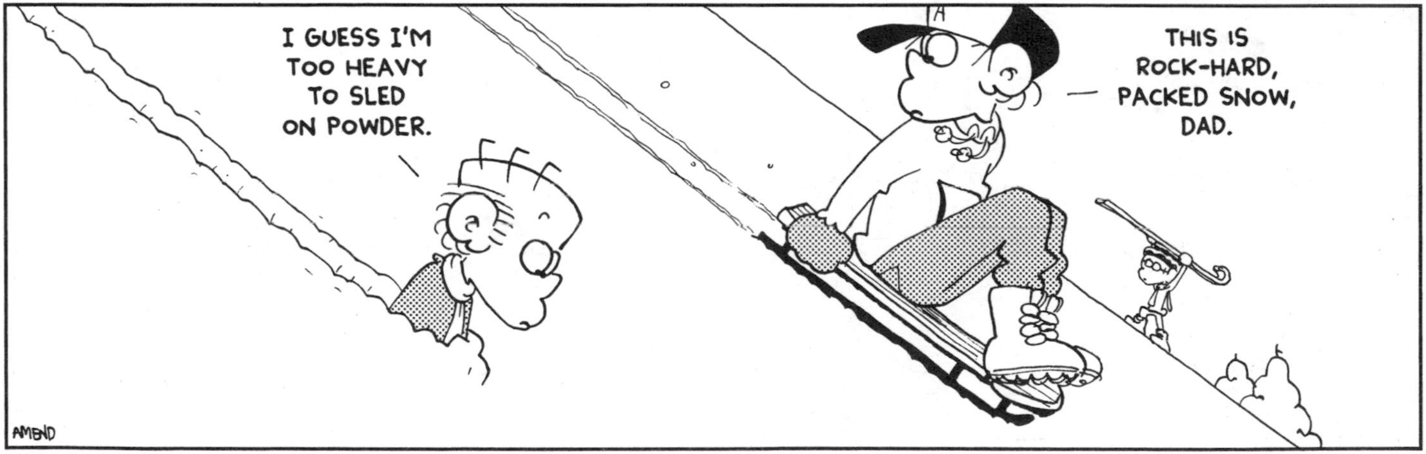
I GUESS I'M TOO HEAVY TO SLED ON POWDER.
THIS IS ROCK-HARD, PACKED SNOW, DAD.
AMEND

BRRR.
BRRR.
BRRR.
AH...HEAT.
I CAN'T BELIEVE YOU RENTED INFRA-RED GOGGLES, PAIGE.
RAISE THE THERMOSTAT AND I WOULDN'T HAVE TO.
THYME
AMEND

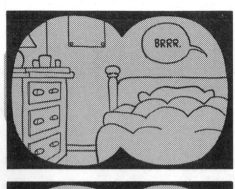

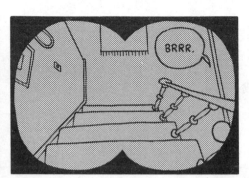

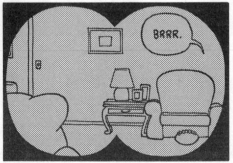

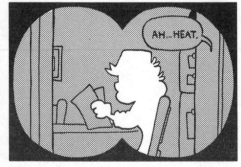

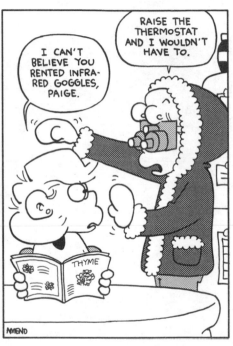

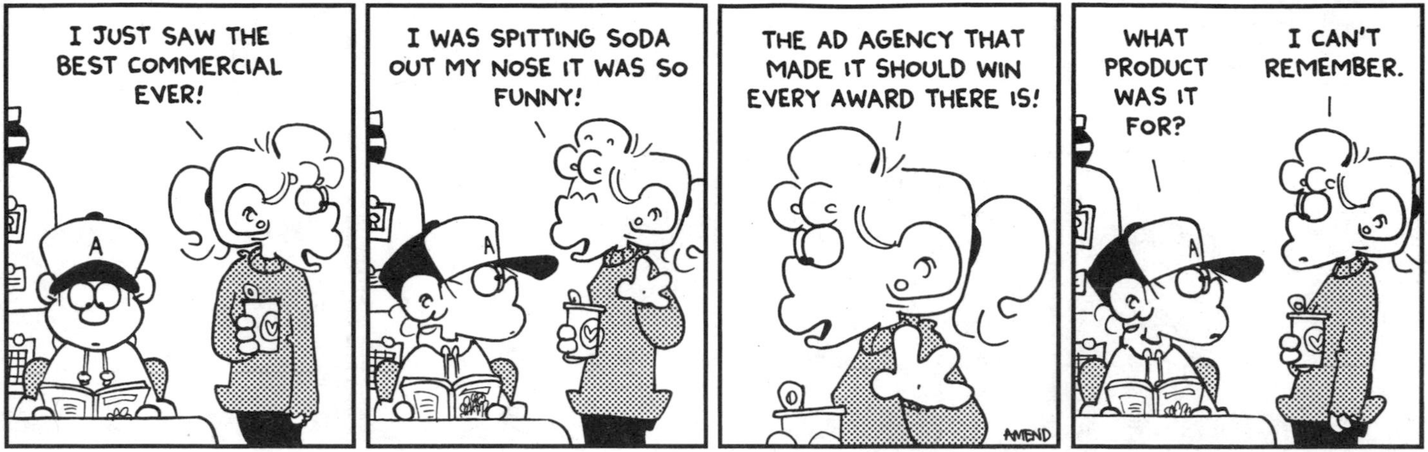
I JUST SAW THE BEST COMMERCIAL EVER!
I WAS SPITTING SODA OUT MY NOSE IT WAS SO FUNNY!
THE AD AGENCY THAT MADE IT SHOULD WIN EVERY AWARD THERE IS!
AMEND
WHAT PRODUCT WAS IT FOR?
I CAN'T REMEMBER.

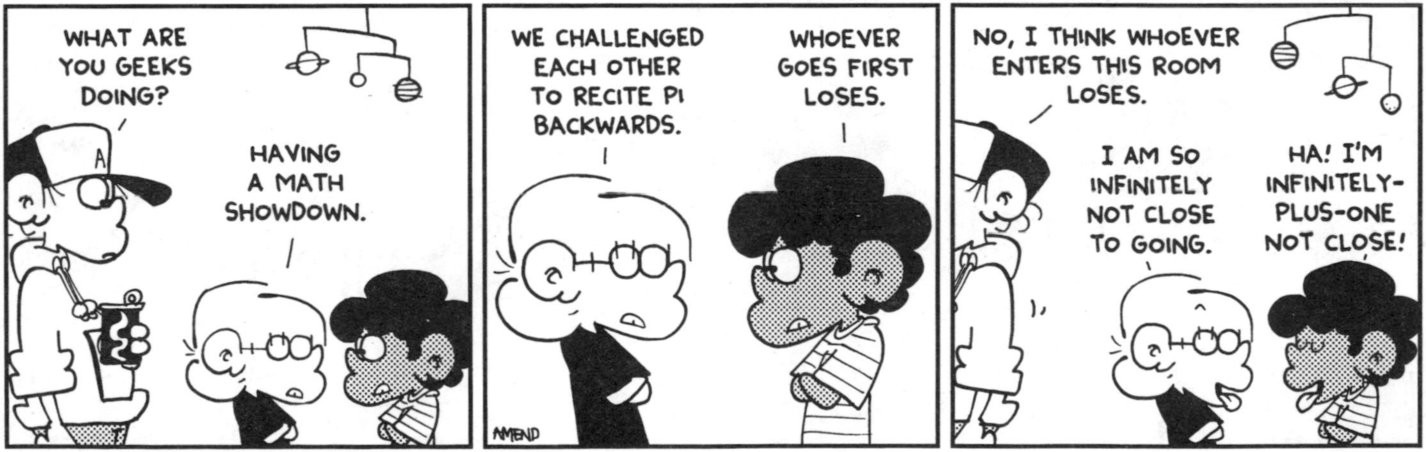
WHAT ARE YOU GEEKS DOING?
HAVING A MATH SHOWDOWN.
WE CHALLENGED EACH OTHER TO RECITE PI BACKWARDS.
WHOEVER GOES FIRST LOSES.
AMEND
NO, I THINK WHOEVER ENTERS THIS ROOM LOSES.
I AM SO INFINITELY NOT CLOSE TO GOING.
HA! I'M INFINITELY-PLUS-ONE NOT CLOSE!

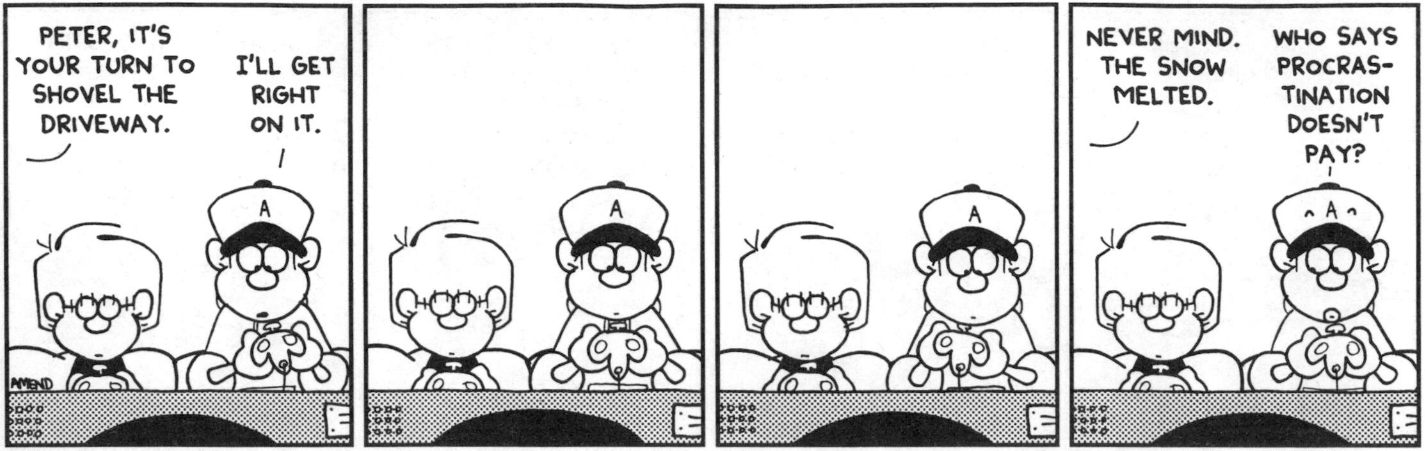
PETER, IT'S YOUR TURN TO SHOVEL THE DRIVEWAY.
I'LL GET RIGHT ON IT.
NEVER MIND. THE SNOW MELTED.
WHO SAYS PROCRAS-TINATION DOESN'T PAY?
AMEND

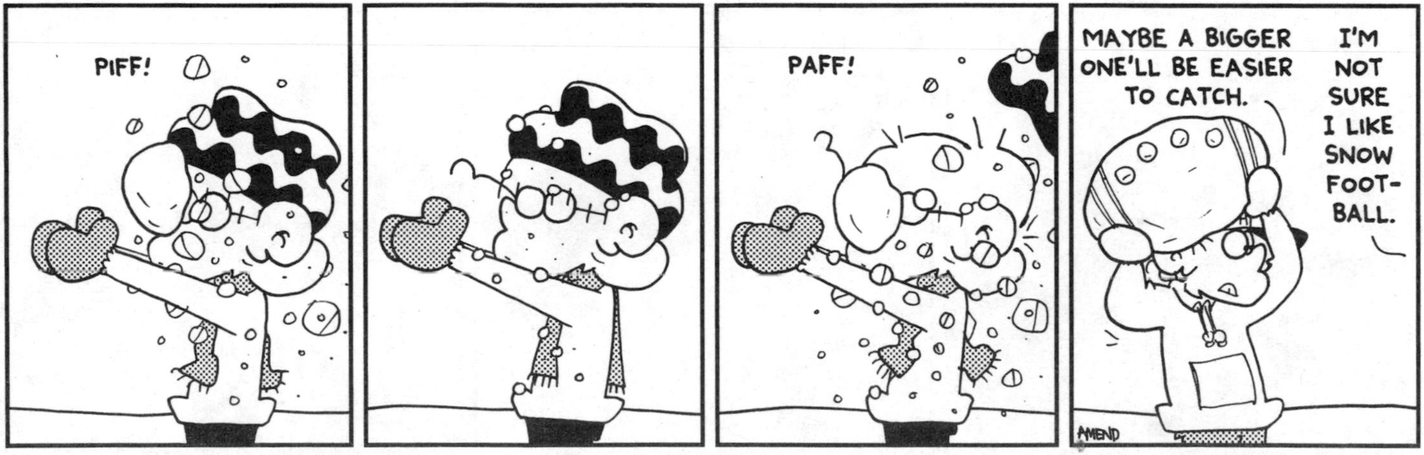
PIFF!
PAFF!
MAYBE A BIGGER ONE'LL BE EASIER TO CATCH.
I'M NOT SURE I LIKE SNOW FOOT-BALL.
AMEND

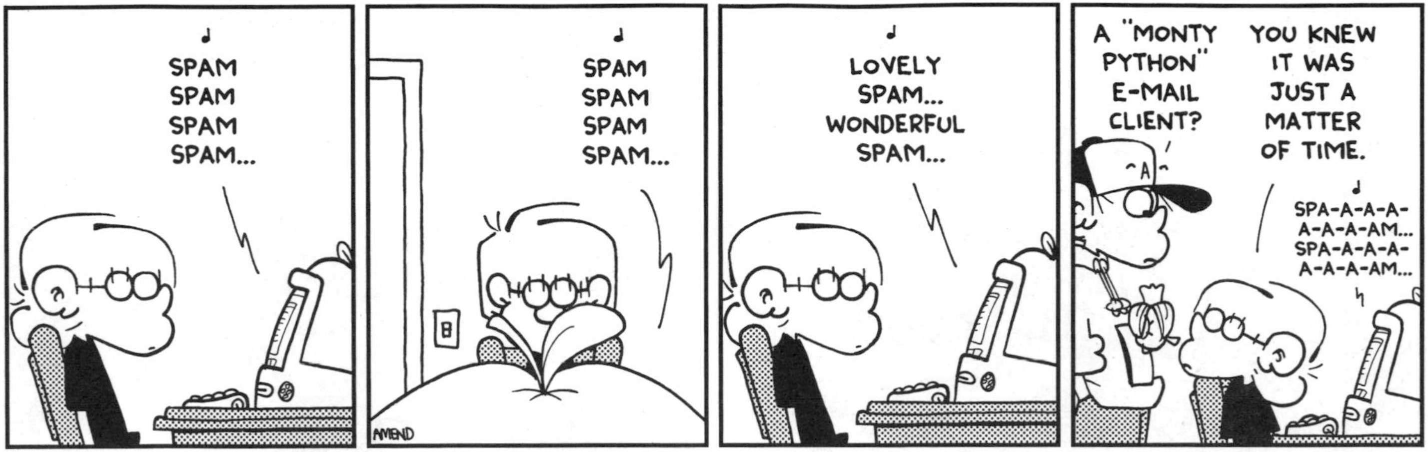
SPAM
SPAM
SPAM
SPAM...
SPAM
SPAM
SPAM
SPAM...
AMEND
LOVELY
SPAM...
WONDERFUL
SPAM...
A "MONTY PYTHON" E-MAIL CLIENT?
YOU KNEW IT WAS JUST A MATTER OF TIME.
SPA-A-A-A-
A-A-A-AM...
SPA-A-A-A-
A-A-A-AM...

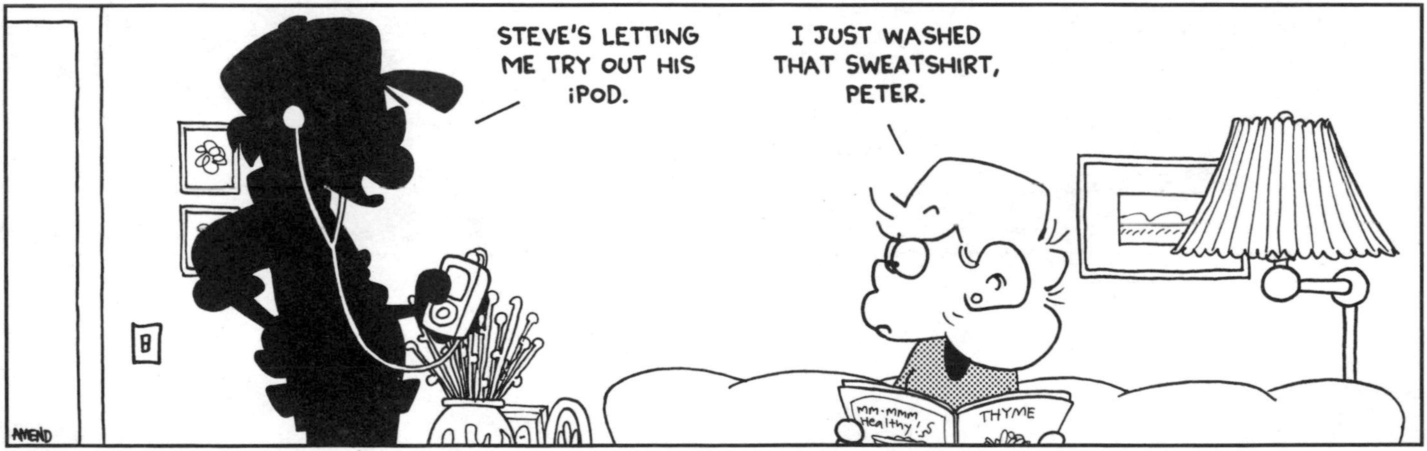
STEVE'S LETTING ME TRY OUT HIS iPOD.
I JUST WASHED THAT SWEATSHIRT, PETER.
MM-MMM Healthy!
THYME
AMEND

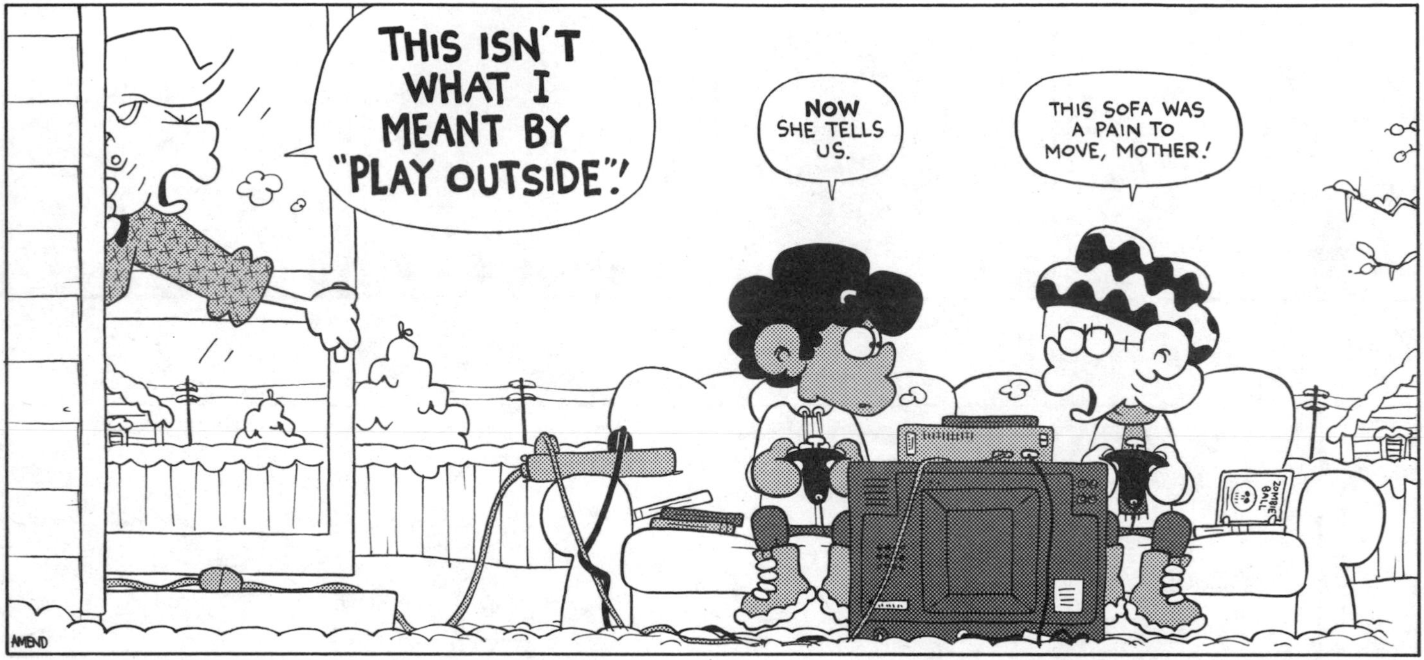
THIS ISN'T WHAT I MEANT BY "PLAY OUTSIDE"!
NOW SHE TELLS US.
THIS SOFA WAS A PAIN TO MOVE, MOTHER!
ZOMBIE BALL
AMEND

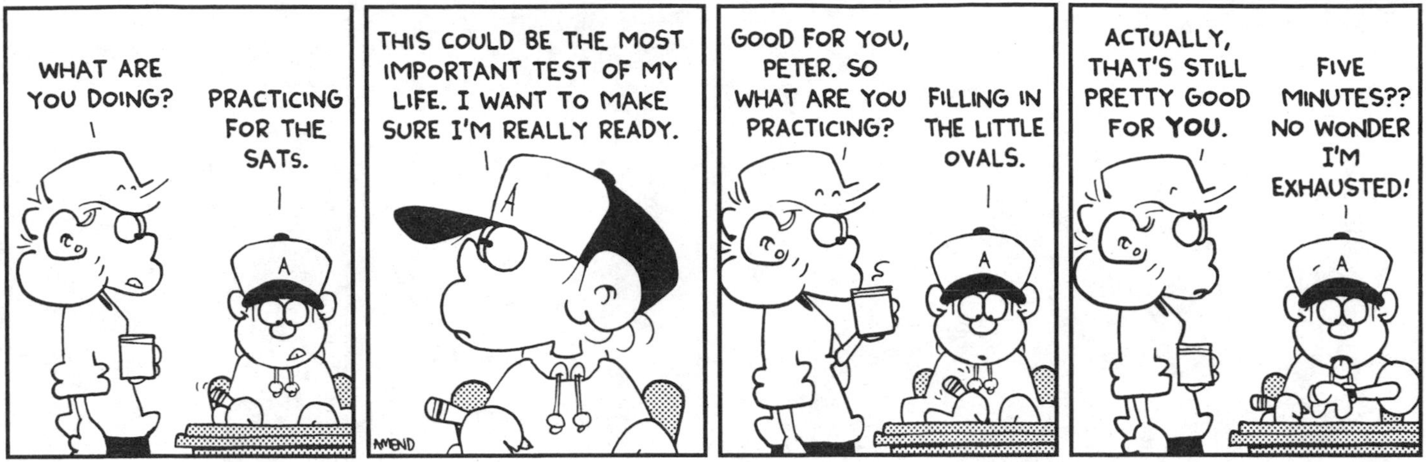
WHAT ARE YOU DOING?
PRACTICING FOR THE SATS.
THIS COULD BE THE MOST IMPORTANT TEST OF MY LIFE. I WANT TO MAKE SURE I'M REALLY READY.
AMEND
GOOD FOR YOU, PETER. SO WHAT ARE YOU PRACTICING?
FILLING IN THE LITTLE OVALS.
ACTUALLY, THAT'S STILL PRETTY GOOD FOR **YOU**.
FIVE MINUTES?? NO WONDER I'M EXHAUSTED!

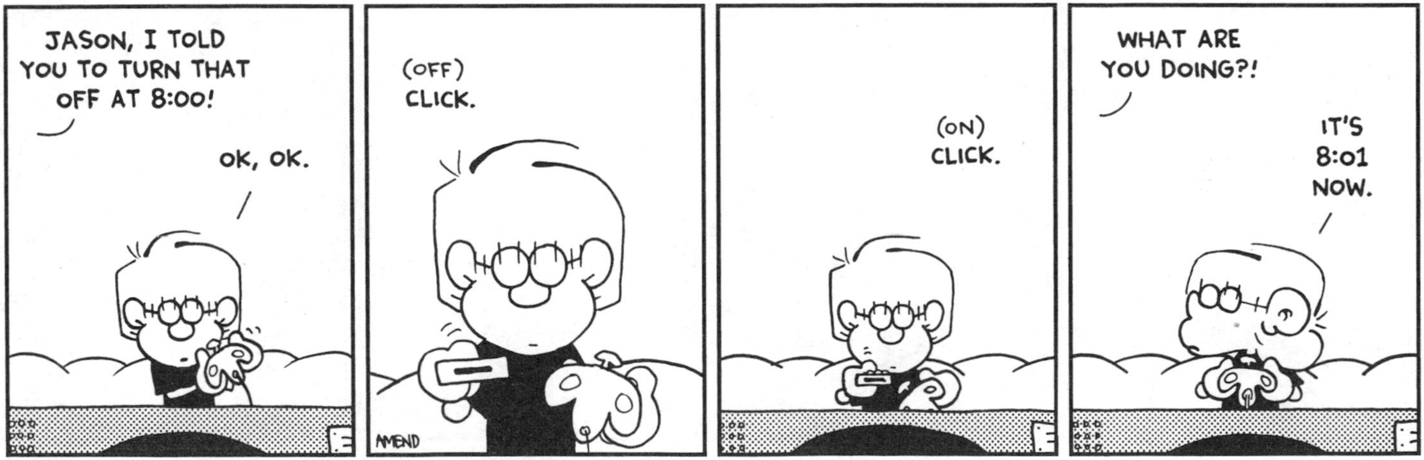
JASON, I TOLD YOU TO TURN THAT OFF AT 8:00!
OK, OK.
(OFF) CLICK.
AMEND
(ON) CLICK.
WHAT ARE YOU DOING?!
IT'S 8:01 NOW.

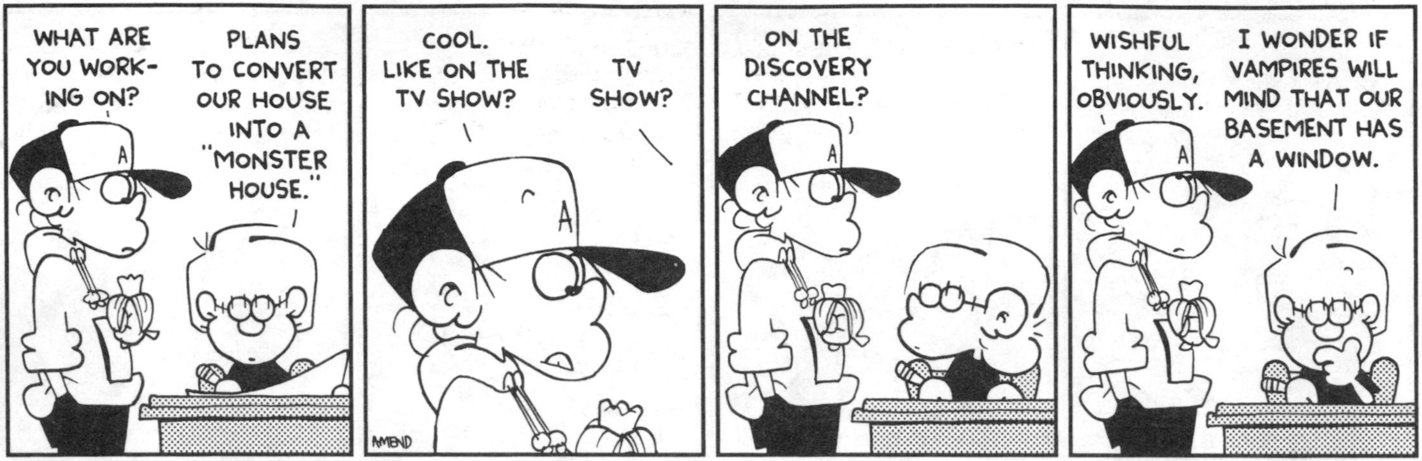
WHAT ARE YOU WORK-ING ON?
PLANS TO CONVERT OUR HOUSE INTO A "MONSTER HOUSE."
COOL. LIKE ON THE TV SHOW?
TV SHOW?
ON THE DISCOVERY CHANNEL?
WISHFUL THINKING, OBVIOUSLY.
I WONDER IF VAMPIRES WILL MIND THAT OUR BASEMENT HAS A WINDOW.
AMEND

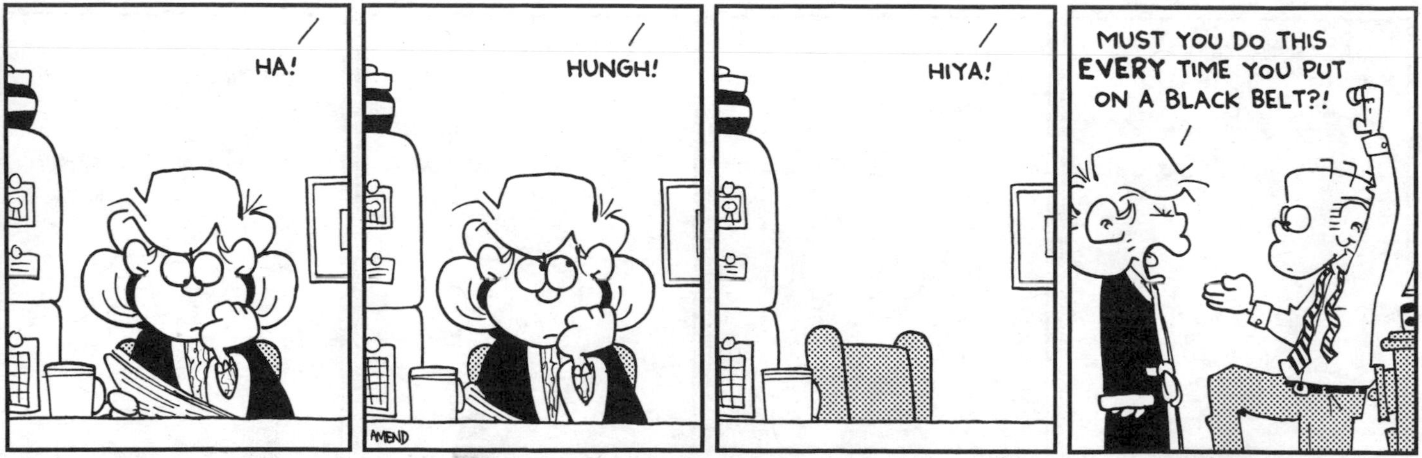
HA!
HUNGH!
HIYA!
MUST YOU DO THIS EVERY TIME YOU PUT ON A BLACK BELT?!
AMEND

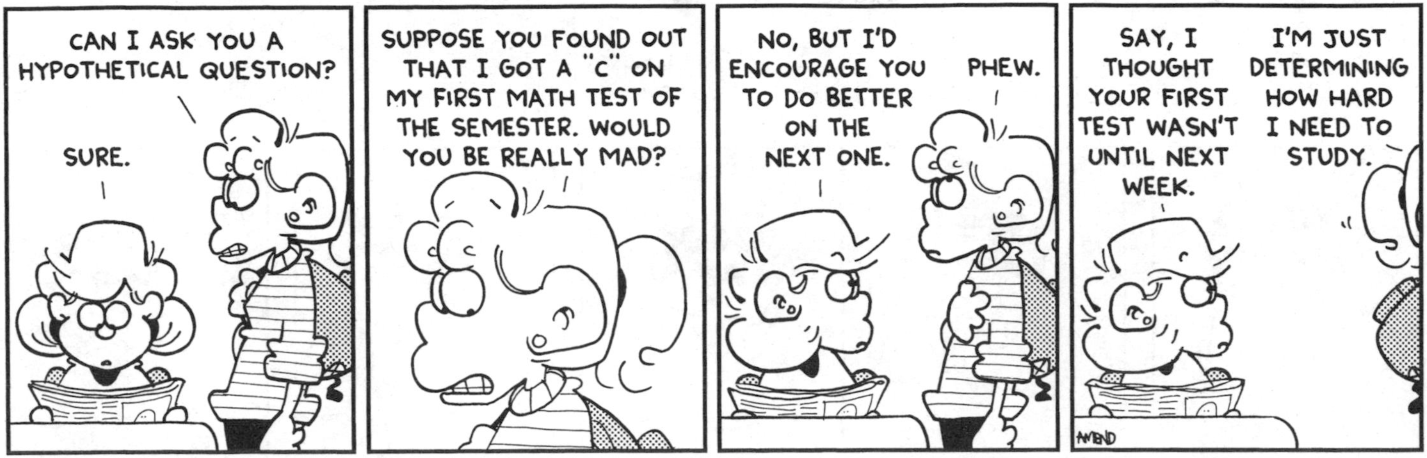
CAN I ASK YOU A HYPOTHETICAL QUESTION?
SURE.
SUPPOSE YOU FOUND OUT THAT I GOT A "C" ON MY FIRST MATH TEST OF THE SEMESTER. WOULD YOU BE REALLY MAD?
NO, BUT I'D ENCOURAGE YOU TO DO BETTER ON THE NEXT ONE.
PHEW.
SAY, I THOUGHT YOUR FIRST TEST WASN'T UNTIL NEXT WEEK.
I'M JUST DETERMINING HOW HARD I NEED TO STUDY.
AMEND

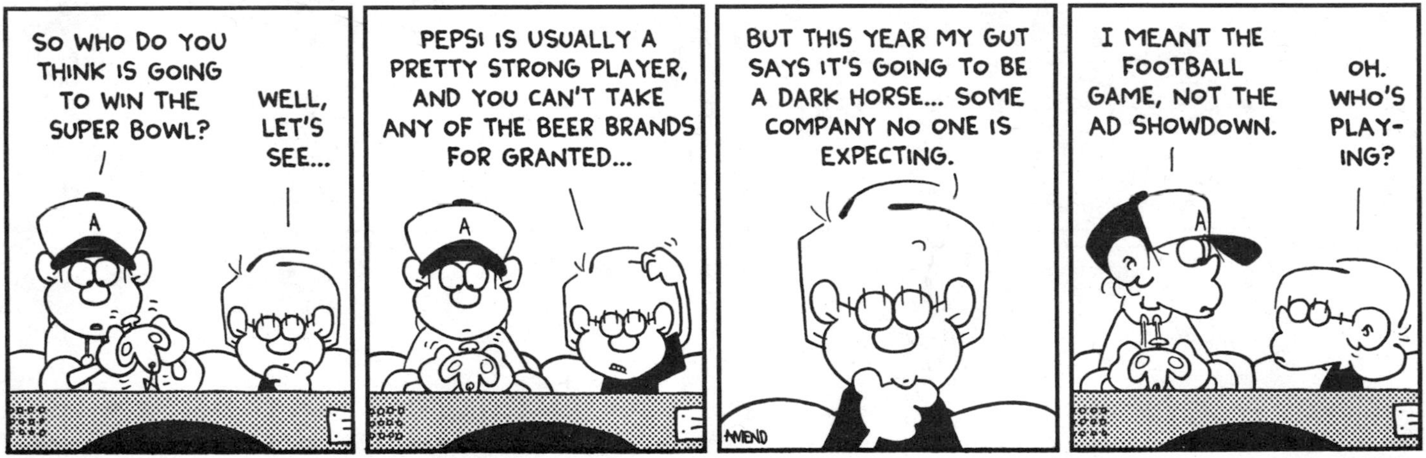
SO WHO DO YOU THINK IS GOING TO WIN THE SUPER BOWL?
WELL, LET'S SEE...
PEPSI IS USUALLY A PRETTY STRONG PLAYER, AND YOU CAN'T TAKE ANY OF THE BEER BRANDS FOR GRANTED...
BUT THIS YEAR MY GUT SAYS IT'S GOING TO BE A DARK HORSE... SOME COMPANY NO ONE IS EXPECTING.
AMEND
I MEANT THE FOOTBALL GAME, NOT THE AD SHOWDOWN.
OH. WHO'S PLAY-ING?

POKE!
POKE!
POKE!
POKE!
POKE!
POKE!
POKE!
POKE!
WE MIGHT NEED TO RETHINK THIS.
TRY A FATTER CUE STICK.
AMEND

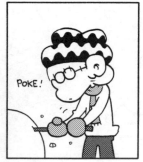

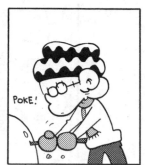

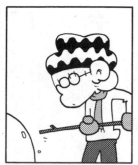

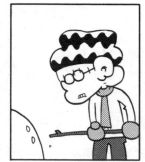

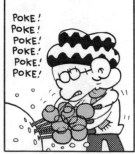

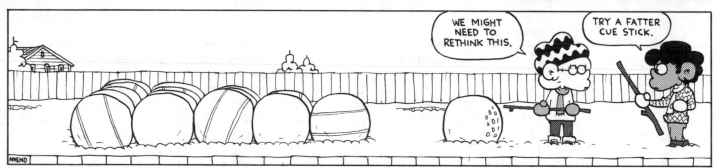

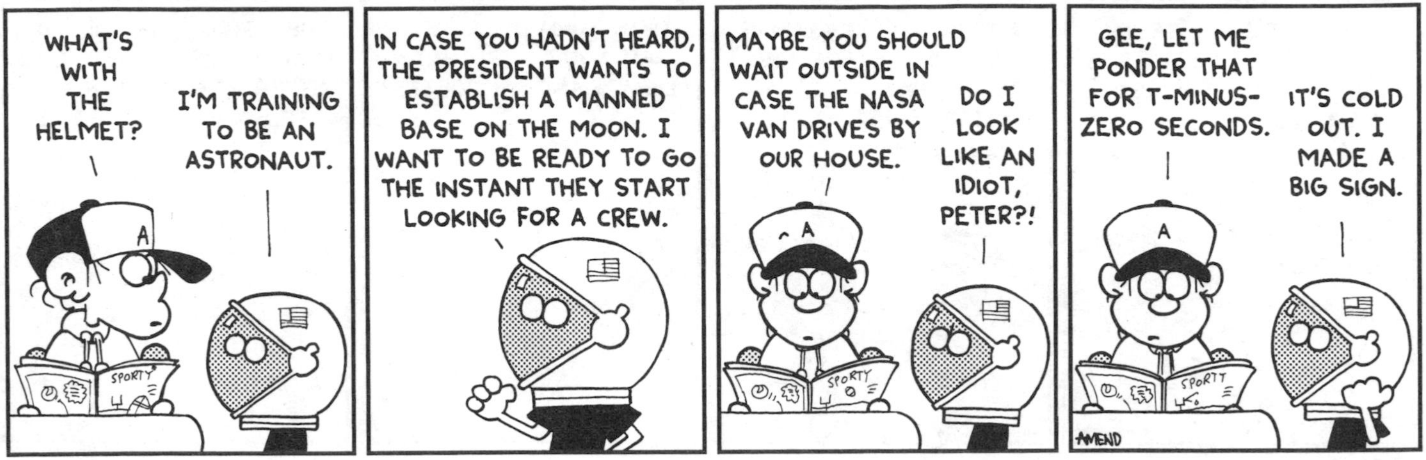
WHAT'S WITH THE HELMET?
I'M TRAINING TO BE AN ASTRONAUT.
IN CASE YOU HADN'T HEARD, THE PRESIDENT WANTS TO ESTABLISH A MANNED BASE ON THE MOON. I WANT TO BE READY TO GO THE INSTANT THEY START LOOKING FOR A CREW.
MAYBE YOU SHOULD WAIT OUTSIDE IN CASE THE NASA VAN DRIVES BY OUR HOUSE.
DO I LOOK LIKE AN IDIOT, PETER?!
GEE, LET ME PONDER THAT FOR T-MINUS-ZERO SECONDS.
IT'S COLD OUT. I MADE A BIG SIGN.
SPORTY
AMEND

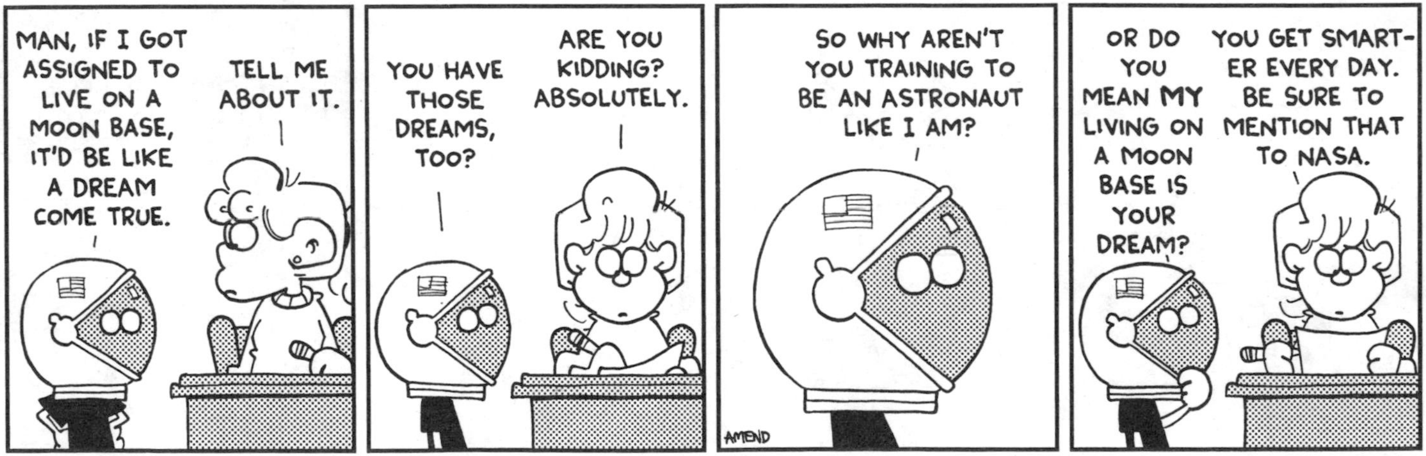
MAN, IF I GOT ASSIGNED TO LIVE ON A MOON BASE, IT'D BE LIKE A DREAM COME TRUE.
TELL ME ABOUT IT.
YOU HAVE THOSE DREAMS, TOO?
ARE YOU KIDDING? ABSOLUTELY.
SO WHY AREN'T YOU TRAINING TO BE AN ASTRONAUT LIKE I AM?
OR DO YOU MEAN MY LIVING ON A MOON BASE IS YOUR DREAM?
YOU GET SMARTER EVERY DAY. BE SURE TO MENTION THAT TO NASA.
AMEND

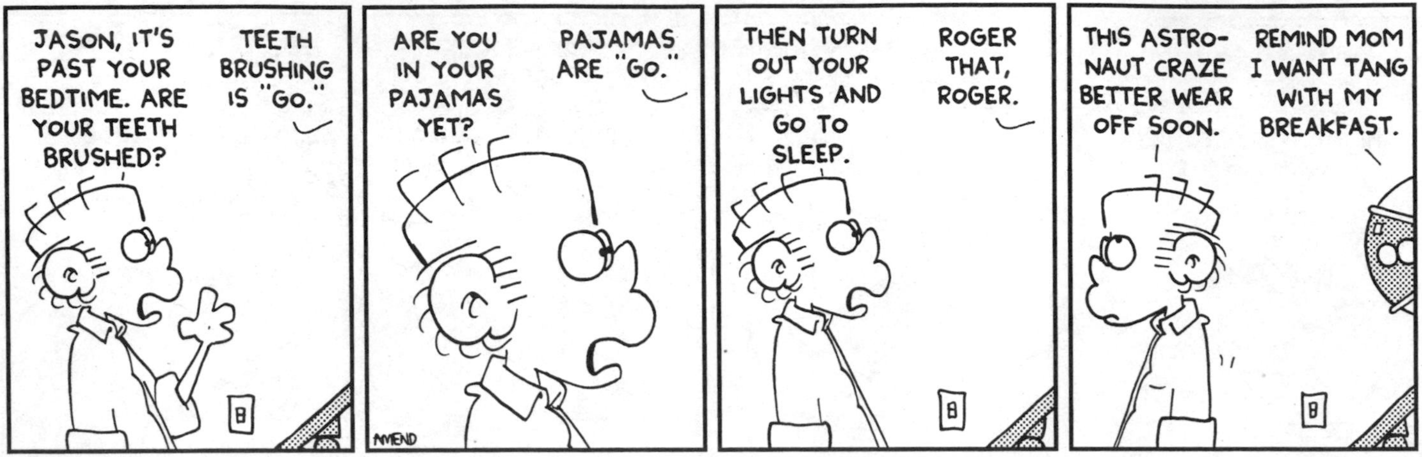
JASON, IT'S PAST YOUR BEDTIME. ARE YOUR TEETH BRUSHED?
TEETH BRUSHING IS "GO."
ARE YOU IN YOUR PAJAMAS YET?
PAJAMAS ARE "GO."
AMEND
THEN TURN OUT YOUR LIGHTS AND GO TO SLEEP.
ROGER THAT, ROGER.
THIS ASTRONAUT CRAZE BETTER WEAR OFF SOON.
REMIND MOM I WANT TANG WITH MY BREAKFAST.

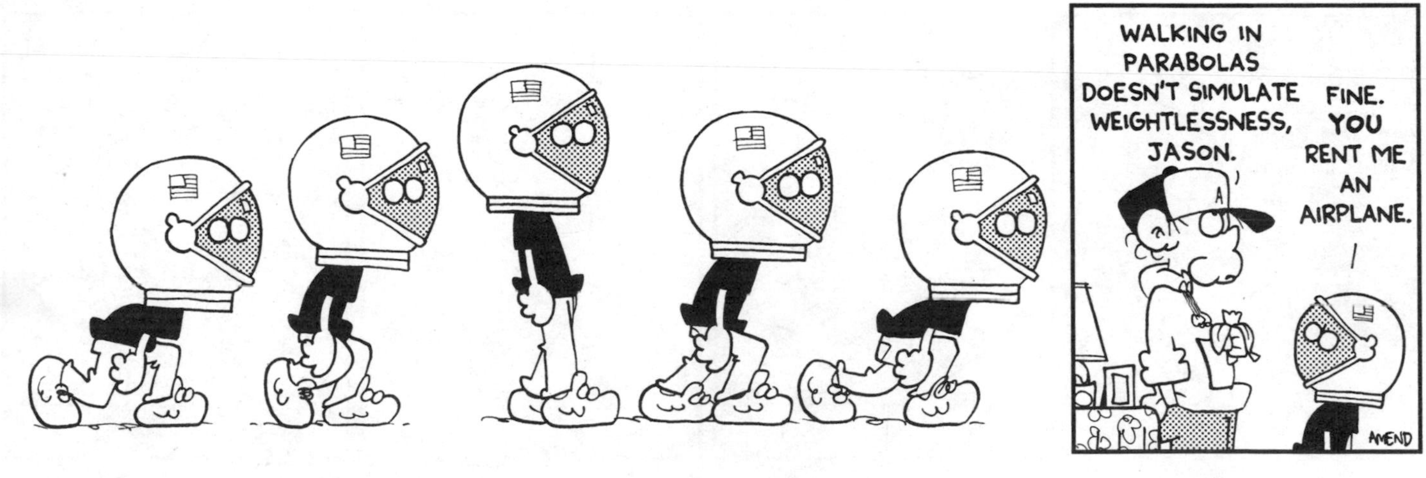
WALKING IN PARABOLAS DOESN'T SIMULATE WEIGHTLESSNESS, JASON.
FINE. **YOU** RENT ME AN AIRPLANE.
AMEND

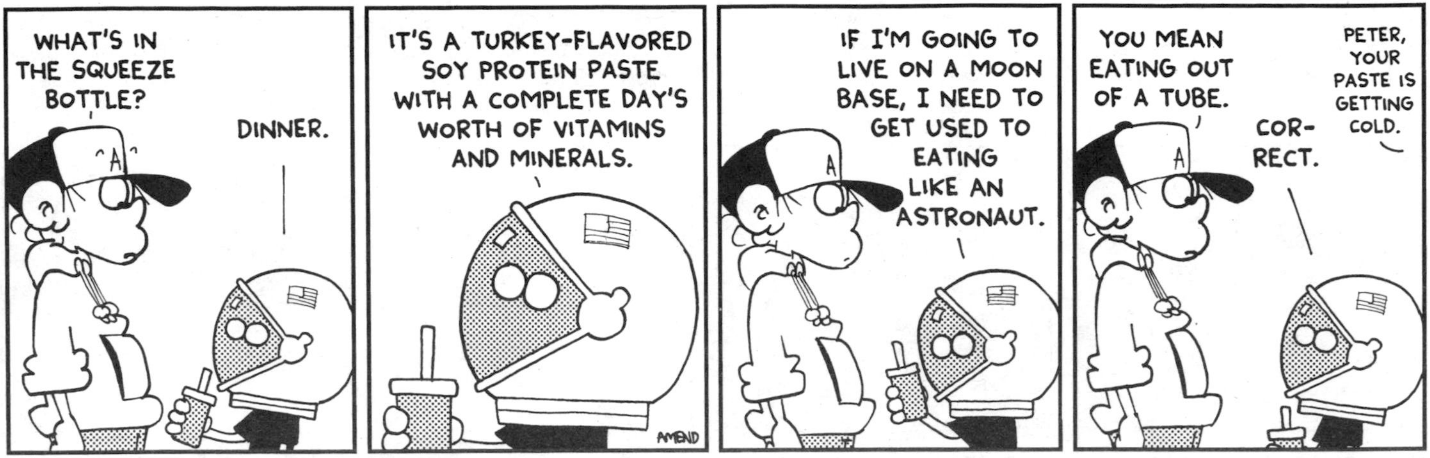
WHAT'S IN THE SQUEEZE BOTTLE?
DINNER.
IT'S A TURKEY-FLAVORED SOY PROTEIN PASTE WITH A COMPLETE DAY'S WORTH OF VITAMINS AND MINERALS.
AMEND
IF I'M GOING TO LIVE ON A MOON BASE, I NEED TO GET USED TO EATING LIKE AN ASTRONAUT.
YOU MEAN EATING OUT OF A TUBE.
COR-RECT.
PETER, YOUR PASTE IS GETTING COLD.

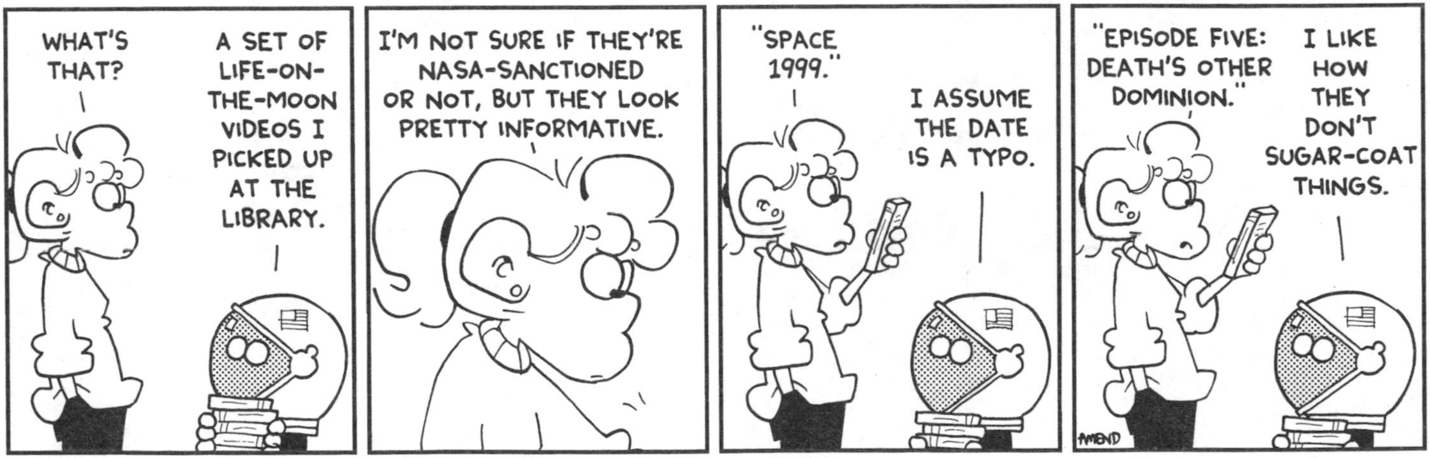
WHAT'S THAT?
A SET OF LIFE-ON-THE-MOON VIDEOS I PICKED UP AT THE LIBRARY.
I'M NOT SURE IF THEY'RE NASA-SANCTIONED OR NOT, BUT THEY LOOK PRETTY INFORMATIVE.
"SPACE 1999."
I ASSUME THE DATE IS A TYPO.
"EPISODE FIVE: DEATH'S OTHER DOMINION."
I LIKE HOW THEY DON'T SUGAR-COAT THINGS.
AMEND

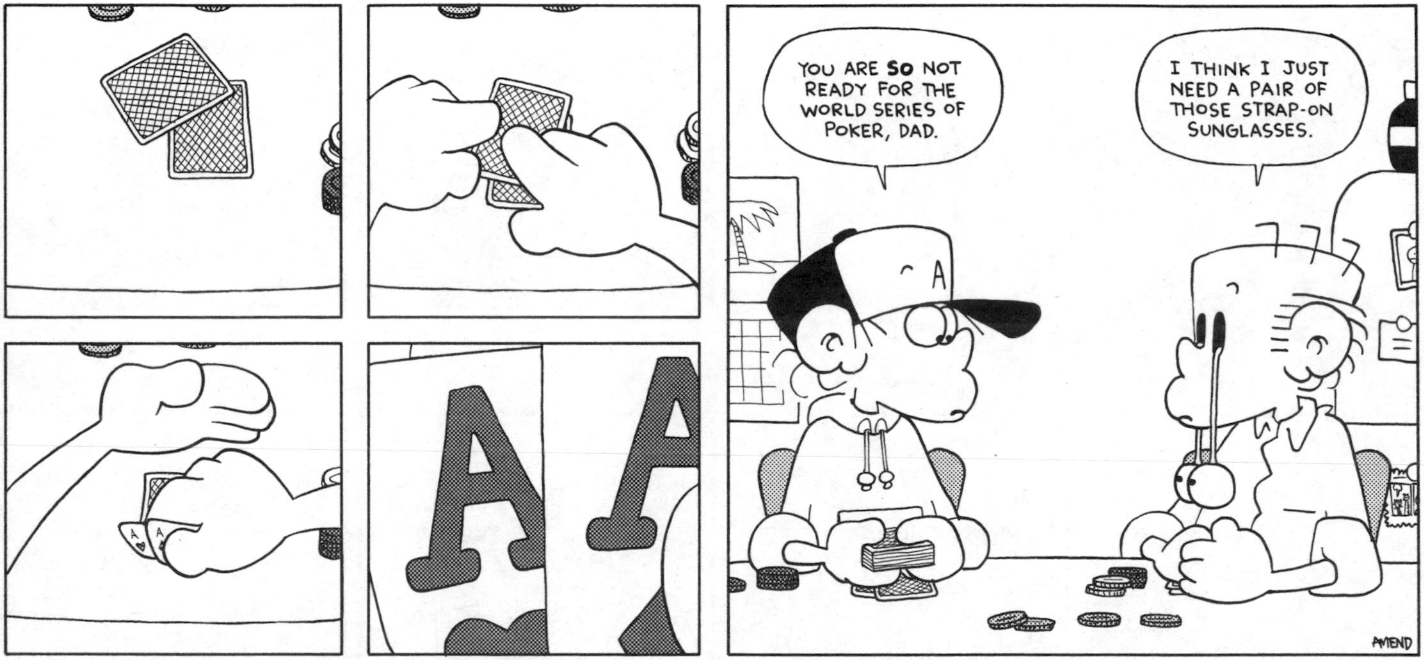

A
A
A
YOU ARE SO NOT READY FOR THE WORLD SERIES OF POKER, DAD.
I THINK I JUST NEED A PAIR OF THOSE STRAP-ON SUNGLASSES.
AMEND

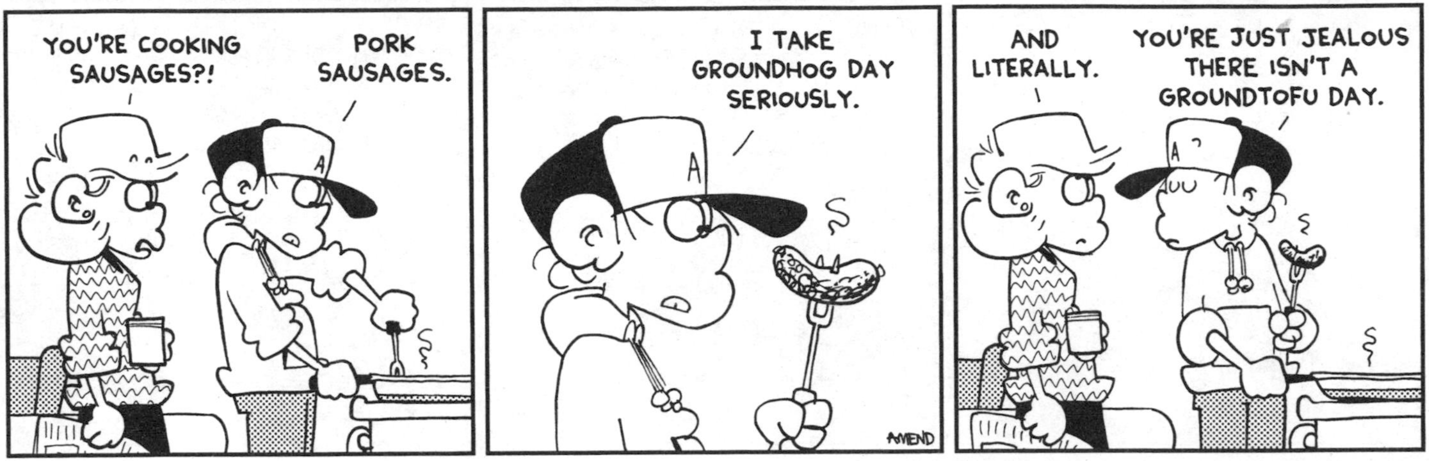
YOU'RE COOKING SAUSAGES?!
PORK SAUSAGES.
I TAKE GROUNDHOG DAY SERIOUSLY.
AND LITERALLY.
YOU'RE JUST JEALOUS THERE ISN'T A GROUNDTOFU DAY.
AMEND

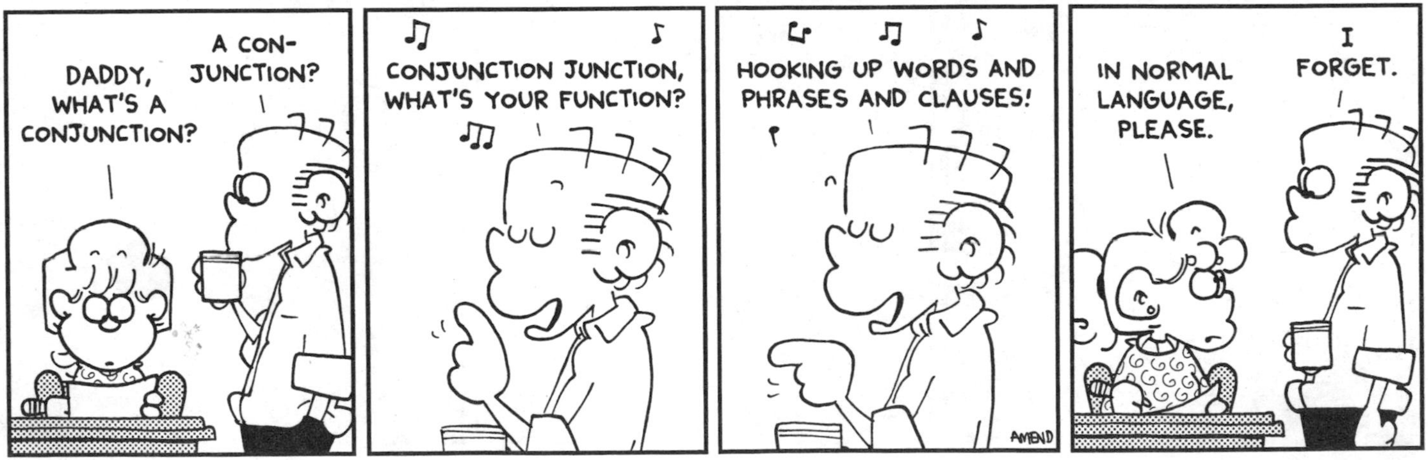
DADDY, WHAT'S A CONJUNCTION?
A CON-JUNCTION?
CONJUNCTION JUNCTION, WHAT'S YOUR FUNCTION?
HOOKING UP WORDS AND PHRASES AND CLAUSES!
AMEND
IN NORMAL LANGUAGE, PLEASE.
I FORGET.

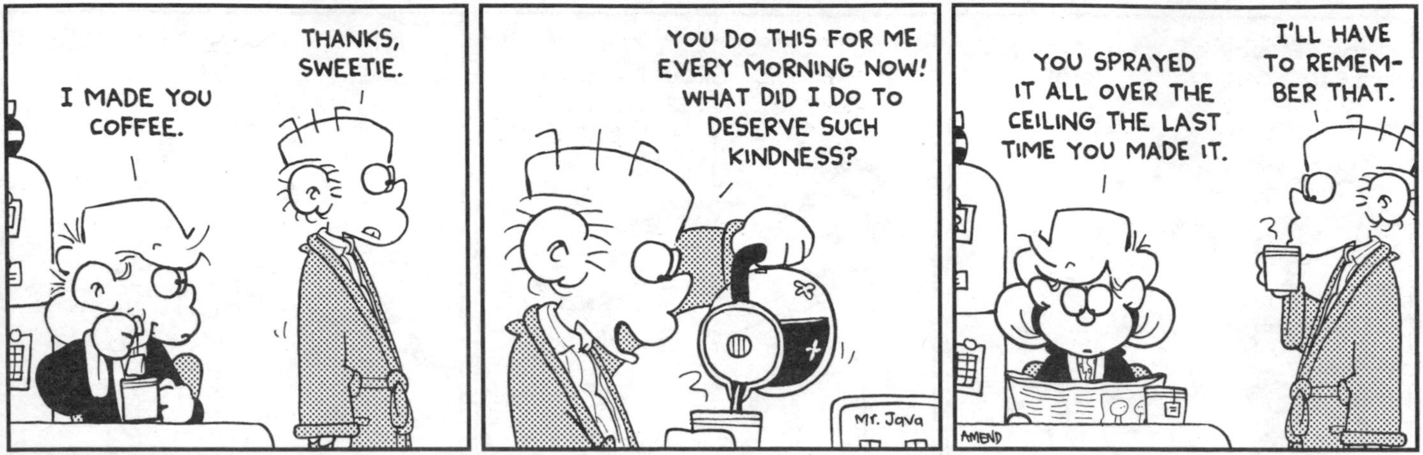
I MADE YOU COFFEE.
THANKS, SWEETIE.
YOU DO THIS FOR ME EVERY MORNING NOW! WHAT DID I DO TO DESERVE SUCH KINDNESS?
Mr. Java
YOU SPRAYED IT ALL OVER THE CEILING THE LAST TIME YOU MADE IT.
I'LL HAVE TO REMEMBER THAT.
AMEND

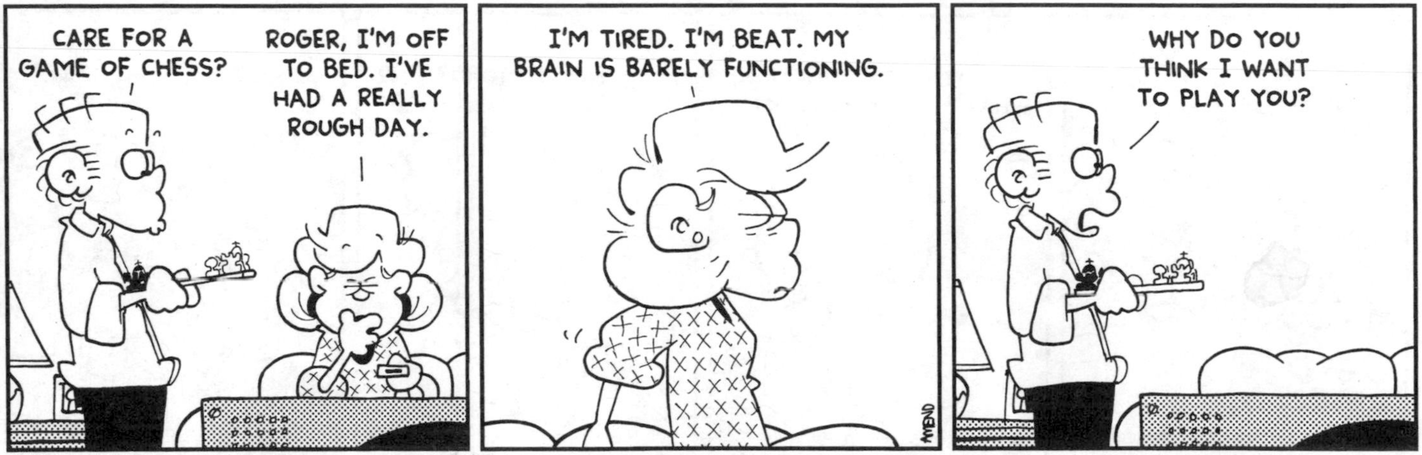
CARE FOR A GAME OF CHESS?
ROGER, I'M OFF TO BED. I'VE HAD A REALLY ROUGH DAY.
I'M TIRED. I'M BEAT. MY BRAIN IS BARELY FUNCTIONING.
AMEND
WHY DO YOU THINK I WANT TO PLAY YOU?

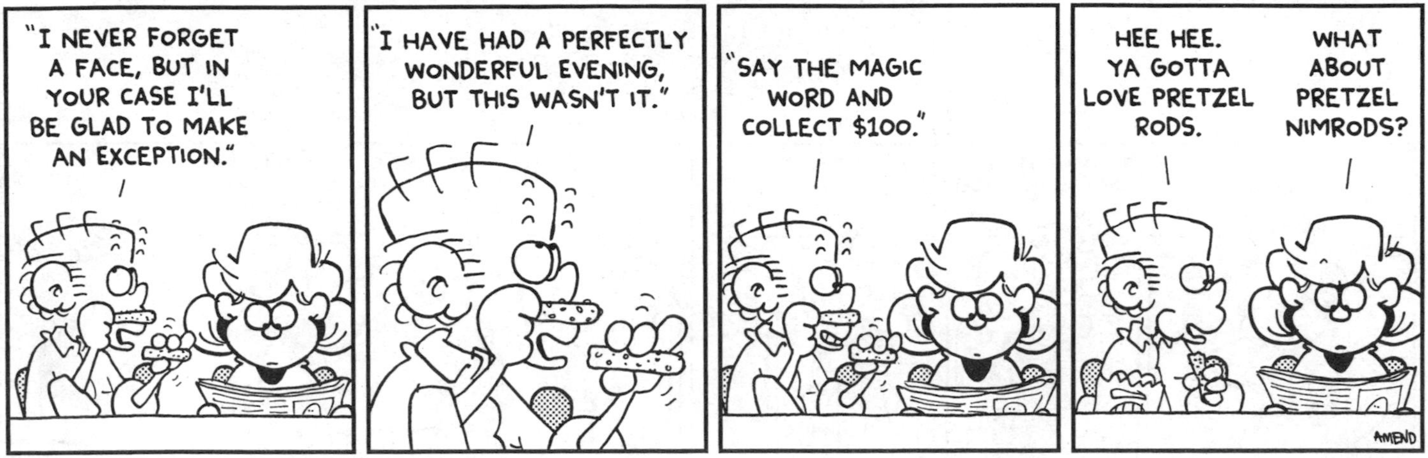
"I NEVER FORGET A FACE, BUT IN YOUR CASE I'LL BE GLAD TO MAKE AN EXCEPTION."
"I HAVE HAD A PERFECTLY WONDERFUL EVENING, BUT THIS WASN'T IT."
"SAY THE MAGIC WORD AND COLLECT $100."
HEE HEE. YA GOTTA LOVE PRETZEL RODS.
WHAT ABOUT PRETZEL NIMRODS?
AMEND

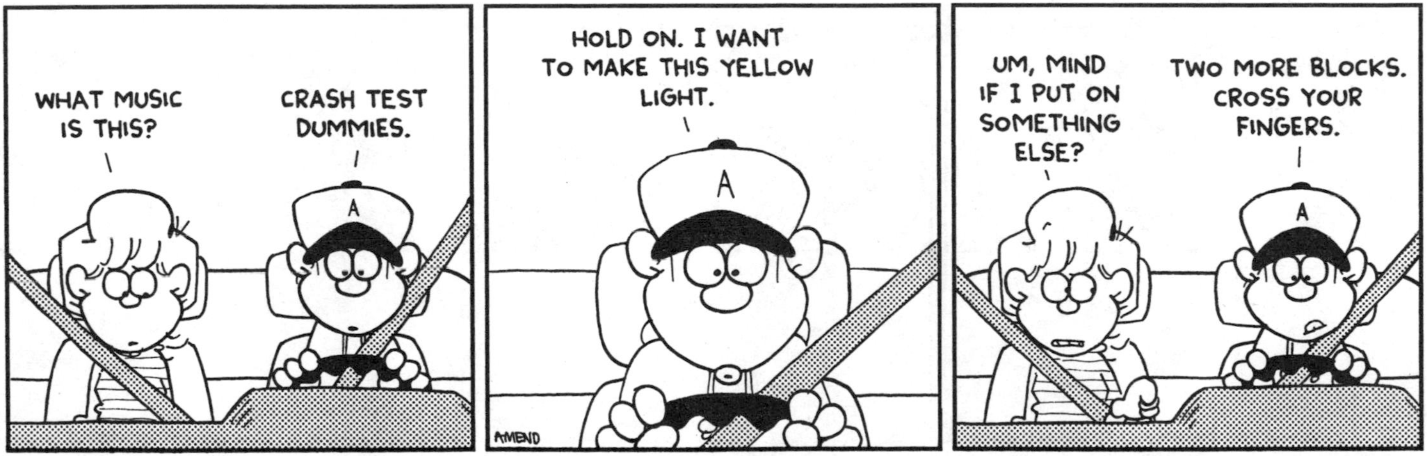
WHAT MUSIC IS THIS?
CRASH TEST DUMMIES.
HOLD ON. I WANT TO MAKE THIS YELLOW LIGHT.
AMEND
UM, MIND IF I PUT ON SOMETHING ELSE?
TWO MORE BLOCKS. CROSS YOUR FINGERS.

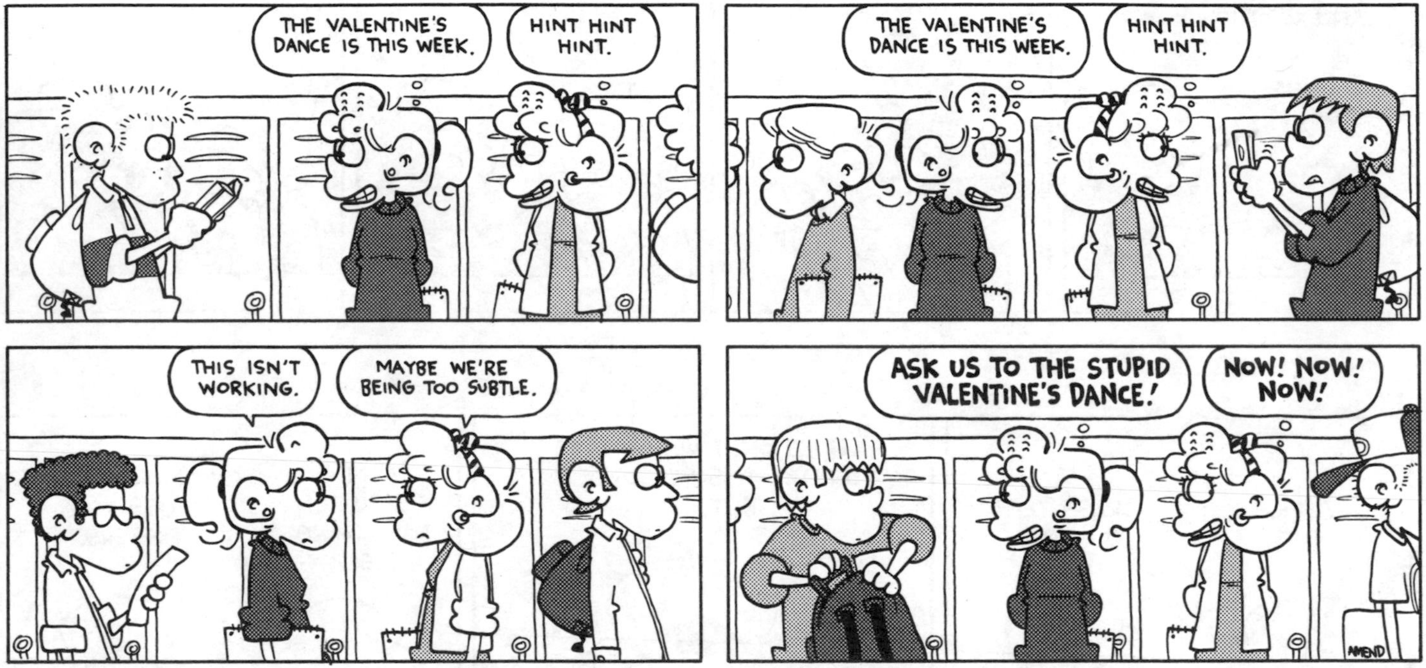
THE VALENTINE'S DANCE IS THIS WEEK.
HINT HINT HINT.
THE VALENTINE'S DANCE IS THIS WEEK.
HINT HINT HINT.
THIS ISN'T WORKING.
MAYBE WE'RE BEING TOO SUBTLE.
ASK US TO THE STUPID VALENTINE'S DANCE!
NOW! NOW! NOW!
AMEND

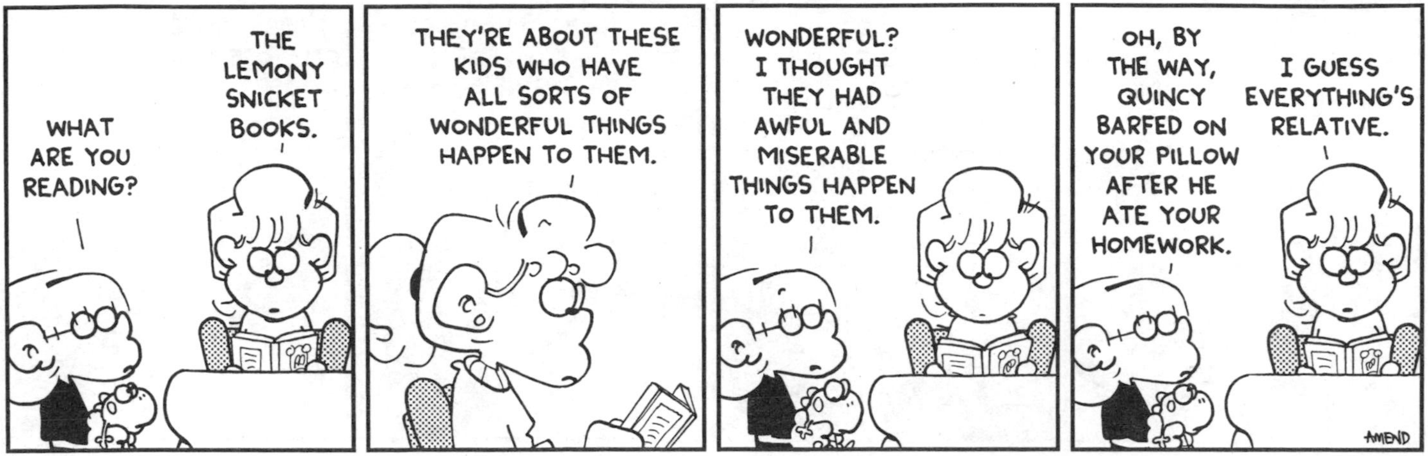
WHAT ARE YOU READING?
THE LEMONY SNICKET BOOKS.
THEY'RE ABOUT THESE KIDS WHO HAVE ALL SORTS OF WONDERFUL THINGS HAPPEN TO THEM.
WONDERFUL? I THOUGHT THEY HAD AWFUL AND MISERABLE THINGS HAPPEN TO THEM.
OH, BY THE WAY, QUINCY BARFED ON YOUR PILLOW AFTER HE ATE YOUR HOMEWORK.
I GUESS EVERYTHING'S RELATIVE.
AMEND

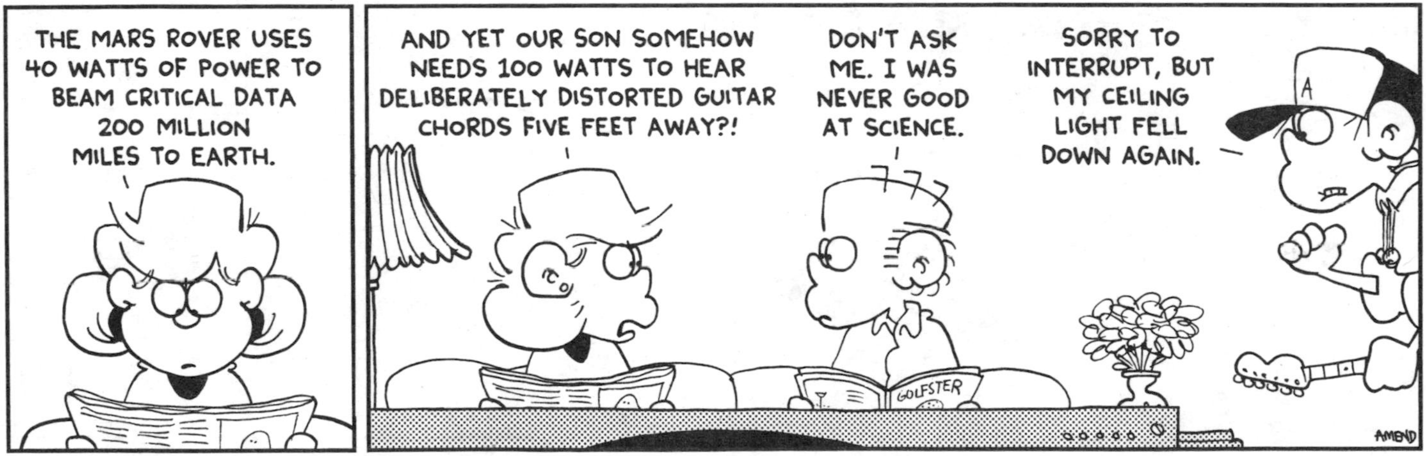
THE MARS ROVER USES 40 WATTS OF POWER TO BEAM CRITICAL DATA 200 MILLION MILES TO EARTH.
AND YET OUR SON SOMEHOW NEEDS 100 WATTS TO HEAR DELIBERATELY DISTORTED GUITAR CHORDS FIVE FEET AWAY?!
DON'T ASK ME. I WAS NEVER GOOD AT SCIENCE.
SORRY TO INTERRUPT, BUT MY CEILING LIGHT FELL DOWN AGAIN.
GOLFSTER
AMEND

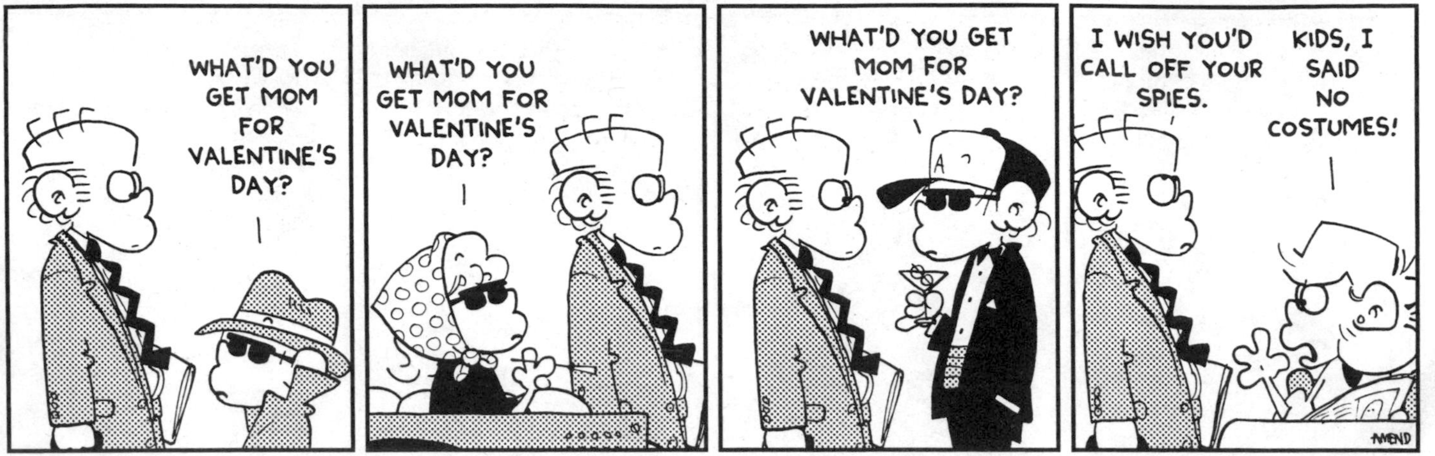
WHAT'D YOU GET MOM FOR VALENTINE'S DAY?
WHAT'D YOU GET MOM FOR VALENTINE'S DAY?
WHAT'D YOU GET MOM FOR VALENTINE'S DAY?
I WISH YOU'D CALL OFF YOUR SPIES.
KIDS, I SAID NO COSTUMES!
AMEND

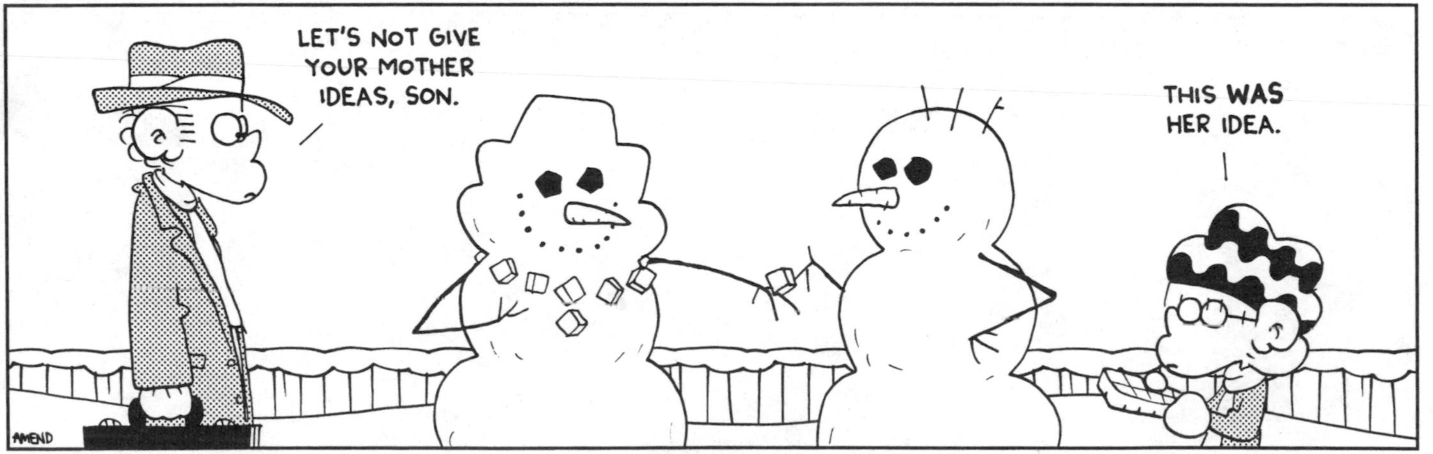
LET'S NOT GIVE YOUR MOTHER IDEAS, SON.
THIS WAS HER IDEA.
AMEND

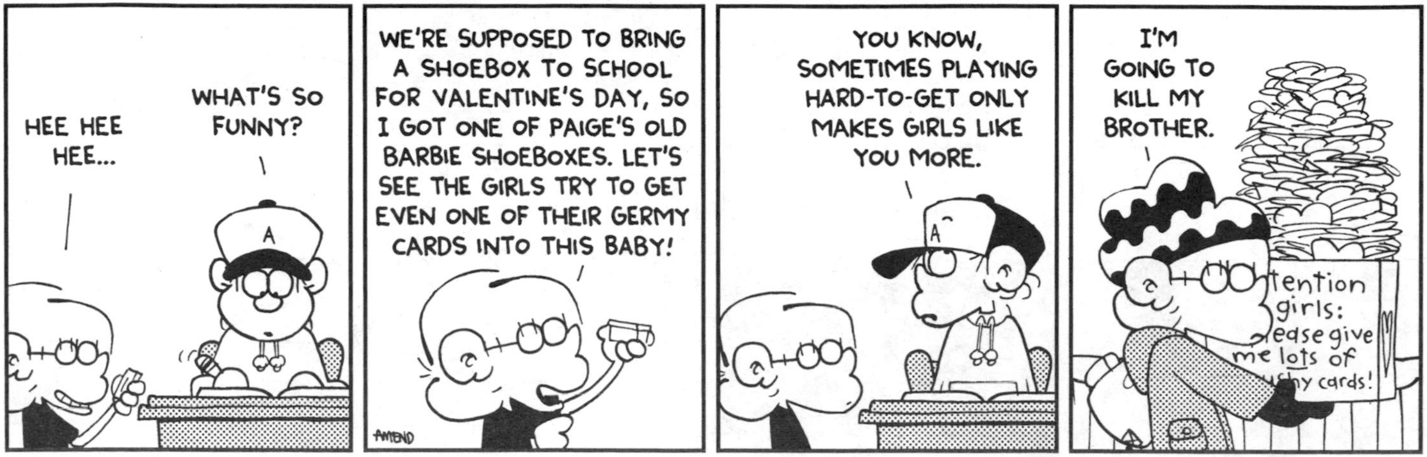
HEE HEE HEE...
WHAT'S SO FUNNY?
WE'RE SUPPOSED TO BRING A SHOEBOX TO SCHOOL FOR VALENTINE'S DAY, SO I GOT ONE OF PAIGE'S OLD BARBIE SHOEBOXES. LET'S SEE THE GIRLS TRY TO GET EVEN ONE OF THEIR GERMY CARDS INTO THIS BABY!
AMEND
YOU KNOW, SOMETIMES PLAYING HARD-TO-GET ONLY MAKES GIRLS LIKE YOU MORE.
I'M GOING TO KILL MY BROTHER.
tention girls: ease give me lots of y cards!

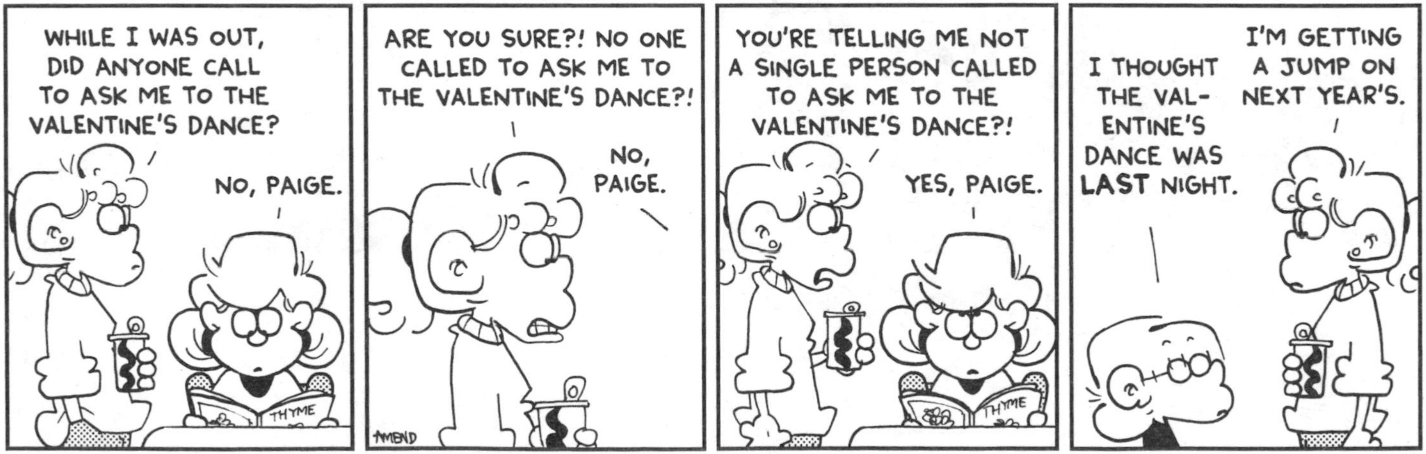
WHILE I WAS OUT, DID ANYONE CALL TO ASK ME TO THE VALENTINE'S DANCE?
NO, PAIGE.
THYME
ARE YOU SURE?! NO ONE CALLED TO ASK ME TO THE VALENTINE'S DANCE?!
NO, PAIGE.
AMEND
YOU'RE TELLING ME NOT A SINGLE PERSON CALLED TO ASK ME TO THE VALENTINE'S DANCE?!
YES, PAIGE.
THYME
I THOUGHT THE VALENTINE'S DANCE WAS **LAST** NIGHT.
I'M GETTING A JUMP ON NEXT YEAR'S.

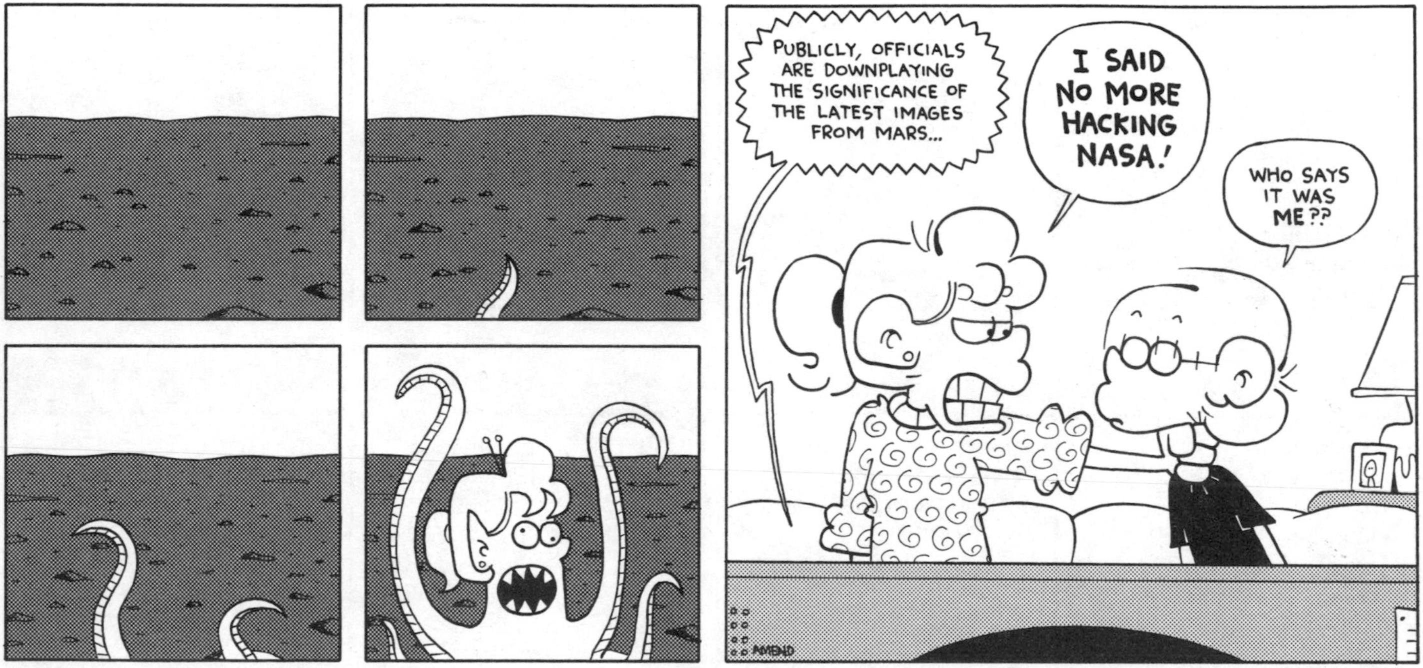
PUBLICLY, OFFICIALS ARE DOWNPLAYING THE SIGNIFICANCE OF THE LATEST IMAGES FROM MARS...
I SAID NO MORE HACKING NASA!
WHO SAYS IT WAS ME??
AMEND

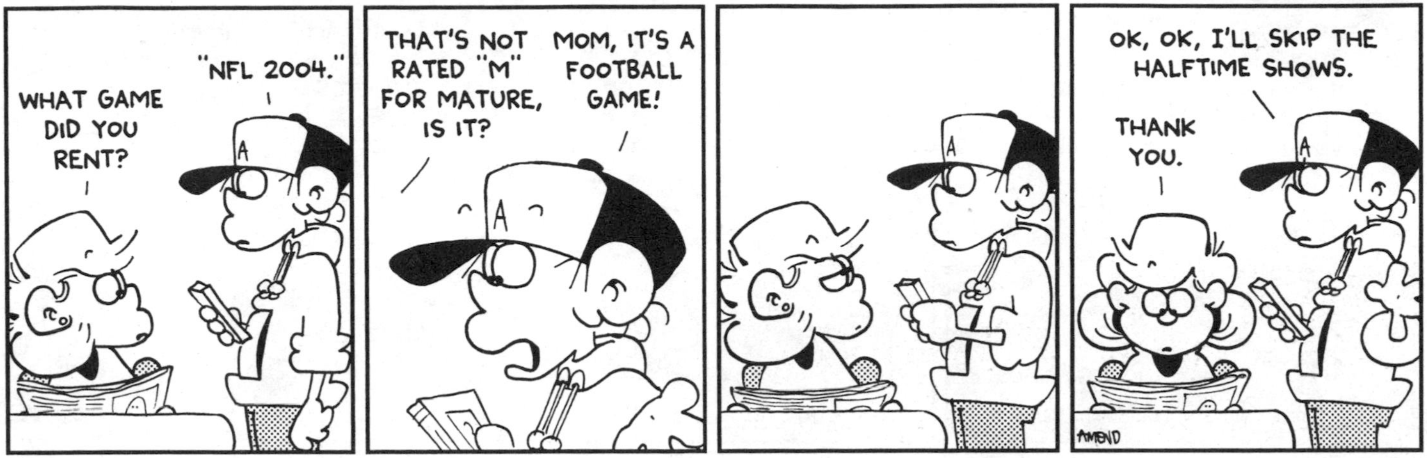
WHAT GAME DID YOU RENT?
"NFL 2004."
THAT'S NOT RATED "M" FOR MATURE, IS IT?
MOM, IT'S A FOOTBALL GAME!
OK, OK, I'LL SKIP THE HALFTIME SHOWS.
THANK YOU.
AMEND

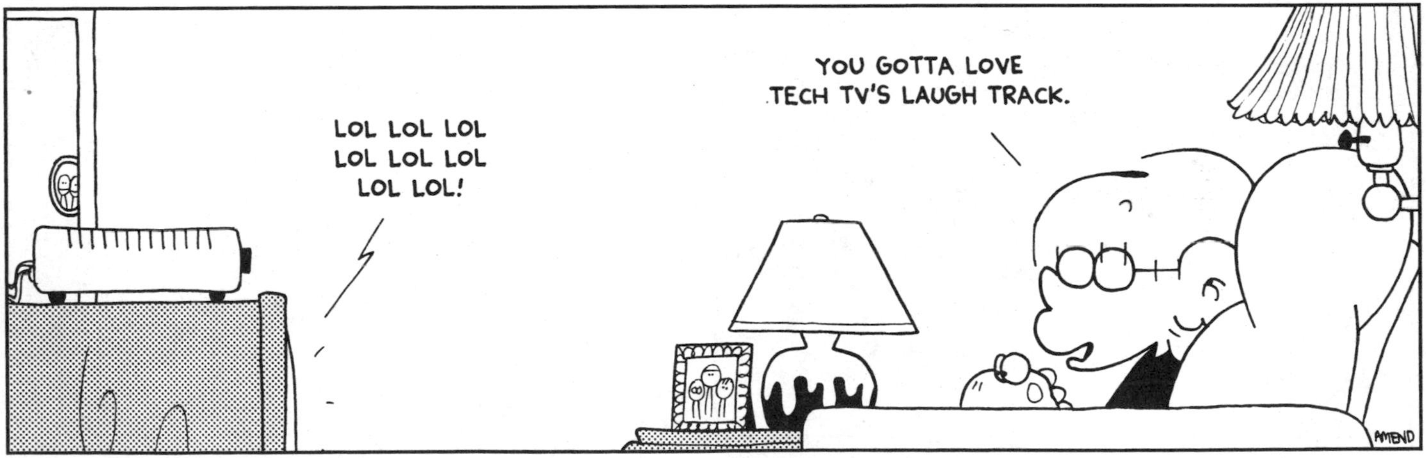
LOL LOL LOL LOL LOL LOL LOL LOL!
YOU GOTTA LOVE TECH TV'S LAUGH TRACK.
AMEND

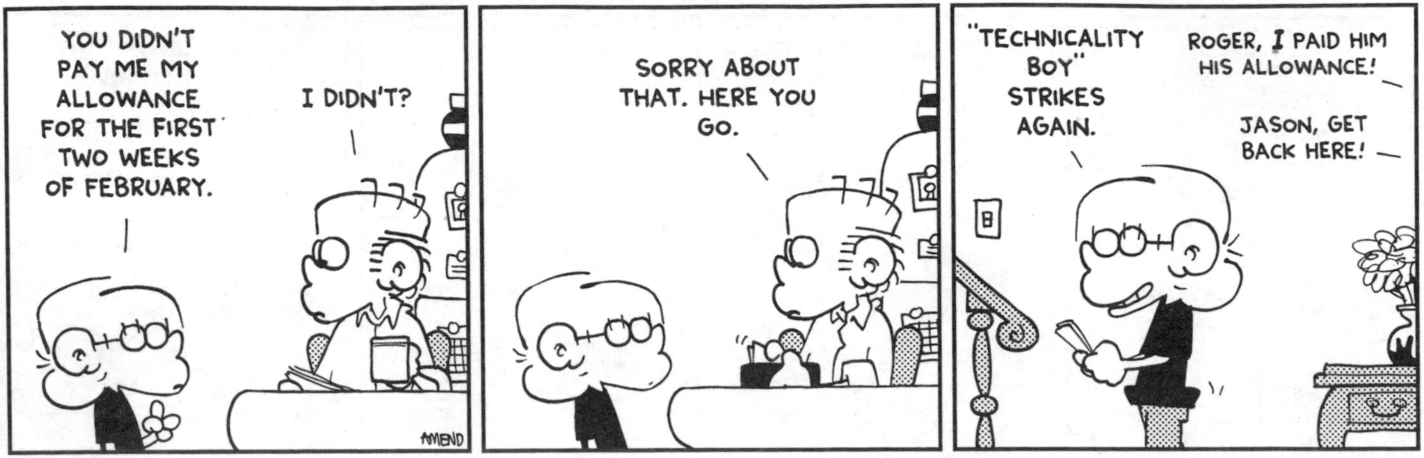
YOU DIDN'T PAY ME MY ALLOWANCE FOR THE FIRST TWO WEEKS OF FEBRUARY.
I DIDN'T?
AMEND
SORRY ABOUT THAT. HERE YOU GO.
"TECHNICALITY BOY" STRIKES AGAIN.
ROGER, I PAID HIM HIS ALLOWANCE!
JASON, GET BACK HERE!

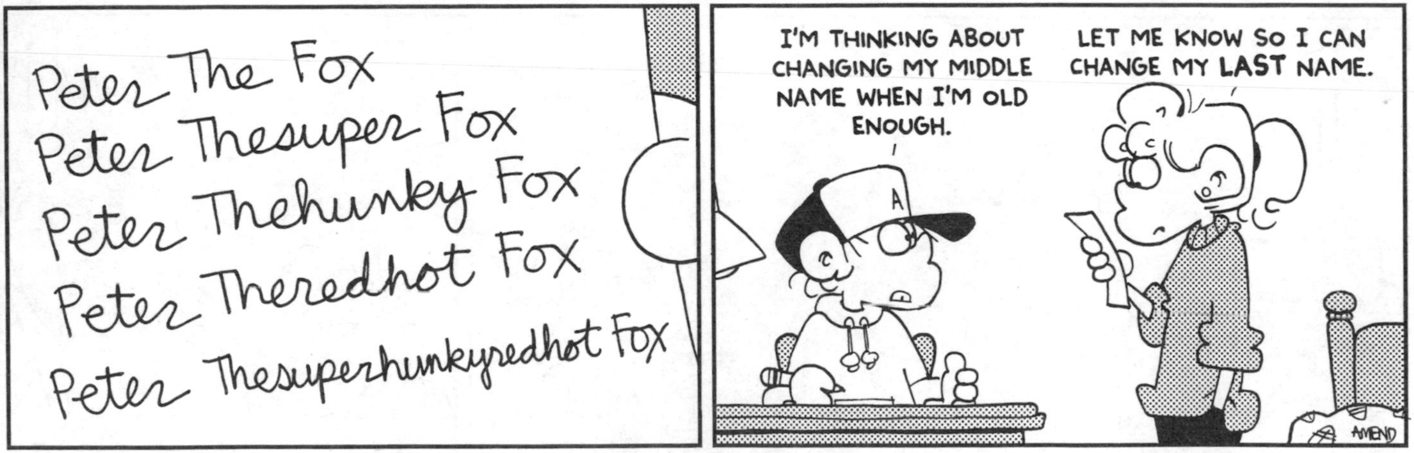
Peter The Fox
Peter Thesuper Fox
Peter Thehunky Fox
Peter Theredhot Fox
Peter Thesuperhunkyredhot Fox
I'M THINKING ABOUT CHANGING MY MIDDLE NAME WHEN I'M OLD ENOUGH.
LET ME KNOW SO I CAN CHANGE MY **LAST** NAME.
AMEND

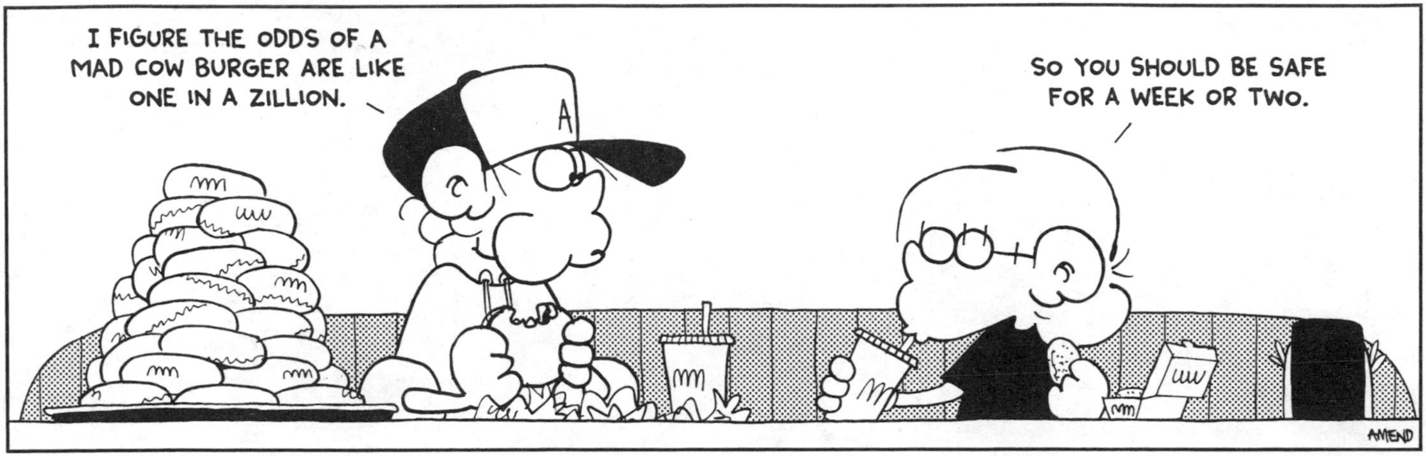
I FIGURE THE ODDS OF A MAD COW BURGER ARE LIKE ONE IN A ZILLION.
SO YOU SHOULD BE SAFE FOR A WEEK OR TWO.
AMEND

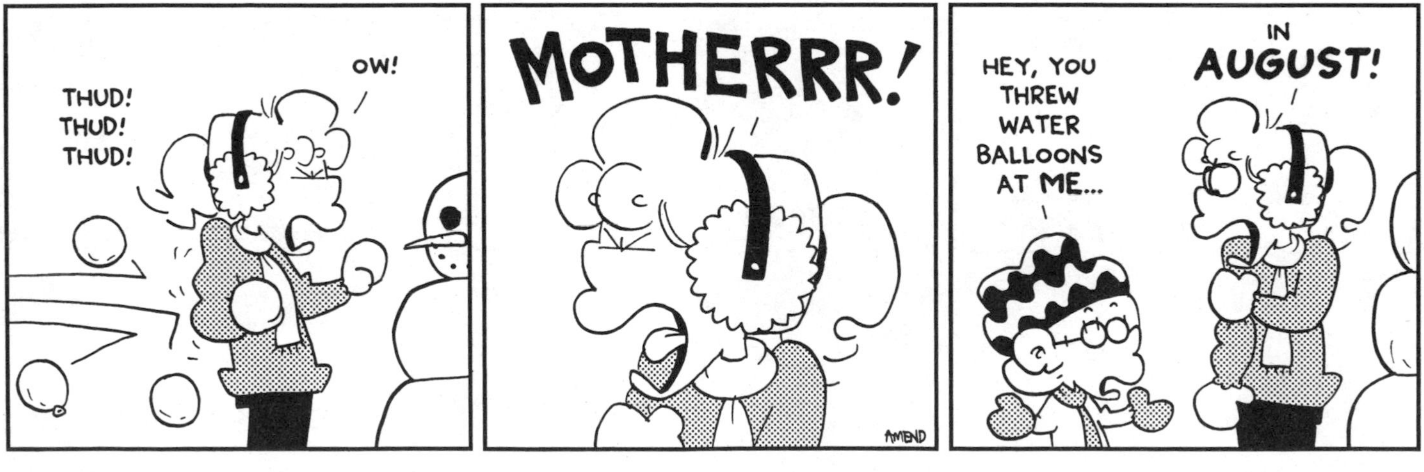
THUD! THUD! THUD!
OW!
MOTHERRR!
HEY, YOU THREW WATER BALLOONS AT ME...
IN AUGUST!
AMEND

UM, THIS IS A LITTLE EMBARRASSING, BUT...
I FOUND THIS WHILE I WAS GOING THROUGH MY CLOSET.
I BOUGHT IT FOR VALENTINE'S DAY AND FORGOT TO GIVE IT TO YOU.
I'M SURE BY NOW THE CHOCOLATES ARE NO GOOD.
DON'T BE SILLY. VALENTINE'S DAY WAS ONLY A WEEK AGO.
WHY'S IT SAY "TO THE MOTHER OF MY TWO CHILDREN"?
I THINK I NEED TO CLEAN OUT MY CLOSET MORE OFTEN.
AMEND

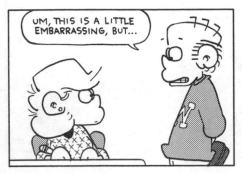

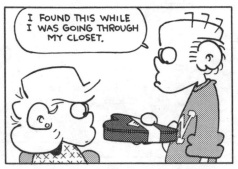

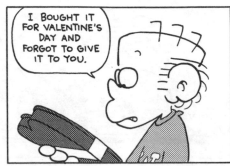

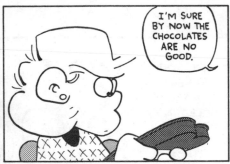

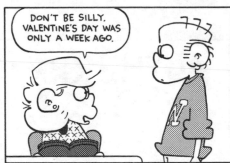

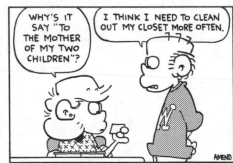

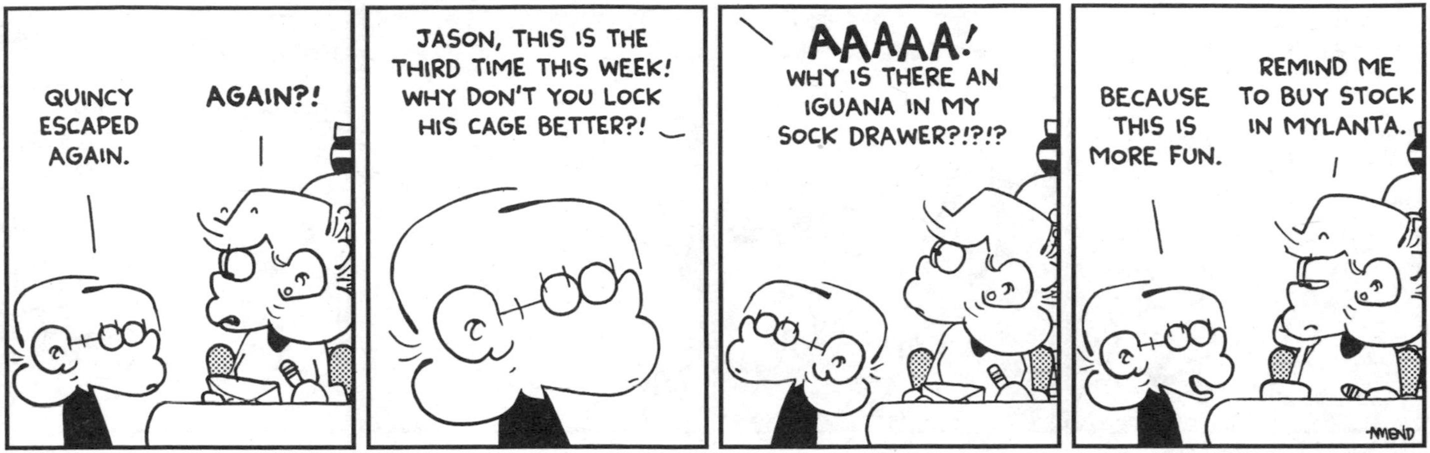
QUINCY ESCAPED AGAIN.
AGAIN?!
JASON, THIS IS THE THIRD TIME THIS WEEK! WHY DON'T YOU LOCK HIS CAGE BETTER?!
AAAAA!
WHY IS THERE AN IGUANA IN MY SOCK DRAWER?!?!?
BECAUSE THIS IS MORE FUN.
REMIND ME TO BUY STOCK IN MYLANTA.
AMEND

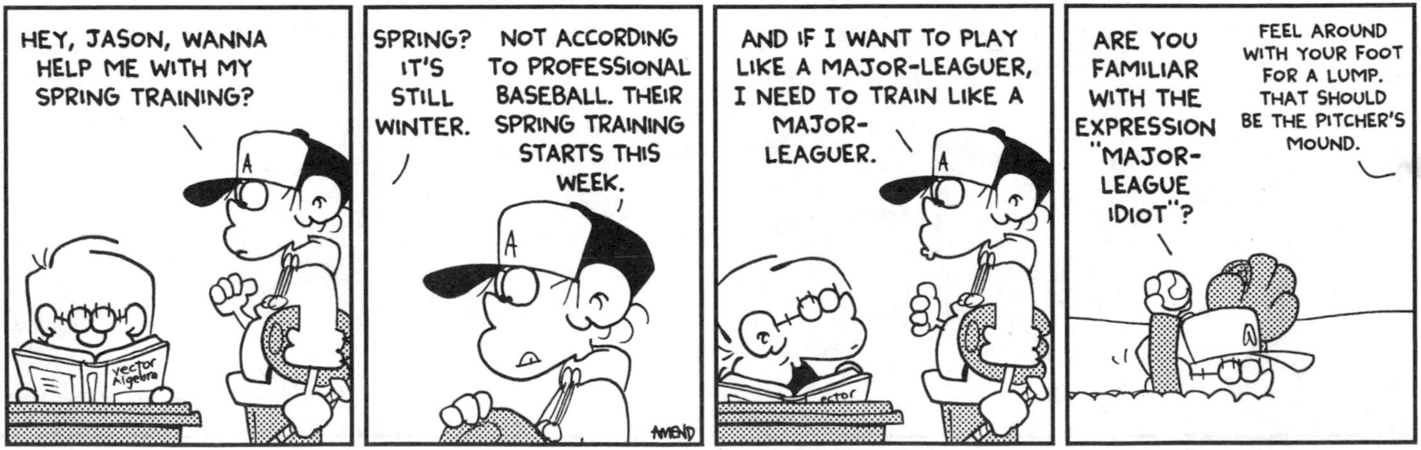
HEY, JASON, WANNA HELP ME WITH MY SPRING TRAINING?
Vector Algebra
SPRING? IT'S STILL WINTER.
NOT ACCORDING TO PROFESSIONAL BASEBALL. THEIR SPRING TRAINING STARTS THIS WEEK.
AMEND
AND IF I WANT TO PLAY LIKE A MAJOR-LEAGUER, I NEED TO TRAIN LIKE A MAJOR-LEAGUER.
ARE YOU FAMILIAR WITH THE EXPRESSION "MAJOR-LEAGUE IDIOT"?
FEEL AROUND WITH YOUR FOOT FOR A LUMP. THAT SHOULD BE THE PITCHER'S MOUND.

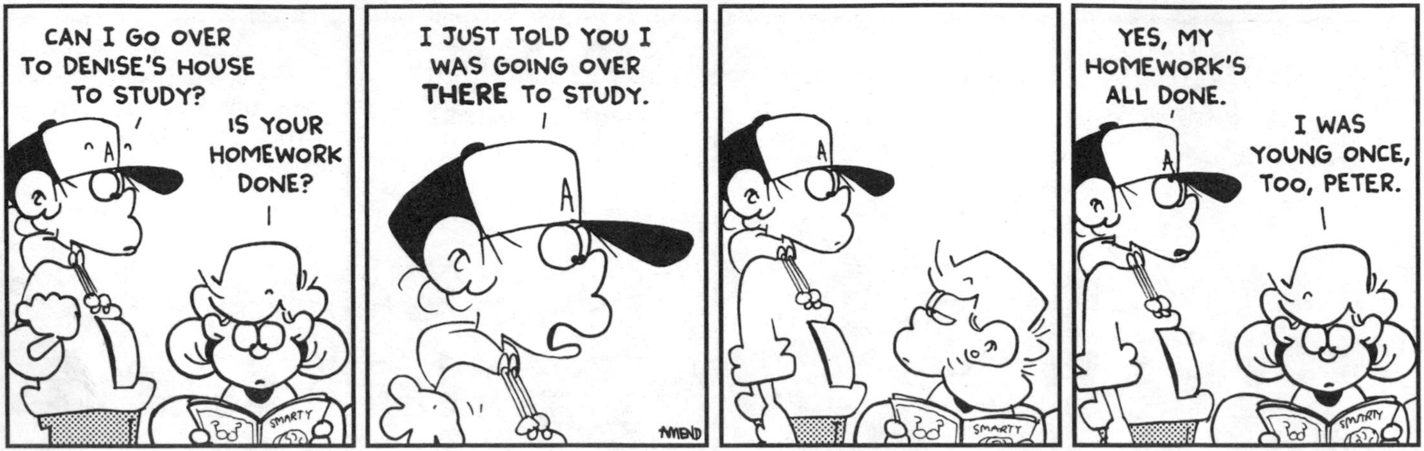
CAN I GO OVER TO DENISE'S HOUSE TO STUDY?
IS YOUR HOMEWORK DONE?
I JUST TOLD YOU I WAS GOING OVER **THERE** TO STUDY.
YES, MY HOMEWORK'S ALL DONE.
I WAS YOUNG ONCE, TOO, PETER.

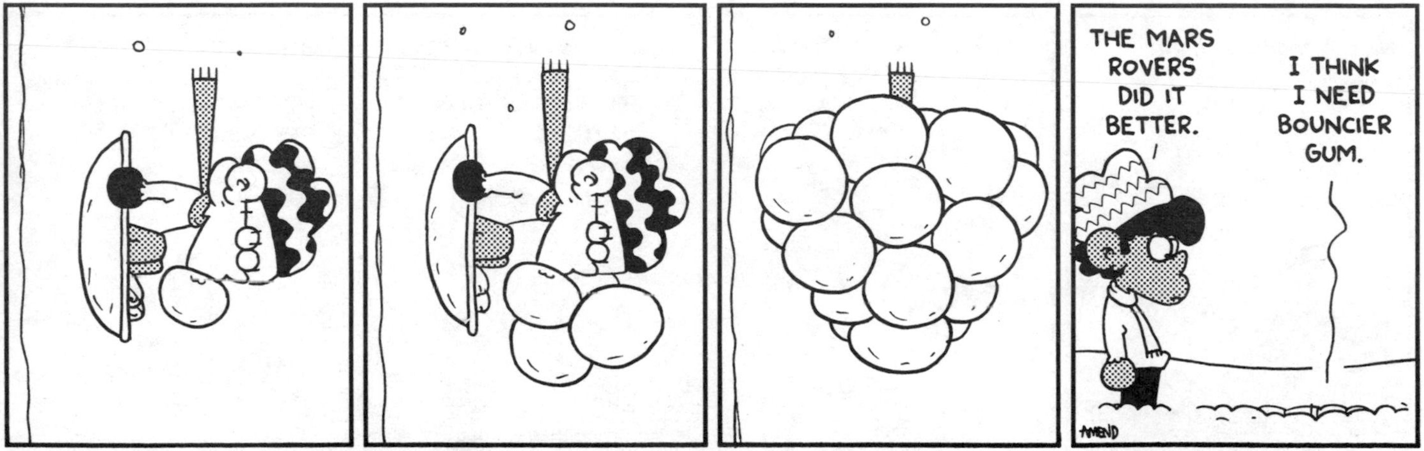
THE MARS ROVERS DID IT BETTER.
I THINK I NEED BOUNCIER GUM.

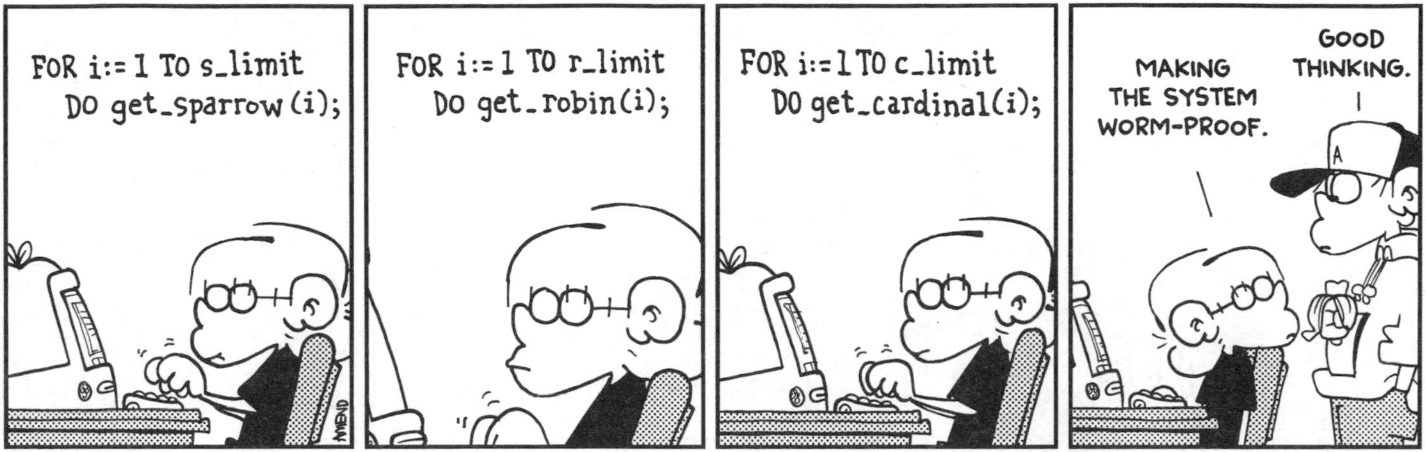
FOR i:= 1 TO s_limit
DO get_sparrow (i);
FOR i:= 1 TO r_limit
DO get_robin(i);
FOR i:= 1 TO c_limit
DO get_cardinal(i);
MAKING THE SYSTEM WORM-PROOF.
GOOD THINKING.

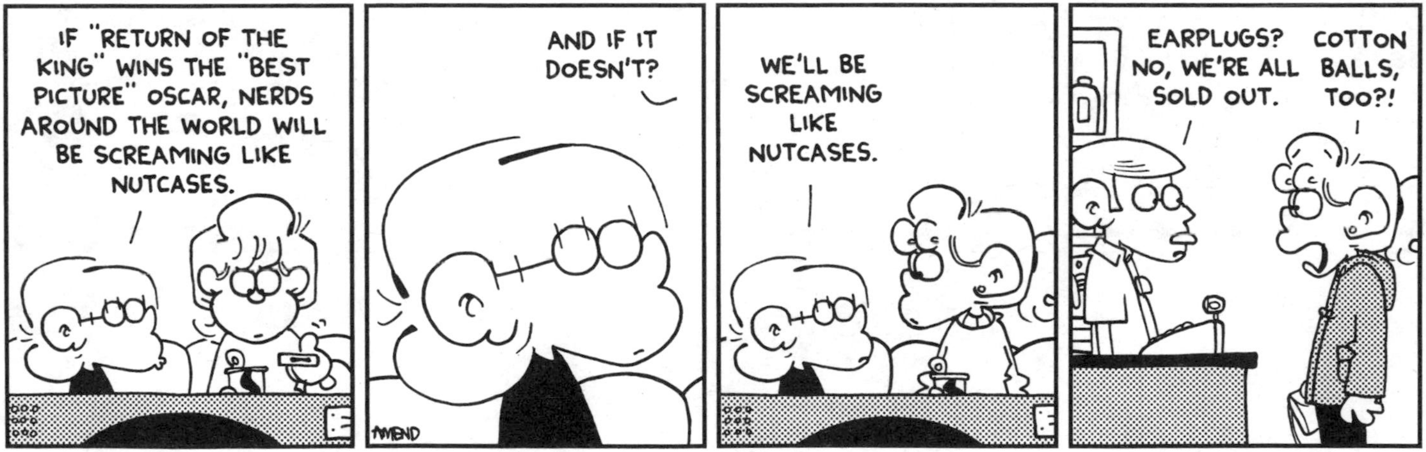
IF "RETURN OF THE KING" WINS THE "BEST PICTURE" OSCAR, NERDS AROUND THE WORLD WILL BE SCREAMING LIKE NUTCASES.
AND IF IT DOESN'T?
WE'LL BE SCREAMING LIKE NUTCASES.
EARPLUGS? NO, WE'RE ALL SOLD OUT.
COTTON BALLS, TOO?!

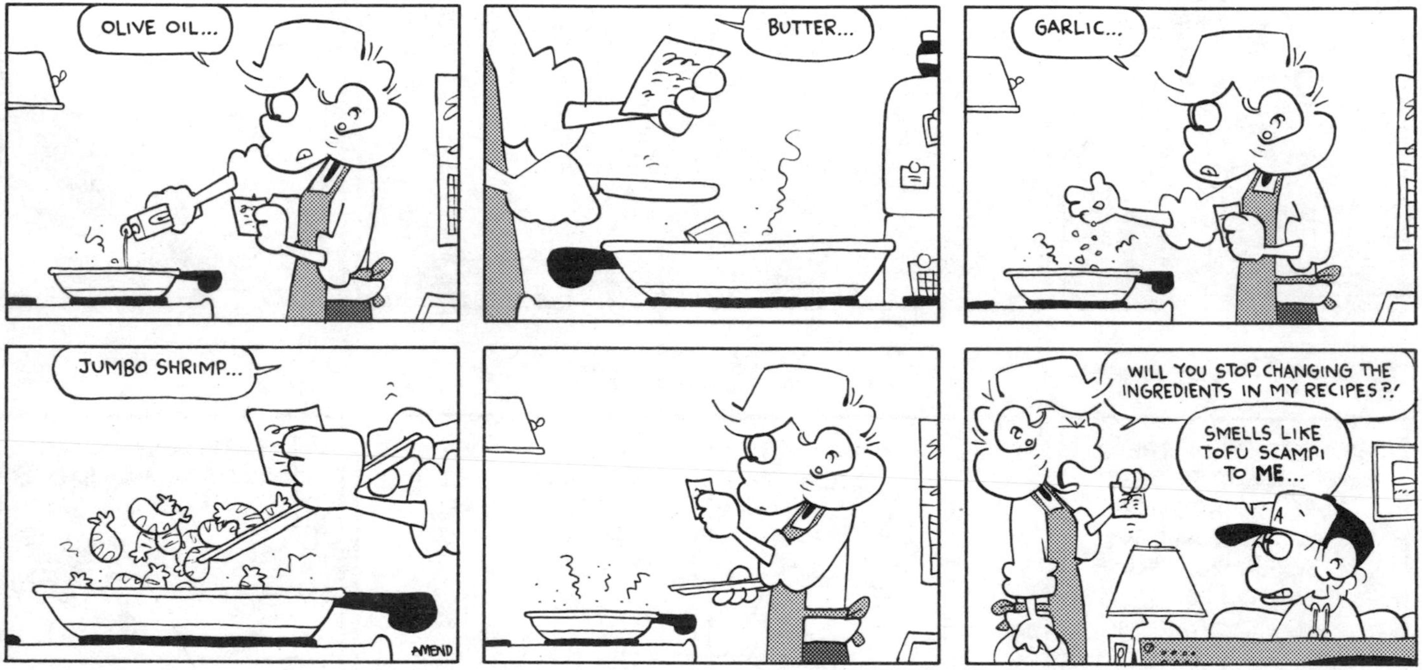
OLIVE OIL...
BUTTER...
GARLIC...
JUMBO SHRIMP...
AMEND
WILL YOU STOP CHANGING THE INGREDIENTS IN MY RECIPES?!
SMELLS LIKE TOFU SCAMPI TO ME...

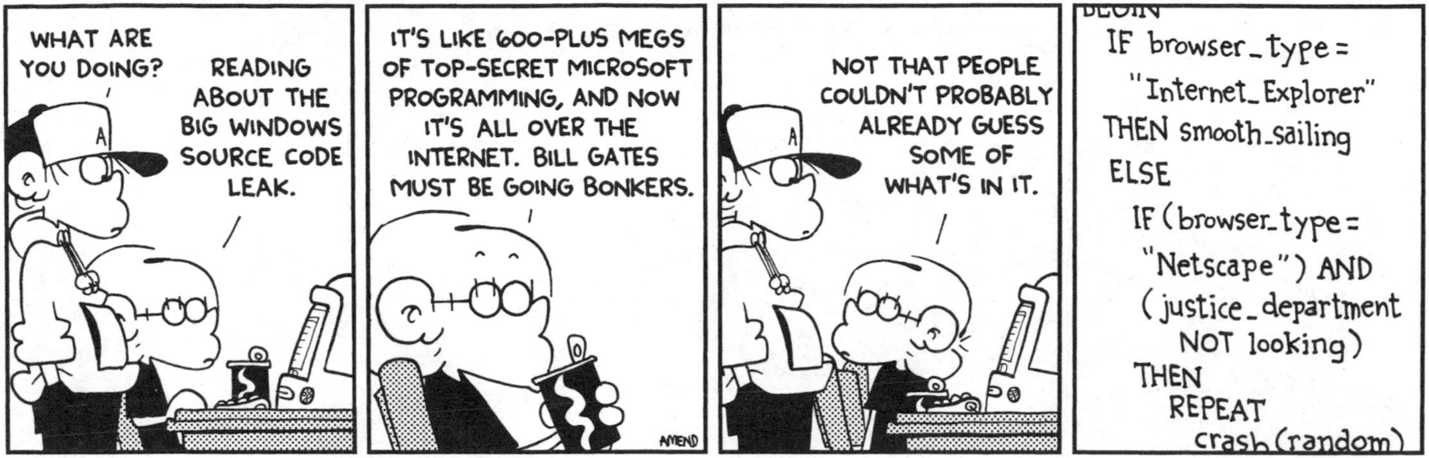
WHAT ARE YOU DOING?
READING ABOUT THE BIG WINDOWS SOURCE CODE LEAK.
IT'S LIKE 600-PLUS MEGS OF TOP-SECRET MICROSOFT PROGRAMMING, AND NOW IT'S ALL OVER THE INTERNET. BILL GATES MUST BE GOING BONKERS.
AMEND
NOT THAT PEOPLE COULDN'T PROBABLY ALREADY GUESS SOME OF WHAT'S IN IT.
IF browser_type = "Internet_Explorer"
THEN smooth_sailing
ELSE
IF (browser_type = "Netscape") AND
(justice_department NOT looking)
THEN
REPEAT
crash(random)

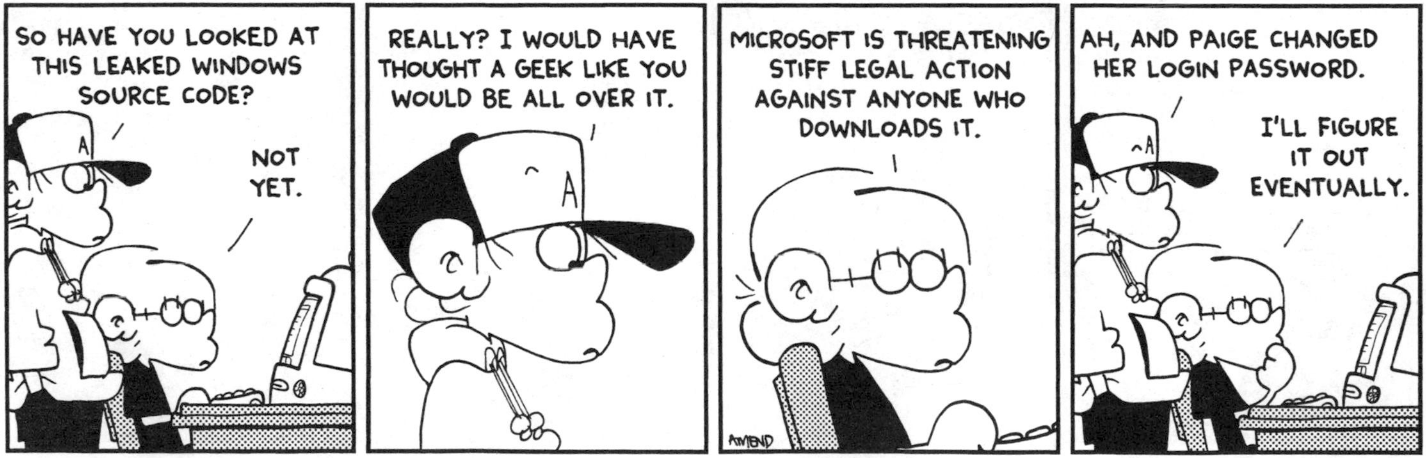
SO HAVE YOU LOOKED AT THIS LEAKED WINDOWS SOURCE CODE?
NOT YET.
REALLY? I WOULD HAVE THOUGHT A GEEK LIKE YOU WOULD BE ALL OVER IT.
MICROSOFT IS THREATENING STIFF LEGAL ACTION AGAINST ANYONE WHO DOWNLOADS IT.
AMEND
AH, AND PAIGE CHANGED HER LOGIN PASSWORD.
I'LL FIGURE IT OUT EVENTUALLY.

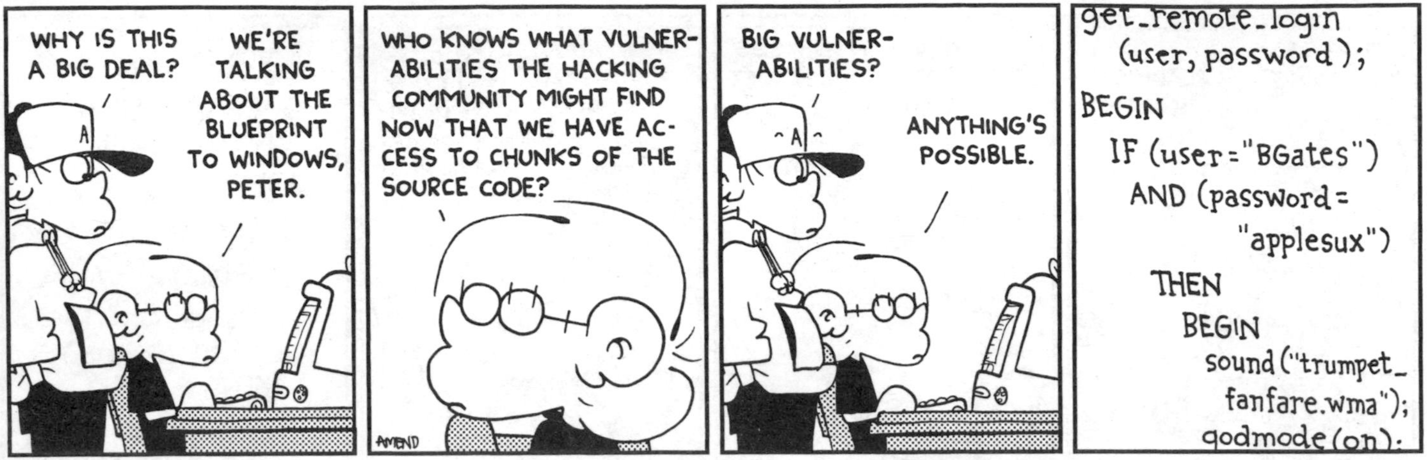
WHY IS THIS A BIG DEAL?
WE'RE TALKING ABOUT THE BLUEPRINT TO WINDOWS, PETER.
WHO KNOWS WHAT VULNERABILITIES THE HACKING COMMUNITY MIGHT FIND NOW THAT WE HAVE ACCESS TO CHUNKS OF THE SOURCE CODE?
AMEND
BIG VULNERABILITIES?
ANYTHING'S POSSIBLE.
get_remote_login
(user, password);
BEGIN
IF (user="BGates")
AND (password=
"applesux")
THEN
BEGIN
sound("trumpet_
fanfare.wma");
godmode(on);

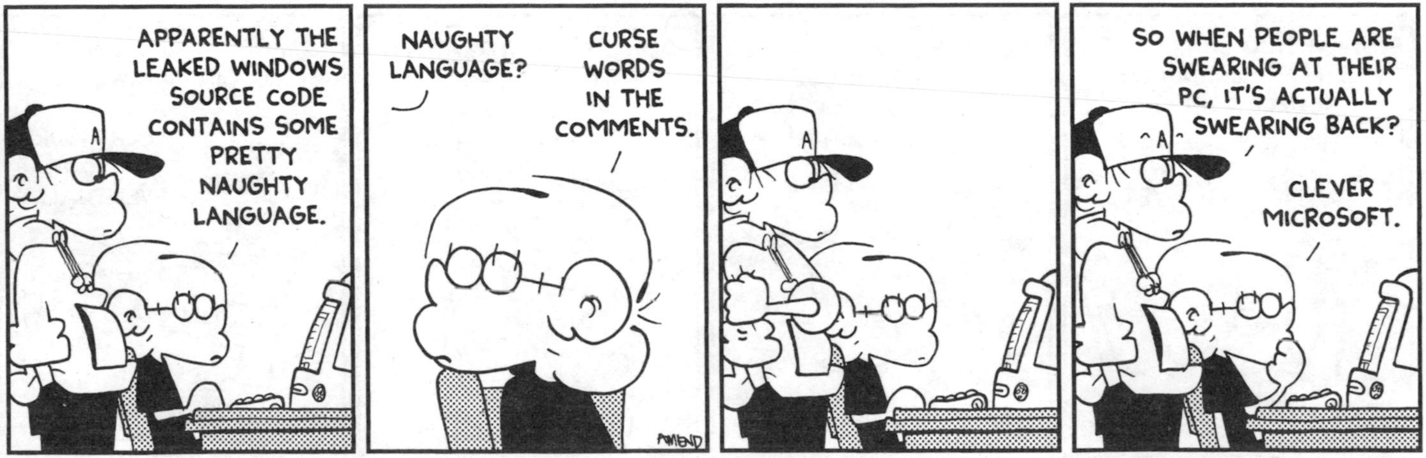
APPARENTLY THE LEAKED WINDOWS SOURCE CODE CONTAINS SOME PRETTY NAUGHTY LANGUAGE.
NAUGHTY LANGUAGE?
CURSE WORDS IN THE COMMENTS.
AMEND
SO WHEN PEOPLE ARE SWEARING AT THEIR PC, IT'S ACTUALLY SWEARING BACK?
CLEVER MICROSOFT.

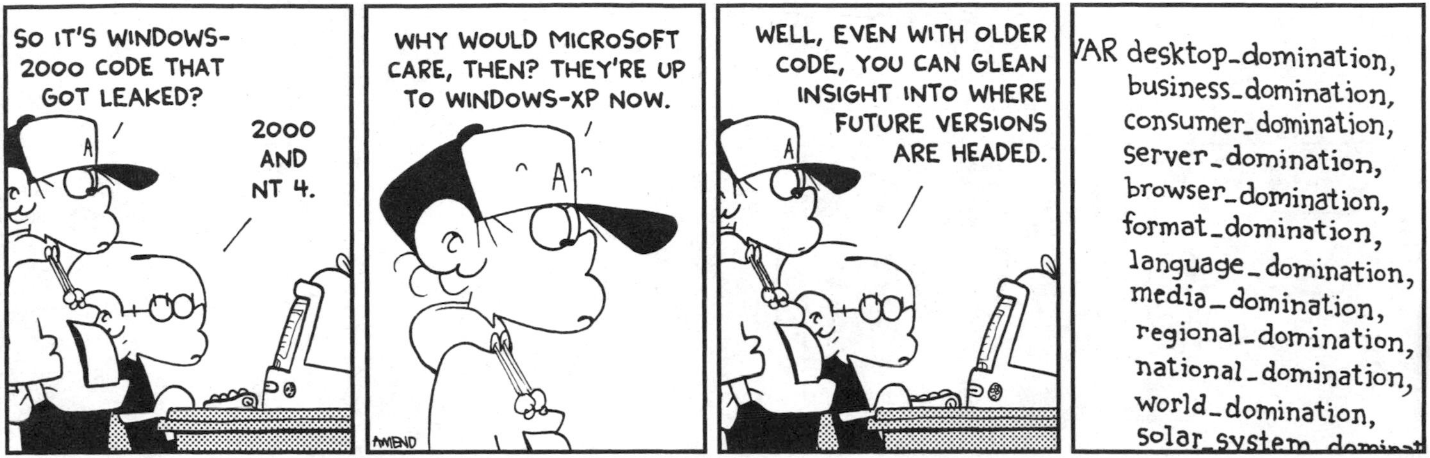
SO IT'S WINDOWS-2000 CODE THAT GOT LEAKED?
2000 AND NT 4.
WHY WOULD MICROSOFT CARE, THEN? THEY'RE UP TO WINDOWS-XP NOW.
AMEND
WELL, EVEN WITH OLDER CODE, YOU CAN GLEAN INSIGHT INTO WHERE FUTURE VERSIONS ARE HEADED.
VAR desktop_domination,
business_domination,
consumer_domination,
server_domination,
browser_domination,
format_domination,
language_domination,
media_domination,
regional_domination,
national_domination,
world_domination,
solar_system_dominat

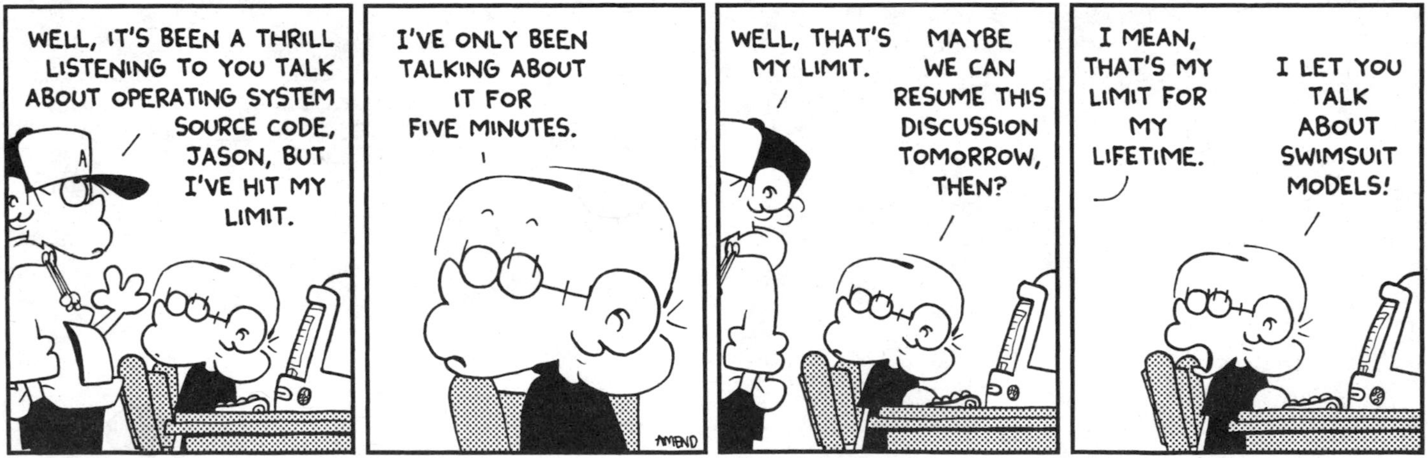
WELL, IT'S BEEN A THRILL LISTENING TO YOU TALK ABOUT OPERATING SYSTEM SOURCE CODE, JASON, BUT I'VE HIT MY LIMIT.
I'VE ONLY BEEN TALKING ABOUT IT FOR FIVE MINUTES.
AMEND
WELL, THAT'S MY LIMIT.
MAYBE WE CAN RESUME THIS DISCUSSION TOMORROW, THEN?
I MEAN, THAT'S MY LIMIT FOR MY LIFETIME.
I LET YOU TALK ABOUT SWIMSUIT MODELS!

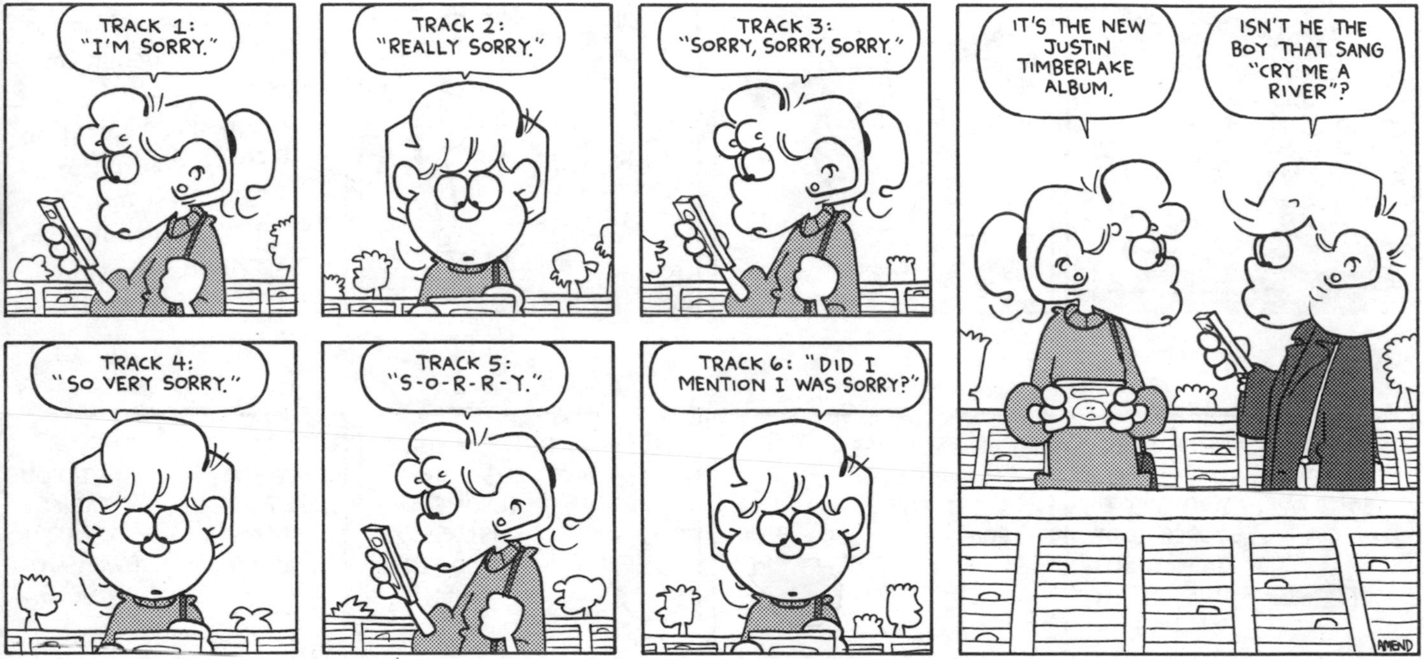
TRACK 1:
"I'M SORRY."
TRACK 2:
"REALLY SORRY."
TRACK 3:
"SORRY, SORRY, SORRY."
TRACK 4:
"SO VERY SORRY."
TRACK 5:
"S-O-R-R-Y."
TRACK 6: "DID I MENTION I WAS SORRY?"
IT'S THE NEW JUSTIN TIMBERLAKE ALBUM.
ISN'T HE THE BOY THAT SANG "CRY ME A RIVER"?
AMEND

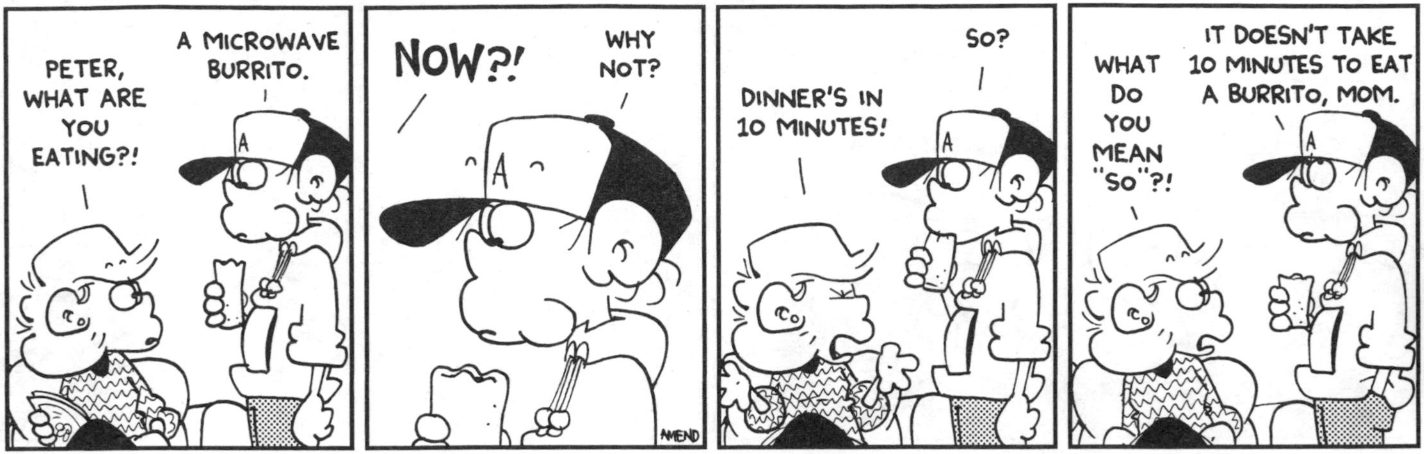
PETER, WHAT ARE YOU EATING?!
A MICROWAVE BURRITO.
NOW?!
WHY NOT?
DINNER'S IN 10 MINUTES!
SO?
WHAT DO YOU MEAN "SO"?!
IT DOESN'T TAKE 10 MINUTES TO EAT A BURRITO, MOM.
AMEND

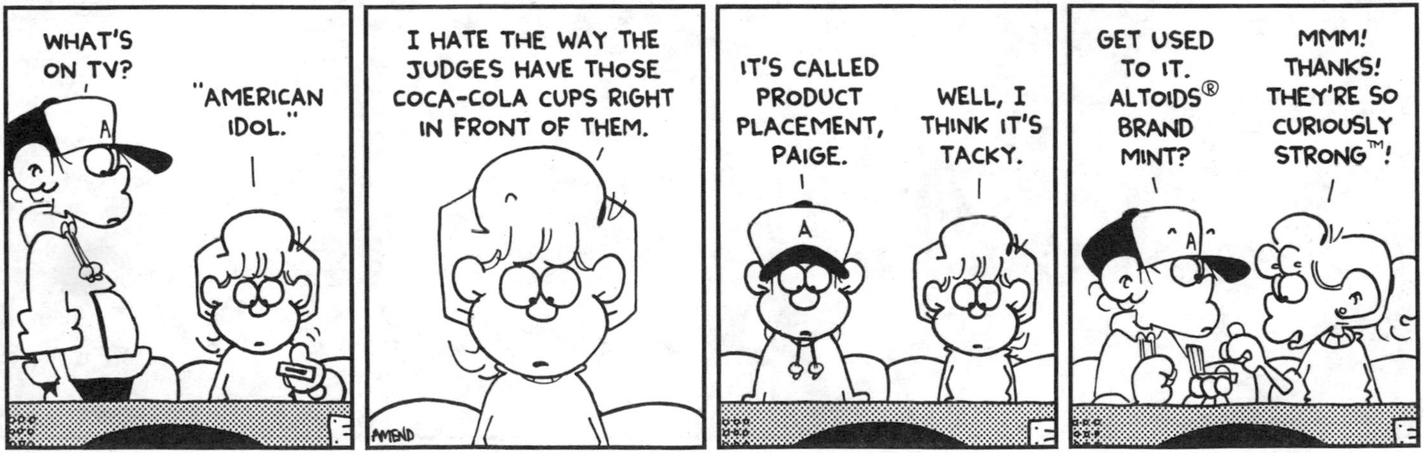
WHAT'S ON TV?
"AMERICAN IDOL."
I HATE THE WAY THE JUDGES HAVE THOSE COCA-COLA CUPS RIGHT IN FRONT OF THEM.
IT'S CALLED PRODUCT PLACEMENT, PAIGE.
WELL, I THINK IT'S TACKY.
GET USED TO IT. ALTOIDS® BRAND MINT?
MMM! THANKS! THEY'RE SO CURIOUSLY STRONG™!
AMEND

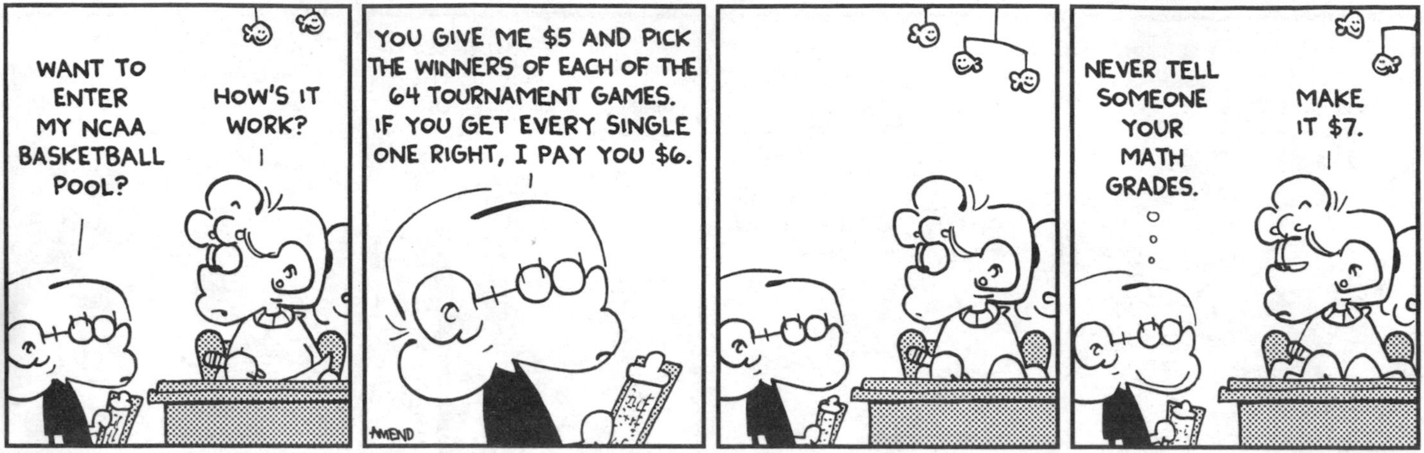

WANT TO ENTER MY NCAA BASKETBALL POOL?
HOW'S IT WORK?
YOU GIVE ME $5 AND PICK THE WINNERS OF EACH OF THE 64 TOURNAMENT GAMES. IF YOU GET EVERY SINGLE ONE RIGHT, I PAY YOU $6.
AMEND
NEVER TELL SOMEONE YOUR MATH GRADES.
MAKE IT $7.

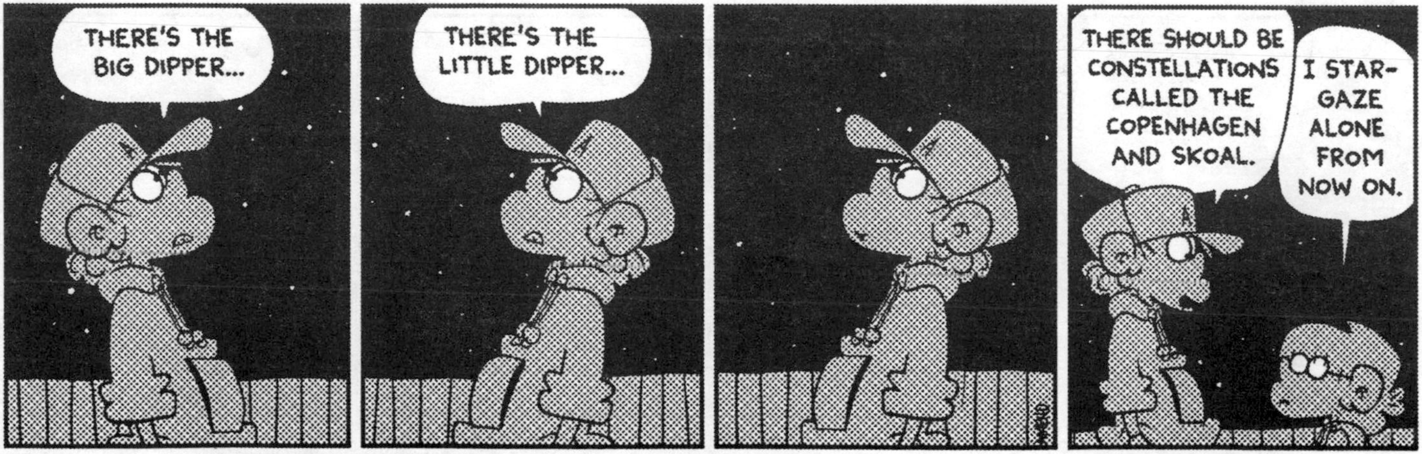

THERE'S THE BIG DIPPER...
THERE'S THE LITTLE DIPPER...
THERE SHOULD BE CONSTELLATIONS CALLED THE COPENHAGEN AND SKOAL.
I STAR-GAZE ALONE FROM NOW ON.

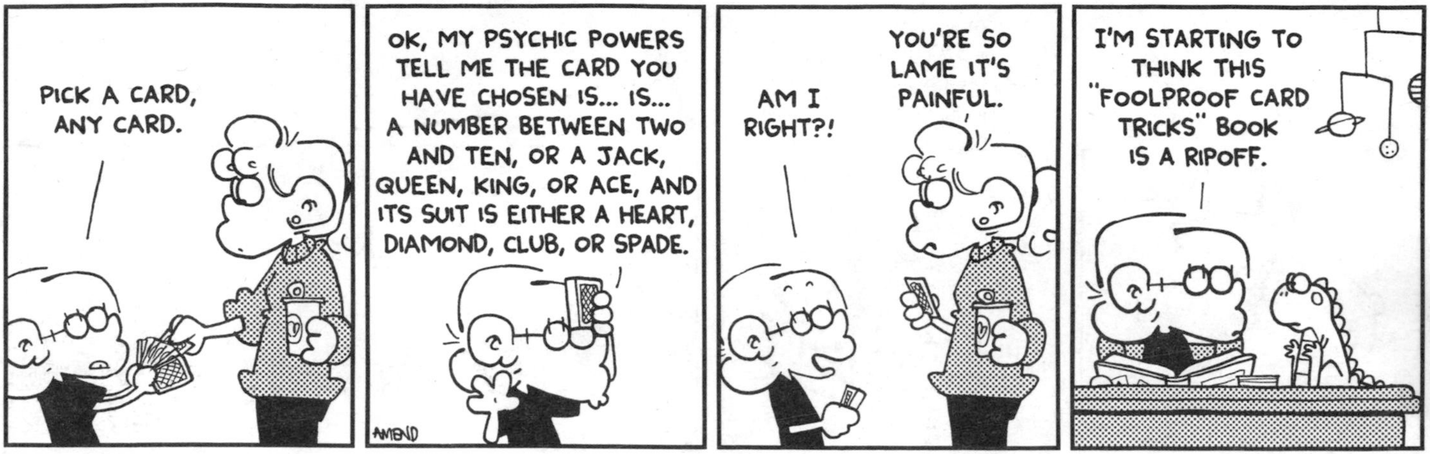
PICK A CARD, ANY CARD.
OK, MY PSYCHIC POWERS TELL ME THE CARD YOU HAVE CHOSEN IS... IS... A NUMBER BETWEEN TWO AND TEN, OR A JACK, QUEEN, KING, OR ACE, AND ITS SUIT IS EITHER A HEART, DIAMOND, CLUB, OR SPADE.
AMEND
AM I RIGHT?!
YOU'RE SO LAME IT'S PAINFUL.
I'M STARTING TO THINK THIS "FOOLPROOF CARD TRICKS" BOOK IS A RIPOFF.

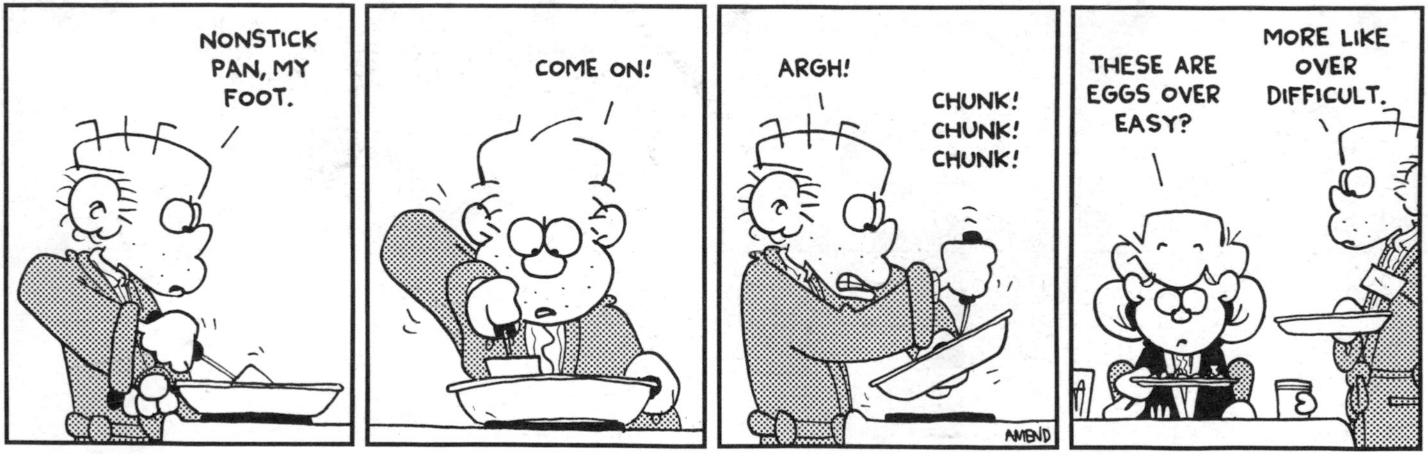
NONSTICK PAN, MY FOOT.
COME ON!
ARGH!
CHUNK! CHUNK! CHUNK!
AMEND
THESE ARE EGGS OVER EASY?
MORE LIKE OVER DIFFICULT.

WHOOPS.
WHIFF
BOINK!
AMEND
SORRY, KILBORN— I THOUGHT YOU WERE LOOKING.
I'VE GOT TO HAND IT TO YOU, FOX — FIRST WEEK OF PRACTICE AND YOU'RE ALREADY IN MID-SEASON FORM.
THANKS, COACH!

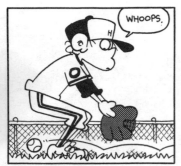

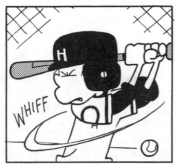

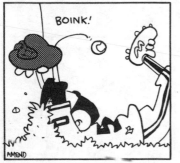

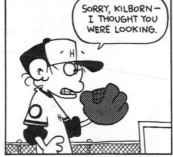

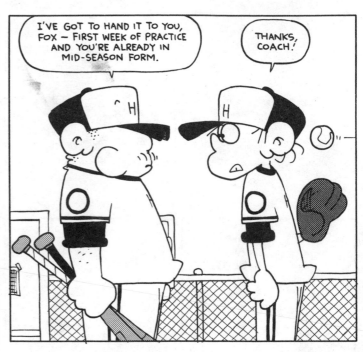